A World in Ruins

A World in Ruins

CHRONICLES OF INTELLECTUAL LIFE, 1943

MAURICE BLANCHOT

Translated by Michael Holland

FORDHAM UNIVERSITY PRESS

New York 2016

The essays in this volume were published in French in *Chroniques littéraires du «Journal des débats»: Avril 1941–août 1944*, © Éditions Gallimard, Paris, 2007.

Cet ouvrage publié dans le cadre du programme d'aide à la publication bénéficie du soutien du Ministère des Affaires Etrangères et du Service Culturel de l'Ambassade de France représenté aux Etats-Unis.

This work received support from the French Ministry of Foreign Affairs and the Cultural Services of the French Embassy in the United States through their publishing assistance program.

Fordham University Press also publishes its books in a variety of electronic formats. Some content that appears in print may not be available in electronic books.

Visit us online at www.fordhampress.com.

Library of Congress Cataloging-in-Publication Data

Blanchot, Maurice.
[Essays. Selections. English]
A world in ruins : chronicles of intellectual life, 1943 / Maurice Blanchot ; translated by Michael Holland. — First edition.
pages cm
"The essays in this volume were published in French in Chroniques littéraires du Journal des débats."—T.p. verso.
Includes bibliographical references and index.
ISBN 978-0-8232-6725-5 (cloth : alk. paper) — ISBN 978-0-8232-6726-2 (pbk. : alk. paper)
1. Literature—Philosophy. I. Holland, Michael, 1950– translator. II. Title.
PQ2603.L3343A2 2015
848'.91203—dc23

2015006038

Printed in the United States of America

18 17 16 5 4 3 2 1

First edition

Contents

A World in Ruins

Introduction

MICHAEL HOLLAND

In 1984, Maurice Blanchot concluded a long reflection on the role of the intellectual with a quotation from René Char's "Letter to Francis Curel," which was written in 1943, before adding: "That improbable date hangs suspended above our heads. Its return is always possible. And it is that date, in my view, which denies intellectuals any hope of disappearing and so shying away from being questioned, from the torment of being questioned."[1]

What exactly did he mean? In certain key respects, 1943 marked a turning point in the war as far as France was concerned. The Germans may have invaded the *zone libre* in November 1942, dispelling any illusions that Vichy France was a reality, but the Allies entered North Africa in the same month, and by mid-1943 the Axis powers had been defeated there. With the creation of the Milice in January, the French authorities adopted the brutal methods of the occupiers. But many of those who were seeking to avoid being sent to Germany as workers under the Service du Travail Obligatoire

(STO) scheme were joining the Resistance. The same month saw the political fusion of the three main Resistance groups in the former *zone libre*, and in May the Conseil National de la Résistance (National Council for Resistance) met for the first time in Paris. Henceforth, Resistance activity would be coordinated and directed, and its geographical range would spread. On other fronts, the war against Nazism was slowly being won. Before it was defeated in North Africa, Germany had already capitulated at Stalingrad in February, and with the fall of Mussolini in July, the Allied invasion of Sicily in the summer and the capitulation of Italy in September, Hitler's army found itself increasingly exposed and overstretched. German troops were obliged to replace the Italian occupying forces in eight French *départements*. Then in October, Corsica was liberated.

Finally, if the authority of the Vichy regime now appeared illusory as Pétain was increasingly sidelined by Laval,[2] this was not solely a sign of German power. In March, General Giraud, a Vichy loyalist who replaced Admiral Darlan as the commander in chief in North Africa after Darlan's assassination in December 1942, declared in a radio broadcast that henceforth, he refused to recognize the armistice or the Vichy regime. His obstructive opposition toward de Gaulle, abetted by Churchill and Roosevelt, had initially delayed the creation of a united French National Committee, but in May he invited de Gaulle to join him in Algiers in order to create a central French authority, and after a series of difficult negotiations, in June he and de Gaulle agreed in a joint statement to set up the Comité Français de Libération Nationale, with both of them sharing the presidency. In August, the Allies recognized this body as the legitimate government of France, and by the end of 1943, thirty-seven countries had done the same.

At the same time, the backdrop to this gradually improving situation was one of widespread and unremitting destruction. The Germans and the Milice brutally repressed Resistance activity. In July, the prime mover behind the unification of the Resistance movements, Jean Moulin, was arrested, tortured, and killed. The Milice embarked on a campaign of summary executions and assassinations; in turn, the Resistance went on the offensive, and its activity became increasingly violent. Groups in Paris carried out organized attacks on the occupying forces, sabotage became widespread, and December saw the start of what became known as the Battle of the Rails, in which railways were the main target. As if reflecting the "total war" declared by Goebbels in February, civil war appeared to be engulfing France.

Furthermore, destruction was now coming from the air. In January, America began daylight bombing raids on German cities, while Britain sent its bombers in at night. The bombing of Hamburg in July caused 30,000 deaths and massive destruction. In November, seven hundred bombers turned Berlin into an inferno. Later in the year, the Allies also began to bomb cities in France. In September, 2,000 people died during the bombing of Nantes. In the same month Paris was bombed for the first time, and in December it was the turn of Marseilles. In all, 7,458 people died in air raids in France during 1943, while in Germany the figure was closer to 100,000.

In France, living conditions had become extremely difficult. In 1943 alone, tens of thousands of people died from malnutrition. And throughout the year, the deportation of Jews continued apace. The "Final Solution" proposed by Himmler at the Wannsee conference in 1942, by which time two and a half million Jews had already been killed, was fully endorsed and accelerated at the Posen conference in October 1943. The Germans took over Drancy, and Jews who had taken refuge in the former *zone libre* were now hunted down. Darquier de Pellepoix, who replaced Xavier Vallat as the Commissioner for Jewish Affairs, declared in August that all Jews should be denaturalized, thus losing any remaining protection afforded them by the French state.

Is this what Blanchot was referring to in his 1984 article? Is the return of destruction on a worldwide scale the threat to which intellectuals must be constantly alert? Is the "world in ruins" that he evokes in the title of the last of his articles in 1943 year a scenario that could always return? Yes and no. Seen from the perspective of someone writing in 1984, the ruinous state to which the war reduced the Western world was indisputably something that this world eventually overcame. After ruin came reconstruction. Even in the worst days of 1943, ruin allowed hope for the future. Indeed, Blanchot himself would appear to have shared that hope.[3] There is no doubt that by 1943 he had left all of his illusions behind. "Jeune France" and the "tragicomedy"[4] of the *Nouvelle Revue Française* were things of the past.[5] As he said in a letter to Francis Ambrière on July 14, he had voluntarily absented himself from all external activity. He saw a few friends from time to time; otherwise he just let the days go by, since what they brought was of little importance.[6] The way the letter goes on is revealing, however: "but what is important will come, it is approaching." And with reference to the July 14 national day, Bastille Day, on which he was writing his letter, Blanchot speaks of "this day when hope is once again allowed." The Germans banned all July 14 celebrations in 1943, but in towns across France thousands of people marched on that day, waving national flags. Blanchot seems to have shared their optimism. In an intriguing passage of the same letter, he writes, "I mentioned those journeys that circumstances sometimes require at the present time and whose consequences cannot always be predicted. So far nothing of that kind has happened yet." Was he considering leaving for London? We do not know that for the moment. But it does seem clear that like everyone, he considered that by 1943 some end to ruin and destruction could well be in sight. On its own, that would allow us to interpret his words in 1984 as an appeal to intellectuals to ensure that the world never again be allowed to become a "world in ruins."

There is more to those words than that, however. In a letter to Vadim Kozovoï in 1981, Blanchot wrote, "I wanted to say something to you about what you said to me so movingly about 'the experience of a glacial world': because that concerns each one of us, and confronts us with a truth that I have been aware of since at least 1940."[7] Though he said no more on the subject, his remark is a reminder of the true significance in his eyes of the ruin and destruction that were wrought by the war: however extensive and all-embracing they were, they were simply surface signs of a destruction that went entirely beyond the limits of the external world, in that it signified the collapse of the entire frame within which Western humanity had related to the world until 1940, the disappearance of the world, the self and the relation between them in an event that from then on Blanchot would term *disaster*. In another letter to Kozovoï he alluded to that experience: "As you know, I am very far from considering myself French above all. During the dark days of the Occupation I was of course aware that danger threatened both a culture and a world that was unaware of its values and was even prepared to abandon them in a cowardly fashion. It was unspeakably painful to feel that there were so few of us who refused the horror and struggled against it."[8] It is precisely the collapse of a culture and a world that for Blanchot, in the prewar period, were inseparable from France and from being French, that the disaster of defeat and occupation consolidated. But the ruin that resulted was more than physical: it extended to the very essence of the world and the self's relation to it. The "horror" that Blanchot evokes was less a response to the human and material destruction that occurred during the Occupation (those who struggled against that were more numerous than the "few of us" to whom Blanchot refers) than a realization that defeat and occupation had actualized the destruction of something that could never be reconstructed, and in the face of which all prospects and all hope were futile. As he wrote in his final article for 1943 with reference to the characters in a novel he was reviewing: "It is thus that the world in ruins—the truth of the world—appears to them, and henceforth they must live without purpose, without hope, as they await an outcome that will itself be merely a ridiculous misunderstanding." If as a Frenchman alive in 1943 he could share the hopes that this year had brought, intellectually such hopes had been impossible since the disaster of 1940.

This is not to say that Blanchot simply resigned himself to defeat and collaboration. Regularly throughout the chronicles that appeared during this year, he would pass trenchant judgment on contemporary affairs. He denounced "politicians who make events happen without understanding their nature," as well as "statesmen who misread the future by repeating the past" and "the oppression inflicted by sovereignty that has become deranged." The writer Charles Péguy, he wrote, had been "spoiled by the use that has been made of this solitary being over the last three years," while great works of the past ran the risk of "collaborating in a grim comedy of rejuvenation" as the regime sought to annex them to its cause. Vichy or what remains of it clearly deserved no respect in Blanchot's eyes. When he evoked Clemenceau, the great World War I leader, he seemed to be recommending his example to the present day: "the celebrated speech by Clemenceau entitled 'I make war' has lost all significance when it is read as a text, but part of its power is restored to it when we imagine its consequences and admire its results."

At a fundamental level, however, the present had somehow fallen outside of the scope of historical time. It was no longer possible any longer to repeat the past or revive what the past had achieved. History must henceforth "take account not just of what was done, but also of what was dreamed of, in vain." History is thus a narrative of delusion. Its only message henceforth is that such delusion is pointless. The article Blanchot devotes to Machiavelli is revealing in this respect, in that it seems to contain echoes of his personal experience. It begins by alluding to the failure of Machiavelli's political career and the imprudent behavior that caused it, before going on: "He was successful in neither his personal ambitions nor his patriotic hopes"; "His dream is to create a national state . . . in the hope that one day, a providential figure . . . will achieve this dream"; "He imagines a state created by tyranny in order to liberate the nation. . . . He entertains the dream of a dictator who will be not only strong enough to form the state, but also selfless enough to disappear once his task is completed"; "the passion of the patriotic visionary . . . makes him identify national greatness as the supreme value." But the true perspective on such ambitions is this:

> Mankind is trapped in a circle of instability in which things begin anew then reach their end in an inexorable cycle. Forms of government repeat themselves according to an unchanging order: As it becomes degenerate, each monarchy gives rise to an aristocratic regime that perishes in its turn as it becomes a democracy, while the corruption of democracy leads to dictatorships that once again turn into monarchies. In this eternal circle, human ingenuity arranges momentary pauses, but the influence of decadent forces always eventually overcomes the feeble powers that humanity possesses, and the precarious edifice collapses in accordance with the same law that once guaranteed its success.

What Blanchot refers to in his article on Tocqueville as "the bitter taste of political upheaval and the ruinous power of history" holds sway henceforth over human affairs. History is at an end. It can merely repeat itself in an inexorable cycle. To live on is now to retreat from everything and "let the days go by," in the knowledge that everything is henceforth without meaning.

In itself, the position that can intermittently be discerned in the articles from this year seems indistinguishable from the sort of nihilistic detachment that so many writers will take with them into the postwar years. In what is clearly a coded response to his friend Claude Roy, who by 1943 was not only in the Resistance but had joined the French Communist Party, Blanchot writes in "French Suite" that what France once was may well "sustain political faith and confidence in destiny" as it has for Roy. But that is not enough to make silence into something to be condemned. As his 1982 letter to Kozovoï indicated, he ceased at some point to consider himself French above all, and the explanation for this is to be found in "French Suite": "Nations change. They belong to a cycle that is greater than they are. They become what they are not only by virtue of their nature, but also as a result of universal changes that alter the face of the world." If we are willing to listen carefully to those who study a nation's past, he goes on, this is what they tell us: "Here is what this people was, and that is what it will never be again." This means that when Blanchot observes earlier in "French Suite" that "the refusal to speak about France . . . may itself also be considered as a characteristic feature of our spirit," he is also revealing that such silence in his case is not a tacit form of national solidarity: it has no meaning and reflects a decision that signifies nothing. Consequently, those who read significance into it (here he seems to be speaking directly to Roy and no doubt others) arouse "bitter anger" in him. In short, France to his mind has definitively ceased to be. The only allusion to any nostalgia for it in the articles from this year is to that felt by Turold, an eleventh-century poet living in exile in Britain. Henceforth, "the ruinous power of history" must simply be given free rein.

This was no mere state of resignation, however. For one thing stood between Blanchot and what he calls "pathetic nihilists who conveniently salvage from their downfall a determination to bemoan it": *literature*. By 1943, Blanchot had begun to acquire status and enjoy recognition in the cultural world that continued to thrive under German occupation.[9] After the publication of his two novels in 1941 and 1942, his critical writing was beginning to command respect. The articles he devoted to Jean Paulhan's *Fleurs de Tarbes* appeared in a slim volume in 1942,[10] and in 1943, to his puzzlement and avowed regret, if what he said at the time and since is to be believed, Gallimard brought out a selection of the "Chronicles of Intellectual Life" with the title *Faux pas*.[11] On July 16, Gallimard founded the Prix de la Pléiade, and Blanchot became one of the judges, alongside André Malraux, Albert Camus, and Jean-Paul Sartre, among others.

As an established novelist and critic, Blanchot was now able to speak with an authority that in all other domains he had relinquished. Repeatedly in the articles that appeared in 1943 he passed severe judgment on the contemporary novel and its practitioners. On occasions that could be pointed: without mentioning him by name, Blanchot scornfully dismissed a novel by Robert Brasillach in May.[12] He consistently condemned realism in the novel and denounced novelists who were too timid to explore what the novel can offer. All of this is summed up when he wrote: "The novel has almost ceased to be a literary genre, because it has abandoned what is arbitrary about formal rules in favor of the no less arbitrary imitation of 'reality.'" He made a similar point elsewhere: "How many novels deserve to be considered as literary works? We have ourselves frequently had occasion to express doubts of that sort, and an examination of current output would tend to encourage such pessimistic theories." And defending the influence of the American novel against critics who saw it as a danger, he wrote: "The current state of our novel is such that it has nothing to lose by venturing down trails that have been so brilliantly blazed by the richest forms of contemporary novel writing."[13] Finally, in "The Pure Novel" he distinguished between existing novel practice and the sort of experiment for which André Gide provides a model before concluding, "the pure novel, whatever its failures, deserves more attention perhaps than well-rounded works of objective narrative. It is in search of the unknown. It demands what it is inaccessible."

Significantly, however, it is not the novel that provides a means of confronting disaster in Blanchot's eyes. It is poetry. Though he was not known as a poet, Blanchot's interest in poetry at this time was marked.[14] On a number of occasions, he invokes poetry for its relationship to ruin. Writing about Jean Tardieu, for example, he pointed to "what makes poetry endure beyond the ruin to which it aspires." Gérard de Nerval's "Artémis" arises from a "deep sense of the ruin of words." And writing toward the end of 1942 about that other "Jeune France" group that brought together some of the nineteenth-century Romantics, he observed: "[they] claim to represent a total form of Romanticism. This does not mean that they are a little more Romantic than Lamartine or Victor Hugo, but that they already exist beyond Romanticism's limits, as a force that, in destroying everything it cannot tolerate, is nothing but a pure image of destruction. They aim to turn literature into the ultimate road to catastrophe."[15] The world of such writers "not only takes the place of the real world where we live our uneventful lives; in the process of destroying that world, it also destroys itself, and having rendered the visible and the invisible equally suspect, it leads the eye beyond the ruins . . . toward a stranger, more unnerving land, toward *something like nothing*, which can only be conveyed to us through a sort of imageless dream."[16]

We see here that for Blanchot, literature as poetry is the only resource left to man, once the past has definitively swallowed up every feature of the known world. But this is not simply because it *reflects* the ruin of all that once was. If poetry yields to the lure of nothing that has ensnared the modern era and acquiesces totally in the destruction of the world, this is not just nihilistic complacency: With the birth of the modernity, ruin and destruction have become the privileged domain of poetry. Something Blanchot says about Rimbaud in 1943 in an article included in *Faux pas* makes this perfectly clear:

> Poetry exists only through what threatens it. It needs to be able to succumb in order to survive. It is reborn only when destroyed. Until the poet of *Illuminations* it had attained its own calling into question only in actual catastrophes, borrowed ruins that to the end remained foreign to it. . . . But with Rimbaud it succeeded in disappearing into a truly poetic, that is to say imaginary, disaster.[17]

Here, in a nutshell, is where Blanchot stood in 1943. He had discovered the *writing of the disaster* that would occupy him for the rest of his life. Until Rimbaud, literature as poetry could only become aware of its own essential destructiveness by looking for objective counterparts to it in the events of history, what he calls "actual catastrophes and borrowed ruins." After Rimbaud it became capable of *true* disaster, which happens not in the world, nor just in the mind, but in language considered as what constitutes poetry's relation to itself. Henceforth and in anticipation, absolute destruction and the ruin of the real world can be as it were embraced and comprehended *as* disaster, because poetry has turned destruction into a new order under the harsh and implacable rule of imagination when it is stripped of all image and becomes pure resemblance.[18] Nothing is always "something *like* nothing." Poets have known this for some time, and now their time has come.

There would seem to be little for our comfort in such an outlook. The poet is a sort of malevolent demiurge, surveying the ruins of our world for signs of imperfection, and endlessly disappointed by our attempts at apocalypse.[19] But the fact remains: Blanchot does not write poetry. The silence he lays claim to with regard to contemporary events is echoed by his silence in that domain. Indeed, after 1942 he would publish no literary writing at all until the war was over. When he did so, it consisted once again of narrative fiction.

How can this be reconciled with his defense of poetry during the Occupation? It is here that Blanchot's true originality is apparent. If nothing is always "something *like* nothing" for poetry, that could simply allow the writer to live in a state of saturnine detachment from a world in ruins. But it also indicates that nothing is never *really* nothing: detachment is never totally possible; something *goes on* in which the writer remains engaged. Consequently, if poetry exposes the mind directly to nothing, it also endlessly defers the advent of nothing by interposing its own processes—referred to by the word *like*—between nothing and the mind. If being a nihilist is pathetic and absurd because to speak of nothing is to place something (language) out of nothing's reach, that same absurdity is transformed by poetry into the very structure of its relation to the world.

It is that *relation*, rather than any form of poetic practice, that interested Blanchot. What he took from it was not the capacity for destruction but the perpetual stepping back *from* destruction that the words "something *like* nothing" encapsulate. In November he wrote, "Who does not sometimes believe that the end of time is near, and that the worst ordeal is about to happen?" That state of imminence, that endless waiting on the brink of destruction, is henceforth the position from which Blanchot will write. And rather than to poetry, whose temporality traverses language in the instant, it is to narrative in its slow-footedness, in the temporization with which it endlessly defers the end, that he will turn for a mode of writing in which destruction will be both embraced and overcome.

Nicholas of Cusa

Amid all the confusion of the fifteenth century, an age of transition that had left the Middle Ages behind yet had still to glory in the brazen splendor of the Renaissance, the name of the cardinal from Cusa remained forgotten for a long time. Though he was one of the major figures of his time, overseeing the affairs of the Church as its leader for several years and using his diplomatic talents to pursue the most delicate negotiations, none of this temporal glory did anything to ensure that the reputation of his writings would endure. He had few readers in the sixteenth century, and if Copernicus and Kepler recognized the originality of some of his views, he was appreciated by philosophers and humanists only thanks to the fraudulence of Giordano Bruno, whose work is borrowed in part from Cusanus, and who is consequently the lucky beneficiary of the latter's prestige and celebrated death. Leibniz showed little knowledge of a body of thought that today appears so close to his own, and as for Descartes, to mention him only once, he demonstrated that he knew nothing about Cusanus at all. In the nineteenth century, Friedrich Schlegel paid homage to him, then German scholarship took him up, and a whole series of historical studies and critical works finally restored him to his rightful place in the history of philosophy. In France, numerous thinkers consolidated Nicholas of Cusa's reputation. First came Lefèvre d'Étaples and his friends, who published and wrote commentaries on his work. Most recently, Maurice de Gandillac has written two major volumes, one devoted to *The Philosophy of Nicholas of Cusa*, the other consisting of a translation of his *Selected Works*.[1]

The historic role played by Nicholas of Cusa is linked to the general direction of this thought. This son of a boatman from Trier (whose name was Krebs) sought persistently to reconcile the Western and Eastern Churches, and he even dreamt of a grand council which would bring together not only Hussites and Greeks, Jews and Arabs, but even Persians and Tartars. In 1437, acting on behalf of Pope Eugenius, he would invite the patriarch of the Eastern Church, Emperor John VIII Palaiologos, to Constantinople along with delegates from the Greek Church and attempt to include in this conciliation the rebellious members of the Council of Basel. Later, when he had become a cardinal, then bishop of Brixen in the Tyrol, the misfortunes of the time confronted him with discord, violence, and even war. The union with the Greeks dissolved. Constantinople collapsed. He advised the Pope to beg Mohammed II to convert, but to no avail. The Turks advanced through Europe "with artillery and new types of weapon," and without a bloody victory it would have been the end of the West. In spite of these events that were so ruinous for his dream, Cardinal Cusanus did not abandon his projects. On the one hand, as the vicar temporal of the Papal States since the election of his friend Aeneas Sylvius as pope, he fought, excommunicated, and planned a crusade. But as a philosopher, he was writing a *Critical Examination of the Quran*, which offered an interpretation designed to familiarize Muslims with the Christian faith. When he died, he hoped he would have disciples. Above all, he thought that men of whatever sort would approach truth through ever more precise approximations, but that they would never reach it because it is inaccessible.

It is clear that with such universalism, with this "concordance" that was not limited to Christendom but embraced Infidels and took account of natural diversity, Nicolas of Cusa broke with the principal tenets of the medieval mind. His dream was not of a universal empire, established dogmatically on force and authority. He imagined rather a sort of Republic without frontiers, whose various manifestations would extend to cover all known lands by means of a religious concordat. Human community cannot be organized hierarchically; whether he be emperor or pope, a leader derives his authority only from general assent, and elections themselves have no significance outside of the discussions that lead up to them, and which serve to make possible a sort of empirical harmony. Every being is a reduced yet real expression of absolute Being. All finite reality carries within it the all-embracing fecundity of the Infinite. It would be sufficient therefore for each individual to develop fully according to his own specific law for universal concordance to be possible. But man's freedom, the pride that makes him more than he is and the idleness that prevents him from being all that he should be, give rise to schisms, spread disorder, and by isolating individuals and groups, expose the State, the community, and the Church to faction and scandal.

The "ecumenicalism" of Nicolas of Cusa clearly appeals to a principle that provides one of the essential features of his thought. The Infinite is immediately and totally present in the finite, and at the same time, the Absolute remains transcendental in relation to all of its manifestations. Those are the two inseparable aspects of a single fundamental argument. All of the problems that he examines directly or indirectly in his different works presuppose this twofold truth: total immanence and real transcendence. What is the mind? A power whose every act posits the absolute as indubitable, yet that comprehends it as what is ungraspable, as a presence that escapes all definition, all precise measurement, all complete intelligibility. What is the world? The external manifestation of Infinite Fecundity, and at the same time, a set of signs that only acquires complete significance because its cause resides in the invisibility of God. Finally, what is God? The pure Unity of which nothing can be said, nothing affirmed and nothing denied, and the root Unity whose life-giving presence can be experienced behind various enigmas in the heart of every creature. These different arguments thus embrace a twofold movement in which the mind posits and then maintains the opposite of what it posits, affirms more than it can affirm, not only goes beyond what it says but only recognizes the truthfulness of this because it is clear that it can also say the opposite.

If we look for those points where Nicolas Cusanus breaks with medieval thought, we may note that first of all, he rejects Aristotelianism by rejecting the traditional use made of the principle of identity. The point of departure for intelligence is a paradox, the sense of something necessarily impossible, "the discovery of a series of fertile contradictions that carry within them the seeds of what can overcome them." Both reason and the mind must become aware of the coincidence first of opposites, then of contradictions. Reality offers us examples of this at every turn, and any person can grasp their profound meaning. From the analysis of geometrical figures or the examination of the infinite series of numbers, reflection derives the mystery of a perfect proportion that eludes all proportion, a quantity that lies outside of any assignable quantity, an absolute wound that is subject to no measurement of any kind. What is more, the existence of the circle and the polygon, forms that are ultimately identical, emphasizes the need to go beyond the principle of noncontradiction. If we imagine an infinite circle, we see that its diameter is identical to its circumference since both are infinite, and that in those conditions, a straight line is no different from a curved one. At the heart of this observation lies a passage to the limit. There is a moment when the polygon turns into a circle, when an angle becomes a straight line, when what is mobile and whose speed can no longer be increased becomes immobile. At that limit, the figure is at one and the same time a straight line and an angle, a polygon and a circle, a limited value and a limitless one. In it, intelligence apprehends the coincidence of opposites.

It is thus through a veritable dialectic that the intellectual process is enacted, and no longer through an effort at definition aimed at extracting what is identical from what is identical, as in Aristotelian reasoning. This passage to the limit presents the mind with a mystery that it can never totally overcome. In itself, the passage remains hypothetical, it is not achieved, it remains as a *terminus ad quem* toward which successive approximations allow us to direct ourselves without its ever becoming actual. It is the perfect sign of immanence. Unknowable as such, what is transcendental expresses itself through the ordered transformations of finite beings as the law of their progression and as the limit that guides them. It is the inexhaustible totality that can be grasped at the heart of the most elementary relation; it is the noncoordinate whose presence appears to thought in the constantly insufficient nature of its own coordinations, and that obliges it to go beyond itself constantly, through renewed conjectures, in an ascending movement that can never reach its peak. Thus it is that the mind acquires the means of its power and the method of its progression. Reason that provides its inner form and that seeks the measurable character of phenomena, brings about a synthesis of opposites. It reveals the successive states of a body and combines colors, speeds, temperatures, and so forth into a law of progression between two "limits." Understanding completes this task and produces a synthesis of contradictory elements. It is understanding that, presupposing the passage to actual infinity, determines an infinite velocity that is equivalent to no velocity at all, an infinite triangle that is simply a straight line and infinite heat that is identical to infinite cold. This synthesis of the large and the small is still just an intellectual synthesis, however. If it is only possible because of the action on the mind of a presence that exceeds all human activity, it expresses the organizing activity of consciousness at the human level, consciousness that make positive use, at the level of relations, of an infinite power that is itself transcendental. In order to go beyond this stage and rise to the level of transcendence, it will therefore be necessary to suspend the highest synthesis of the mind and, beyond all mental representations, acquire a presentiment of the inaccessible essence of the Infinite in itself.

Maurice de Gandillac, from whom we have borrowed these analyses, has shown that Nicholas of Cusa's thought was close to that of Meister Eckhart and the Rhineland mystics. It may even be said that Cusanus's system expresses at the level of logic and even of physics some of the demands [*exigences*] for which the Thuringian master had provided a mystical formulation, with an admirable sense of the absolute. But the cardinal remains impervious to any sort of inner experience in the strict sense. The nonknowing [*non-savoir*] that he arrives at is not the result of a complete denuding of the soul, as it is for Meister Eckhart; it does not signify the anguished death through which the soul renounces everything, even God, and casts itself into an abyss where it is ready to lose everything and to lose itself. The nonknowing, "the learned ignorance" of the master Cusanus, is the conclusion of a dialectical process in which discursive knowledge, having affirmed, denied, and then combined affirmation and negation in a synthesis and finally suspended that synthesis in order to go beyond it, naturally reaches the Ungraspable. What is interesting about this way of thinking is the fact that while it claims to preserve absolute transcendence, it is seeking to identify the pathways that remain open and allow it to be reached; it wants the mind, through the activity that is peculiar to it, to have the same experience of God as that for which the mystics impose total passivity on the soul; it replaces nonknowing considered as a break with discourse and the sacrifice of all thought, with a discursive nonknowing that is the culmination of a progression and the expression of a continuous development. As a result, in spite of the precautions which defend it, transcendence in Cusanus's doctrine appears constantly fragile and under threat. It lies beyond all series, but the abyss that signifies it is not that true abyss that only those who leap into it with a sense of the uncrossable can ever truly cross. It presupposes that the mind possesses everything it requires in order to understand it, at least negatively, without being dashed to pieces.

Among the significant features of Cusanus's philosophy, it is therefore necessary to stress the capacity of consciousness that is both a source of existence and a source of value, and that, in the process of reflecting on itself, constructs out of sense data on which it imposes limitations an increasingly intelligible universe that is a match for man. With all necessary care, Maurice de Gandillac identifies the links that can be made with Kantian idealism. He insists, too, on the importance that Nicholas of Cusa attaches to mathematical knowledge; to know one must measure, and also weigh if possible; even sensuous qualities, were we to be able to penetrate their nature, would reveal themselves to us as determined by a network of mathematical formulas. One of the dialogues of the *Idiota* shows that air has weight, and that by adding together the mass of the smoke and that of the ashes, we should be able to discover the original mass of a burned object. Last, mention should be made of what is one of the Cardinal of Cusa's best-known achievements: the fact that he not only posited the motion of the earth and the ultimate destruction of the stars, but he also denied the very idea of a fixed point, of a single central reference point for all cosmographical relations. This position makes him a more modern precursor than either Kepler or Copernicus.

The influences on the Cardinal were numerous. The Neoplatonists, Pseudo-Dionysius the Areopagite, the Rhenish school, the mathematicians of his time, not to mention the nominalist tradition, all provide his thought with more than just points of departure and often supply the very themes that it combines. Moreover, as a man of action who was responsible for the Church during the years when the world trembled, and who was obliged to go on endless journeys, he had very little time to let his work mature, and it will require the enforced leisure of a period spent in the fortress of Buchenstein for him to clarify the significance of his mathematical discoveries. The form of his works is therefore not perfect. Their vocabulary is always vague, and their mediocre Latin, with its laborious combinations of words, makes one yearn for a less hasty philosophical language. Nonetheless, to read the treatise on *Learned Ignorance*, the dialogue of the *Idiota*, the treatise on the *Vision of God*, and the dialogue of the *Bowling Game* is to discover everything one could expect to find in a mind that has boldly distanced itself from Aristotelian logic, that has the acutest of scientific intuitions, that discovers a sort of monadology before Leibniz seemingly as an amusement, amidst the labors of a difficult reign, during the years when the Turks capture Constantinople and Gutenberg invents the printing press.

—January 6, 1943

The Correspondence of Madame de La Fayette

No book can ever have been put together with greater care than the one that has brought together Mme de La Fayette's correspondence for the first time.[1] It contains all the explanations one could wish for, and the only inaccuracies to be found in it are of the sort that neither erudition nor delicacy of taste can remedy in the case of a subject that is open to so much conjecture. The present edition was produced by the late lamented André Beaunier. He devoted copious notes and all kind of patient study to it, so as to make the order in which he presented the letters nearly definitive. Then, in twenty-four little notebooks, he reproduced extracts from memoirs and letters, with the aim of clarifying the obscure allusions contained in a text with which he was admirably familiar. His work has been continued and completed by the current editors. It will give its readers the utmost pleasure.

It is quite remarkable that Mme de La Fayette's letters have never been brought together before. They were known about. Various publications had drawn attention to the main elements, but the correspondence as a whole remained scattered across a range of rare or inaccessible works. It is true that what has survived seems very slim alongside what was actually written. Brief notes penned with no literary intention, business notes or hasty expressions of friendship are more or less all that has come down to us. Moreover, Mme de La Fayette was a reluctant correspondent, or at least she claimed to be. Numerous letters of hers exist only in order to tell people that there will be no letter, while others, like those of Mme de Sévigné, denounce the folly of writing ("Your taste for writing to everyone," she writes to a friend, "still endures; I have lost mine in the case of everyone; and if I had a lover who required letters from me every morning, I should leave him"). But such coquettishness did not prevent Mme de La Fayette from sending as many as and even more letters than most of her contemporaries. Some were about art. These were more extensive and more polished. The others, written without any frills, waste no time on the pleasures of fine style. Those are the ones that we still possess.

They are perfect, and though lacking style, their style is extraordinary. People have sometimes preferred them to those of Mme Sévigné; and who could not find them preferable, provided one values sobriety more than grace, sharp delivery more than imaginative effort, elegance of tone rather than elegance of figure? They lack neither delicacy nor refinement, but what is delicate and refined about them is combined with a firm, proud movement, and we enjoy it while feeling that it is utterly natural. Haste is her best ally, and also anger or sharpness of temper. In such cases, the negligence is incomparable, and it is enhanced by an invisible art that reaches its goal in a few deft moves. Other letters are less spontaneous. While still a girl, she writes to Gilles Ménage in a studied manner, seeking and finding stylistic flourishes that she puts on display. With Pierre Daniel Huet, that soul of refinement, she is also sometimes less simple, and her letters to Mme de Sévigné are curiously influenced by the latter's correspondence, and become more playful, flighty, and picturesque than they usually are.

But in almost every case, her nature has the upper hand. After one or two precious turns of phrase she reverts to the detached concision, the cutting pride and the truthfulness that is entirely a matter of movement and tone, and that constitutes the essential perfection of classical art.

These discontinuous fragments nevertheless allow us a sense of the continuity that links together the various periods of Mme de La Fayette's life. Her long friendship with Ménage is a joy to consider thanks to the mixture of badinage, seriousness, and real affection it contains, to the nuances that time brings to it and to the twists and turns one guesses it contains. What is more, theirs is the only correspondence that extends over such a long period and that gives the impression of being complete. Without it, we would just have a few scattered notes. Ménage, who was initially her teacher, is for Marie-Madeleine de La Vergne a mind that she admires, and who, thanks to his influence in the world of letters, represents in her eyes the knowledge and literary talent that she would like to possess. What is more, the thirty-eight-year-old professor is in love with the fifteen-year-old girl, as he has been, more or less successfully, with many another lady. (He was the cause of what Mme de Sévigné called her "martyrdom.") He showers her with elegies, madrigals, and letters in Latin or Italian; he asks for her opinion more than he offers her advice; he writes the name "Laverna" everywhere. The first part of the correspondence is thus devoted to a charming exchange of civilities. The girl is full of attentiveness and admiration. She guards this friendship jealously and is proud of it. She wants it to be even more faithful and more certain. She is critical if it appears too hasty or not prompt enough. She is anxious about what might weaken it. In all, she shows as much candor as she does coquettishness, diffidence as well as sincerity, and when she is reproachful, her words take on a sharp, almost imperious tone. (On September 12, 1656: "A letter informs me that you are in love with Mme de Montbazon. Tell me a little about this . . . for though I am merely your friend, I am convinced that a mistress would be detrimental to me, as I believe all mistresses are to friends." And on January 30 1657: "You often write to me with such haste that I would almost prefer not to have any letters from you at all.")

When Marie-Madeleine de La Vergne becomes Countess de La Fayette, her relations with her former teacher do not change. She continues to live far from Paris, she displays the same contented affection for the man who sends her the latest books—*Clélia* or the *Almanach of Love*—and she is totally devoted to him. However, Mme de La Fayette has to manage her husband's affairs. Litigation, in which she proves a both stubborn and canny adversary, takes up much of her time. She is constantly engaged in petitioning, organizing procedures, and studying verdicts. Ménage does what he can to further her interests, and the letters she sends him reveal the attention to her affairs and the somewhat selfish concern for herself with which contemporaries sometimes reproached her, and about which La Rochefoucauld himself appears to have had cause to complain (when his grandson married the young Mlle de Louvois, in a match arranged by Mme de La Fayette in order to obtain the favors of the minister). Then the La Fayettes came to Paris. The letters Ménage received were now no more than brief notes designed to fix up a meeting or respond to an invitation. But their friendship remained strong. It would even seem that she allowed the genial man of letters to become occasionally too gallant in his use of language, whereupon Mme de La Fayette would tartly call him to order; this is the only case of such severity to be found in her correspondence. ("But are you aware that you will not see me again, if your friendship increases so intensely. You know perfectly well what limits I have placed on it. In your letter you write so fondly that were you to send me similar ones too often, I would scold you very sharply. Take great care not to make us fall out once and for all. I do not believe that love casts spells, but I do believe that the brain can become quite giddy.") Their relations continue on a friendly basis, with one or two setbacks. It is generally Ménage who loses his temper. He becomes annoyed and stops writing. The tone is that of a misunderstanding that subsides or a quarrel that leads nowhere. Then everything settles down again. This goes on until January 1661, and on that date we read a rather brusque, rather cold note, which will be the last she sends him before a silence begins that will last for twenty years.

At that time Mme de La Fayette had been separated from her husband for six years. The correspondence does not shed any light on their separation. The only allusions there are to her marriage are there in order to underscore the excellent nature of their relations. (To Ménage in 1656: "Taking care of my house occupies me and provides me with numerous distractions; and since in any case there is nothing that aggrieves me, since my husband adores me and I love him dearly [this nuance is perhaps merely a matter of delicacy], since I am the absolute mistress in my own home, I can assure you that I find the life I lead to be an utterly happy one, and I ask God for nothing other than for it to continue.") André Beaunier believed, like Émile Magne and Harry Ashton, that this separation could be explained without assuming there was any drama behind it. M. de La Fayette returned to the Auvergne to administer his estate. Mme de La Fayette stayed in Paris to look after her children, her court cases, and her social life. Their differing inclinations and the reason that governs their relations provide the explanation for a distance that was less remarkable in those days than it is now. On the subject of the friendship between the Countess and the Duke de La Rochefoucauld, the correspondence is no richer in allusions. A letter to Mme de Sablé at a time when Mme de La Fayette did not yet enjoy the confidence of the writer offers this judgment on the *Maxims*: ("It is precisely because your 'maxims' [Mme de Sablé's] are honest and reasonable that I wish to read them, and that they convince me that all people of good sense are not as convinced that corruption is everywhere as M. de La Rochefoucauld is.") Another letter mentions the rumors that the closeness of their relations has given rise to ("I hate to death the fact that people of his age [she is referring to a youth, the Count de Saint-Paul, who is moreover the illegitimate son of de La Rochefoucauld] can believe that I ever engage in dalliance. I fear we must appear to them to be a hundred years old as soon as we are older than them, and they are quite ready to be astonished that they are still dealing with people. . . . In any case, I don't want him to think anything, except that he is one of my friends.") In the rest of the correspondence there are numerous references to the duke as her dearest friend and most esteemed confident, and when he dies in March 1680, we learn of his friend's grief only through the descriptions that Mme de Sévigné has left us in several letters. During these years, while living the life of a society lady, the countess actively looks after her interests. The letters from Louvois, of which there are quite a few, are brief, formal, and conventional, and their purpose is solely to respond to requests concerning the young La Fayette, who was now the colonel of a regiment. Or else they correspond to the actions that Mme de La Fayette undertakes on behalf of Madame Royale, the Duchess of Savoie, whose emotional life is complex while her political situation is unfortunate, and whose former companion at the Visitandines convent acts as her go-between in royal circles. Then the Countess becomes the author of *Zayde* and *The Princess of Cleves.* As one of her correspondents puts it, she has wealth, she has dignity, she has unequaled merit, and the greatest and finest reputation in the world.

But finally old age comes, and with it frailty and bereavement. Her husband is dead; the Duke de La Rochefoucauld is dead; her best friends pass away. (She writes to Mme de Sévigné with admirable verve: "You are old, the grounds of Les Rochers are overgrown with woodland, catarrh and pneumonia beset you, you will grow bored, your spirit will sadden and decline: all of that is certain.") Concern for matters of the soul has given way to care for the heart. The Countess feels the need for spiritual guidance; the Abbé de Rancé writes to her; the Abbé du Guet alerts her to the languishing of her conscience in language of the grandest style; she herself discusses spiritual salvation with her friends. It is then that her friendship for Ménage is reawakened. The old man of letters, now well past his seventieth year, is crippled and suffers from quite serious infirmities, but he still receives visitors, and his mind remains alert and curious. The last letters that pass between the two friends are among the most touching that one could ever read. Mme de La Fayette talks of nothing but her ailments and her friendship, but one never tires of hearing her repeat: "I have my vapors; it is a devil of a condition, the vapors; I have a serious cold in the head; I have pains in my stomach and pains in my heart; I am astonishingly thin; I have an obstruction in my bowels"—all of which is said with such unaffected style that one would willingly read a hundred notes in this vein. For his part, Ménage sends her the news that he hears about. He recalls the accolades of yesteryear. Even with one foot in the grave he is still zealous and still faithful. It would be impossible to find a greater degree of humanity and sentiments more worthy of note in such slight correspondence. It is appropriate that the last letter of Mme de La Fayette's that we know of should be addressed to that friend of a lifetime, three weeks before his death, and should honestly discuss the affairs of the world as if they could go on forever.

It would have been gratifying had the correspondence of Mme de La Fayette also been that of the author of *The Princess of Cleves*; but we must resign ourselves: the Countess's discretion on the subject of her works was as great as her restraint when it came to matters of the heart. She mentions *Zayde* once to Huet, who has the task of correcting and improving it; and *The Princess of Cleves* once to the chevalier de Lescheraine, in order to disown it most artfully: ("Personally I am flattered that people suspect it is by me, and I believe I would admit to the book, were I sure that the author would never come and ask for it back.") To Ménage she makes one mention of the latter novel, recognizing that she alone is its author and that La Rochefoucauld and Segrais had nothing to do with it, apart from a small amount of correction. Finally, to Lescheraine she also says this about her book (while disowning it): "I find it very agreeable, well written without being excessively polished, full of admirably delicate things and deserving of more than one reading. Above all, what I find in it is a perfect imitation of the world of the court and the way people live there. There is nothing novelistic or recherché [*grimpé*] about it, and indeed it is not a novel: properly speaking it consists of memoirs and that, I am told, was the title of the book, but it was changed." All that has long been known about, and simply teaches us what we know already. A few years ago, André Beaunier published a hitherto unknown manuscript entitled *The Triumph of Indifference*[2] and cautiously attributed it to Mme de La Fayette. It is a conversation against love between two girls, one of whom trusts it, while the other complains of the unhappiness it causes and prefers an attitude of "happy indifference." Is this dialogue by the future author of *The Princess of Cleves*? It is alert, written in flowing language and somewhat muddled in its reasoning; but there is nothing to corroborate this doubtful attribution. However, the correspondence provides two clues. In 1653, when she is twenty, Mlle de La Vergne writes to Ménage: "I am delighted that you are not capricious. I am so convinced that love is an uncomfortable thing that I am full of joy that my friends and I are free from it." But is that any more than a flash of wit? Ten years later, in a letter to Huet, she acknowledges that she has just written "on the edge of a tablecloth" "a disquisition against love" (and she intends that this should not be divulged to anyone). Thanks to what she confides, even though it proves nothing except that Mme de La Fayette enjoyed indulging in flirtatious casuistry in an era when everyone did likewise, we may assume that we are in possession of a sort of preparatory version of *The Princess of Cleves*. It is a pleasant thought, and one that is attractive enough to be believed.

—January 13, 1943

The Book

It is generally acknowledged that civilization is based on both a respect and a disdain for the book. Someone who is exclusively interested in the printed word shows undue reverence toward signs and pure values, but the burning of libraries will always be the calamity that foretells the death of the mind. To burn a book, to write a book: It is between those two actions that culture inscribes its conflicting oscillations. This dual movement extends even to the way a work is considered. Someone who is presented with a printed work is tempted to relate to it either by deriving a set of intellectual values from it, or by considering it as a thing, an object to be contemplated from without. In the first case, thought consumes the book, reduces it to naught, transforms it into itself in a process that rejects all of its material substance; in the second case, the book seeks to become an idol and lets itself be admired without allowing the gaze to make it visible to thought.

As Paul Valéry has observed, these altogether simple remarks determine the overall development and destiny of written works.

They must choose between being read and being seen. Reading makes demands of its own that are almost exclusive. When the eye goes from one line to the next in an infinitely repeated movement, fixing on one then on several words and in no time linking this provisionally isolated group to another associated one, it is effectively blind to the signs it perceives. As soon as it sees what it thinks it sees when an incident such as an abnormal letter or a word out of place exposes the eye to the physical presence of the forms that it is scanning, reading is impeded and the mind is distracted from what it is doing. Reading is possible only when vision is unaware that it is vision. In its everyday mode, this requirement is governed by conditions that can be easily understood. The readability of a text must conform to the basic laws of optics. The shape of the letters, their volume, the length of the lines, the size of the gaps can all be rigorously determined according to elementary physiological experience. For texts, there is an ideal level of clarity and precision that can be accurately measured using technical calculations.

A text that is read differs from a text that is seen through the pleasures it brings and the conditions it presupposes. It is always possible to consider a book as an object and a page as a combination of black and white shapes. The eye receives a set of impressions that it either enjoys or dislikes. It does not seek to transform them, and it apprehends them immediately in their simultaneous arrangement while linking this directly to no particular convention and requiring only that it give pleasure. Whereas before it only perceived signs that had already metamorphosed into ideas, now its sees patches and pure forms; and whereas it was continuously in motion, going tirelessly and imperceptibly back and forth, from one word to the next, one line to the next, in pursuit of the ever incomplete totality of meaning, now it remains motionless in order to perceive the distinct elements that have been assembled in accordance with the laws of a rigorous art into a harmoniously constructed whole. This new way of seeing conflicts in numerous ways with the demands imposed on us by reading. A readable text is a material reality that fades, one that, rather than seeking to endure through the admiration it elicits, is only admirable if it offers itself for immediate destruction and leaves behind no residue. A text designed to appear, on the contrary, is required to be so visible that it is unassimilable by the mind, making it attentive to its physical appearance and its tangible presence through being persistently indiscreet.

These two tendencies between which the book is divided are not totally foreign to each other. They combine by seeking to reconcile what is conflicting about them. They allow the need to read and the wish to see to seek, through a studied harmony, the alliance that will grant them mutual satisfaction. The mind that sacrifices the book to reading in an ideal manner nevertheless needs signs to bring it alive by appearing in a distinct form—for example, a word set in different type, italic say, gently urges the mind to give it special treatment; another, through the capital letters that magnify it, slows down the attention for a fraction of a second and becomes visible the better to make itself understood; similarly, the overall elegance of a text and the pleasure it gives the eye can help intelligence do a better job of changing the little symbols in whose midst it is active into ideas or memories; the joy of seeing stimulates the effort at understanding; there are some books that the mind seizes hold of sensuously before appropriating them for itself through reading, that it possesses in a manner that is not entirely mental, and that it feels it would understand less, were they less handsome and less a source of delectation for the eye. Furthermore, literature has sometimes required that in order to be readable it must also become visible. Linked through the ear with song, its ambition has been to transform the abstract values that every language carries within it into appearances governed by the eye. A poem of whatever sort, however closely attuned it may be to music alone, is made out of space, forms a figure that is not random out of the irregular lengths of its lines, expresses itself not only in words and sounds but in images. The poetry of the calligramme exaggerates this alliance that verbal movement seeks to forge with the concern for plasticity that may be found in any printed sentence. (It should nonetheless be noted that this ambition did not have to wait for Guillaume Apollinaire in order to emerge; its presence can be observed from one century to another; in the sixteenth century, for example, in a book by Geoffroy Tory, the typographical composition is used to represent the objects that the text names.) And one of the most renowned works of French poetry, Mallarmé's *A Throw of the Dice*, is founded on the material enchantment of words, the physical significance they receive from minute changes to their font, the complex aspiration through which the word in its written form seeks to make contact simultaneously with the primary senses and in so doing, impress the mind with its ideographical value.

The example of *A Throw of the Dice* shows not just that printing is an art, but that as a consequence, poetry is no different to printing itself. That is a glorious claim, and it should be enough to put the pure mind to shame for the scorn with which it disdains "the physical aspect of books." Present in every printer who studies the physical layout of a book, in the engraver who seeks the value of a letter, in the compositor who harmoniously distributes the intensity of white and black, there is a Stéphane Mallarmé, that writer for whom the task of poetry consisted in linking spatial quantities to letters variously deployed, the precise layout of a page to the rhythm of a sentence and the evocative power of words. The printer is an artist who aims to turn the two opposing ways of becoming attached to a book into a necessary alliance, who succeeds in making reading a profound experience by making it inseparable from a material presentation that is in itself handsome and well judged, and who always composes the abstract imagery of a book so that it accords with the meaning it expresses and the ease of exercise that it offers the mind.

The art of the book is thus closely linked to the shape and harmony of a civilization. It expresses what that civilization is, and perhaps it is the case that a work judges the era with which it is associated by its form as much as by its content. In this regard, the very fine volume that the Éditions du Chêne have just published in the "Tradition française" series with the title *The Book*,[1] and which examines the development of French publishing with reproductions of the finest items in the Bibliothèque Nationale, will be both "read" and "looked at" with the greatest of pleasure. The studies it contains reveal that in the sixteenth century, the book attains a state of perfect equilibrium that in other eras will be no more than a memory. In those days, the printed page is clear and strictly ordered; it can be read in the elegant typeface that artists such as Tory, geometers such as Oronce Fine, or engravers such as Claude Garamond designed with sensitivity and precision in equal degrees; it can be seen in illustrative elements such as borders, vignettes, bands, fleurons, and "florid lettering" that are incorporated into the text and distract the eye only so as to accustom it effortlessly to a long period of uninterrupted reading; last, it is constructed using well-proportioned margins, harmonious line spacing, and a constantly sustained alternation between white and black. Although illustrations remain important and are often the work of the greatest artists, the printed book has broken free from the seductions of illumination. Whereas in the fifteenth century the manuscript is the model to be imitated (the outline of the letters, the use of abbreviations, the dissymmetry of the titles confine the freedom of the calligrapher's hand within a mechanical regularity), in the era of Guillaume Budé's *De Philologia* or the *Chronicle* of Gérard d'Euphrates, the printer takes the decorative forms that adorn the text from the basic elements of printing and skillfully combines the ornamental possibilities that the variety of characters and fonts provides, with culs-de-lampe and ruled borders. After the middle of the sixteenth century, when the Pléiade is emerging and Ronsard is already marked out for glory, this perfect equilibrium finds expression in works that are destined to endure.

The early years of the seventeenth century are less auspicious. The rules that place restrictions on book publishing and the privileges that guarantee the security of the corporations are not always favorable to an art that is wary of traditions that are too stable. The masterpieces of the great writers are generally published in a very mediocre fashion. Indeed, almost without exception, the finest texts, even those that enjoy immediate success, must wait for succeeding centuries to grant them the outer apparel they deserve. However, the founding of the Royal Printing House gives a certain style to the main publications. A new font, the famous University font, is born. Splendid magnificence and grandiose truth replace the sensuous harmony of which the previous era had provided the finest examples. There is a certain monotony, but also a noble, authentic beauty in these serious editions that present religious works in solid quarto form, amply printed and decorated with restraint. The eighteenth century sees the art of printing tend more toward illustration, and Boucher, Moreau le Jeune, Fragonard, Eisen, Gravelot, and Choffard bring to it every possible grace. This is the age when, contemplating the abundance of prettified books, Grimm wrote in his *Literary Correspondence* of August 1764: “Gentlemen, you are too preoccupied with going into print. If you do not stop, we shall very soon be saying that you are selling us M. Eisen’s pretty images in order to pass off your verse, which is not pretty in the least.” But at the same time, the great printer-booksellers such as Didot and Panckoucke are achieving technical progress that will never be matched. The illustrative engraving cannot be more perfect than it is then. Typography aspires to a geometrical regularity that reflects an acme of precision and taste. The “Didots” created by Ambroise-Firmin Didot in 1775 turn every page into a finished design. Nothing could be more regular or more sober. This sobriety persists throughout the nineteenth century, eventually becoming monotonous and dry until the rebirth of Elzevir around 1850 once more allows grace and embellishment to find fortune.

The art of the book in the nineteenth century and probably also in the twentieth is not only remarkable for its extraordinary diversity, but for the increasing role that illustration plays within the text. It is striking that the illustrator, be he Delacroix or Célestin Nanteuil, seeks a deep harmony with the work he is illustrating, but has no time for the harmony created by precise page-setting; he wants the image to be at one with the spirit of the book, but not with its material shape. The architecture is no longer preserved. The composition falls apart. The book is a fine object in its parts, but it no longer exists with the incontrovertible reality that the works of previous eras lent it. It may also be noted that the new processes that allow color reproduction and make available to the printed book the effects that transformed ancient manuscripts into works of art can also tend to pose a threat to the unity of the work, and risk expunging its intellectual efficacy entirely. Between the engraver who uses only blacks and whites and the writer who merely uses a little ink, there is what amounts to an agreement over means: each of them creates a world with almost nothing. On one side, the entire image is suggested with only a few strokes of the pen; on the other, out of what is most abstract in its design, from a few letters that are uniformly shaped, the inner music of the line is born. But color, used as a mechanical means of reproducing images, breaches this agreement between the mind and an art that resembles it, and through the extraordinary facility with which it can be used, it creates more problems for printing than it provides solutions. This is in fact the sort of enigma to which all technical progress gives rise. It was fashionable several years ago to foresee in the way that works are transmitted and reproduced a whole range of unbelievable innovations, the end of the most ancient customs, and even the disappearance of the book. Today, it would appear that these changes have been put off until later, and if the book is in danger of disappearing, it is not because progress requires it.

—January 20, 1943

A Novel and a Tale of War

The importance of Alexandre Vialatte's novel *Faithful Shepherd* deserves to be stressed for several reasons.[1] First of all, Vialatte the man, Kafka's translator, occupies a significant place in literature. To be associated with the writer who created the most solemn and incontrovertible images of human destiny is a merit that far exceeds the minor glories one may acquire through one's own writing. And then there is the fact that *Faithful Shepherd* is a novel about war. But it is a novel that, instead of giving a realistic portrayal of war, absorbs it more profoundly into an inner adventure, describing it indirectly through the effects that it has on a mind that is suddenly expelled from itself and exposed to a devastating truth. Last, the theme of this book is one of those to which contemporary literature has most consistently been drawn. It expresses one of the sole authentic concerns of our times.

War novels, that is to say novels written after a war by those who took part in it, are sometimes good but are rarely of great literary significance. The reasons for this are plain to see. It is very clear in the case of such novels that reality, be it major or minor, can offer the art of the novel only the illusion of a subject. It provides elements, details, and the opportunity to reproduce it in fiction. But that is all. It is commonly thought that a writer borrows subjects from real life (as it can be observed objectively) and then transforms them according to the laws of his heart and the form of his art. This is simply not the case. The subject of a work, which is to say its cause, the grain of its images, and the truth of its narrative, is always linked to an inner discovery. It only has meaning within the specific content of an imagination. It takes shape only in relation to a problem that, experienced inwardly, provides "everyday events" and actual circumstances with their sole source of consistency.

Vialatte's book is a novel that does not represent war or an aspect of war, but describes it as a fatal occurrence for an individual mind, an ordeal whose consequence is that things have become hidden and lost their structure. Who is this Shepherd? Brigadier Shepherd of the French army, number 2404, a man whom fatigue, hardship, cold, sickness, and the horror of a situation he cannot comprehend gradually make obscure in his own eyes. For several days he has been marching alongside men who, like him, have been taken prisoner. Why is he there? What has happened? How can he account for events that have no meaning for him? Marching is an excruciating ordeal. His legs swell up; his head is constantly aching; thirst sends streams from which he cannot drink flooding across the road; incoherent memories threaten his lucidity. What is the meaning of all that? Where is this experience leading? The predominant feature of his wretched state is the enigma that conceals it. His suffering and his discomfort are extreme, but they appear as fatigue and suffering only because they lack any meaning. The truth of events would seem to be linked to their incomprehensible nature. Everything is a problem; everything requires the weary mind to come up with an interminable series of reasons. Shepherd's hallucinations do not trouble him, for he knows they are the product of exhaustion. And yet one of them obsesses him. It is the face of one of his former comrades. He sees it over and over again. It, too, has the look of an enigma about it. He recalls that one day, this Planier entrusted him with a secret that he begged him never to divulge. The more he thinks about him, the more it seems that Planier has come back in order to renew his instruction. That is no doubt absurd, but in the midst of the all the chaos this intrusion is perhaps not without its importance. To respect a command, to keep a secret, yes, that matters. In any case, he was wrong to neglect this instruction. One ought not to forget a friend's wishes. And the secret has indeed been forgotten. He cannot remember it. He does not know what it is he must not tell. He racks his brains in an attempt to remember. He goes round in circles, but to no avail. While he is totally absorbed in these thoughts, the column reaches a town in Alsace. It is here that Shepherd once sat his exams. Now he has returned, defeated and a prisoner. It is pathetic, an appalling sham. Who is responsible for it? Who created these uncanny coincidences so persistently? During the night, Planier's ghost comes to him again. It is a preposterous situation, but it at least provides him with a distraction from more terrifying dreams. The mind cannot bear having nothing to do; it abhors a vacuum, requires duties it can fulfill. And so he clings to this final instruction: He must rescue from the debacle a secret that he does not know, the way a child saves a doll from a burning house.

A little later on, Shepherd wakes up in a cell with a stone floor. Through the bars on the window he sees a little old man dressed like a circus performer, running back and forth along a white wall. He can hear the sound of an accordion. He is alone. What an odd business! Where is he? What do they want of him? Why is his situation becoming more ominous by the day? At first he was in a huge, guarded prison yard, then in a solitary room, and now he is in a jail that is a sort of tomb. Has he done something wrong therefore? Is he guilty of some indiscipline? Did he try to escape? He looks at his wrist and sees that they have removed his identity disc, the one that stated that he really was Brigadier Shepherd, number 2404, the tag that is never removed, not even from dead men. How strange. Something truly abnormal is happening. Perhaps he is mad. But he knows perfectly well he is not mad. He has had visions that were caused by fatigue. He experienced the brief frenzy of the retreat. None of that can erase someone's reason. If he is not mad, therefore, he is the victim of inexplicable scheming; someone has it in for him and he doesn't know why. It is as if he has been mistaken for someone else. Like Kaspar Hauser, who was locked up in a cellar for seventeen years and eventually killed, without ever knowing what his crime was, he seems threatened with having to pay for a misunderstanding which he will never know anything about. In whose eyes is he so important, then? What makes him a problem? What about Planier's secret? Yes, after all, is it not that secret, the one that came back to him in exceptional circumstances? What if it were a state secret! You don't come across state secrets every day, but all it takes is for a friend to be indiscreet and you find yourself implicated forever in a truth that leaves you crushed. So that is what it has come to. He is expected to disgrace himself by revealing something. He has been thrown onto a stage set, into a comic-opera prison, with that ridiculous old man gesturing pointlessly at him amid the sounds of a carnival, laughter and shouting, in order that the wearisome emptiness of things should make him fail to carry out his orders. It is all too clear. He must lose his final reason for living. There is no way out now. Brigadier Shepherd will therefore defend himself by committing suicide. He tries to reach the blue bulb that lights the upper part of the vaulted ceiling. The ceiling is too high. He stands his bed on its end and places a chair on it, making every effort to construct this ridiculous pyramid before climbing up it with infinite care. At last he takes hold of the bulb. He crushes it. He slashes his arm. The blood flows. The show is almost over.

The last two sections depict the long road that must be traveled in order to emerge from a situation that not even death can resolve. Shepherd's wound is not fatal. He is in a hospital for the insane; the treatment, the waiting, the confinement, the nightmares, the ghost of his mare Pantalona on which he tries desperately to flee, Planier's ghost which is always there, the feeling of being rather out of his element in this entirely closed-up house, whose very window panes, stained blue, forbid the sun from shining, all this swinging between delirium and misery makes the hope that is the only thing that could restore him to the true world of things become more remote with each passing day. One night, he dreams he is escaping. After painstaking preparations, he scales the prison wall, runs into a wood, and crosses a river. No one is keeping watch. It couldn't be easier! But it is too easy. You can't achieve liberty without overcoming obstacles. He shouts; he defies the guards. No one comes. What should he do? He is so bewildered that he goes back to the camp; anxiety has become a prison for him, and this prison casts such a long shadow that it follows him wherever he tries to flee. Such is now his fate. When he is freed, he cannot believe in his freedom. When he is reunited with his wife, he is on his guard. You can't just decide to return to a place that you willingly abandoned by yielding to fate. Gradually, however, he calms down. The enigmas begin to fade. The shadow of Planier grows more remote. And it is Planier himself whom he thinks he sees at a café terrace. Is he still crazy? But no, it really is Planier. Well then, what about that secret? he asks. Naturally, the other fellow has forgotten it. Too bad, says Shepherd: "I was foolish enough to link it to some other matters." But this encounter brings about his final deliverance. He has followed the order to the end. He has been faithful to his absurd task. He is saved.

This outcome lacks the authenticity of the story itself. That is because such situations cannot be resolved. They are resistant to all solutions. What makes them true is the fact that there is no way out. As soon as you recognize the absurd, you have to obey it desperately, despite the fact that nothing can cause greater suffering than to obey it. Perhaps you have to be mad to follow its commands, but if you betray them you become the most inconsequential and superficial of people; you are more vacuous than the craziest of men. It would be a complete mistake to see Vialatte's book as merely the novel of a madness brought on by the chaos of war. It is important not for its description of an abnormal psychological state, but because that psychological state appears to express the situation of every human being, and because that situation remains true, regardless of the frenzied circumstances in which it is revealed. Brigadier Shepherd, loyal to a nonexistent secret, has no doubt lost touch with common reason; he displays all of the symptoms of a rather incoherent persecution complex; he has yielded to the temptation that offers misfortune a refuge in solitary insanity. But along with this mental disorder, we are also shown what appears as its reverse, something like the inverted image of the world on a retina: a possible meaning for the order we think we inhabit. Vialatte's hero forms an infantile view of the absurdity that has suddenly become visible to him through a tear in the fabric of reality. He invents a secret, and allows its importance to grow inordinately. He sacrifices himself in order to save it. But compared to the nonsense that has suddenly been revealed to him, his delirium is the epitome of order and harmony; it is infinitely closer to reason than what reason could say about that fundamental incoherence, were it ever to fathom it. He is mad for having held back from madness such as that, for having been unable to focus without either image or myth on the unrelenting purity of the despair that he once encountered. It is that truth that gives Vialatte's book its importance. Written in precise tones that could preferably have been even more sober, even freer of any lyrical superstition, it is made up entirely of familiar details and of circumstances that are almost banal. It leaves no room for the extraordinary. That is what makes it strange.

It is possible to compare Vialatte's novel to the book that Antoine de Saint-Exupéry has just published with the title *Flight to Arras*.[2] In a narrative such as this, from which fiction is excluded, the absurd also has its part to play. The reconnaissance mission over Arras that Captain Saint-Exupéry is asked to fly in the midst of the debacle is a total absurdity. The risks could not be greater, and the results will be totally pointless. The reconnaissance will be of use to no one. Its results will not be transmitted. They will not be made use of. They will never reach a headquarters that has forgotten its orders and will perhaps no longer even exist. With a few highly expressive touches, Saint-Exupéry describes the nonsense of a war that is out of control. We assume that defeat has overwhelmed the high command with problems, that it is inundated with the things it has to do, that it is sending its infantry, its artillery, its tanks, and its planes all over the place while in a state of exhaustion and feverishness where everything is gambled in a single throw. Not at all. The debacle does not generate problems, but conceals them. It is not fever that prevails but unease. No one knows what to do and there is nothing left to do. Everything is mired in an atmosphere of futility and boredom. Saint-Exupéry tells the story of his absurd mission, which requires him to fly into the jaws of death for no other reason than this: Right to the end, a war—even if it is out of control—has to look like a war. The pages he devotes to these episodes of folly have the simple pathos, the raw, immediate expressiveness that made *Night Flight* such a powerful book.[3] In midflight, when the danger is most intense, the pilot begins a meditation that is basically an attempt at seeing off the absurd. His victorious return is also a return to the most reasonable thoughts on the subject of civilization, humanism, and the meaning of French tradition. What is interesting about these thoughts comes from the perilous action during which they came into being. That is why they are unsullied by any political slant, and striking for the honesty of their judgment.

—January 27, 1943

Charles-Louis Philippe

Does the memory of Charles-Louis Philippe live on in the minds of the reading public? In the homage that is regularly paid him by the literary world after more than thirty years of posterity, it is possible at least to see the mark of a reputation that does not fade. Though he died young, he has gone on living among friends thanks to whom he has enjoyed an extended existence. He has been given a second life through the friendship of André Gide, Léon-Paul Fargue, Paul Fort, and Jean Giraudoux. Beyond the grave, he has pursued the career he would have had, if typhoid and meningitis had not effectively cut it short when he was thirty-five. Instead of books by him we have had books about him. And readers today do not read *Father Partridge*, *Poor Marie*, or *Bubu of Montparnasse*, which are in any case out of print, but Jean Giraudoux's study or the book that Émile Guillaumin has just devoted to him with the simple title *My Compatriot Charles-Louis Philippe*.[1]

In the brief pages with which he prefaces the book, Daniel Halévy is right to say that it differs from all the others. It is delightfully simple and supremely engaging. It is a homage paid by sincerity to sincerity, by innocence to innocence. It talks of literature as if it were free of all vanity. Moreover, it is not lacking in shrewdness. Émile Guillaumin is someone about whom Daniel Halévy has frequently written, scrutinizing him with the aid of the profound, ingenuous gaze that he casts over everything. He is thus well known to the literary world. The countryman from Ygrande in the Bourbonnais, who is the author of several respectable books, was the natural choice when it came to writing about the clog maker's son from Cérilly. As his compatriot and his friend, born as he was with no literary experience, drawn like him to literature by a serious urge to write, and just as faithful as he was to his origins, even in the pursuit of an art that appeared to oblige both men to betray them, he sometimes gives the impression that he is telling the story of Charles-Louis Philippe using his own existence. His life is the biographer. It tells us a story that duplicates the one he provides us with. In some of its broad outlines, at least, for Philippe immediately assumed a role in literature that Guillaumin never wished to have.

One of the most touching passages in the book concerns the first visit that the writer from Cérilly pays to the countryman from Ygrande. They do not know each other very well. Charles-Louis Philippe's reputation is only just emerging. But he lives in Paris, and he is a Paris writer. Such an enormous advantage is something that his host finds intimidating. He lives on the farm, among his family, and he is afraid in case some incident will spoil this occasion. Will his plain-speaking father not make some remark about the trouble such an exceptional visit has put them to? Will he not allude to meals that last far too long, to the fact that work in the fields is being delayed? And as for his grandfather, who speaks only in patois and bluntly says what he thinks, will he not also let rip with some dreadful outburst of frankness? Poor Guillaumin is anxious. But everything goes off smoothly. His father, who fought in 1870, tells the story of the siege of Paris. His grandfather talks about witches. And a few minutes later, having retired to his room with his guest, the young countryman is able to read him a few pages of a manuscript, while his guest listens and silently approves.

With that sense of what is unique that allows him to express the truth through what is self-evidently paradoxical, Jean Giraudoux has said that Charles-Louis Philippe was an exception in our literature. It is certainly true that there was something about his vocation that placed it in a class of its own, and if the singular nature of his career appears less visible to us today, this is because a whole tradition of literary artifice has succeeded in concealing what was original and rare about it beneath arbitrary imitations. What is exceptional about Charles-Louis Philippe does not come from his origins. If he is the son of a clog maker, if he comes from a poor family, he very soon escapes the confines of his village, and first as a pupil at the lycée in Montluçon when he was eleven, then as a boarder at the lycée in Moulins at the age of seventeen, he is destined for the École Polytechnique and fails to get in not because he is penniless, but because he is in poor health. Nor does what us exceptional about him stem from some malign fate that, by placing insuperable obstacles in the way of his career as a writer, obliged him with tiresome tactlessness never to forget what he was. For though on leaving the lycée he goes through a difficult period, and though in Paris the job that he finds at the Town Hall allows him to live, but little more, he shares this condition with the majority of writers whose beginnings are traditionally modest. When he starts writing, none of his dealings with either publishers or readers brings him any noteworthy misadventures. He does not receive the Prix Goncourt, but this failure leads to greater fame than any trivial success would have done. No one treats him any differently from the richest of bourgeois writers. He is admired and loved, and it is only his untimely death that focuses attention on what might be considered unjust about a life that was basically one of contentment.

What is exceptional about Charles-Louis Philippe might perhaps come from his art, from a degree of repugnance that he may have felt at the idea of making use of what is aristocratic about all literature in order to express sentiments that bear no relation to aristocracy. But nothing could be further from the truth. The art that in his hands provides an echo of what is natural and instinctive is entirely literary. Discovering Mallarmé no later than his other writer friends, he is as enchanted as they are by this revelation. He likes Tolstoy, but he ranks Claudel higher than anyone, and his preciosity, the boldness of his figures, his attention to words and the precision of his language are all, along with his love of writing, the gift of a vocation that appears totally unaffected by his origins. Like any French writer, he is imbued with culture. He is classically educated. He may have been mistreated at school by prefects, but he won major prizes too, so that the laurels bestowed on him by literature merely continue that admirable tradition. He may well be a clog maker's son, but he belongs to the same caste as his friends Valéry Larbaud and André Gide, because for him as for them, no writer can exist without recognizing that closed and exacting realm which is the domain of images and words. He is thus entirely equipped to become a writer just like any other. His origins are humble, but he receives the same training as the Symbolists or Parnassians. He is attached to his village and to the simple folk he knew there, but his tastes incline him toward hermetic poets or foreign novelists. He is at home wherever literature is resplendent. What is missing in order for him to join the class of those who have no class, who no longer care if they are a general's son like Hugo or a queen like Marguerite de Navarre or a rope maker's daughter like Louise Labé, but who are all the descendants of troubadours, Maurice Scève or Shakespeare? Why does he give the impression not just of not being a proletarian writer, as others from whom he is nonetheless quite different will be called later on, but of not being simply a writer either? What makes him different when everything seems destined to make him blend in?

The fact is, he is faithful: faithful to his class not because of its miseries or the injustices it endures, but out of a feeling of sympathy that is his indelible gift; faithful also to the art he has chosen, and from which his affinity with what is natural and simple will never make him deviate. In fact, there are two ways for a writer to distance himself from the humblest realities and betray popular sentiment. He can enter literature as if it were a brotherhood, with its rules, its customs, its own particular nobility that supersedes all others, and through his mastery of those formal refinements called style, or the literary expression of a sentiment, let himself be stripped of his plebeian origins. That is generally what happens in classical literatures. But it is also possible for a writer to enter literature by rejecting its refinements. By feeling that he is a countryman or a worker before all else, he can reject the purity and perfection of literature that appear like the heritage of a noble and bourgeois culture; being faithful to his class makes him unfaithful to what is classical in literature; in order to express faithfully what he is, he seeks to break away from refined modes of expression. That is, of course, the ideal of populist and proletarian schools of writing. In both cases there is a jettisoning of original truths and tendencies. The classical writer has at his disposal the instrument that would allow him to translate both the dignity and the baseness of the common people without betraying them, but he has allowed the source that could reveal their authenticity to him to dry up. Sympathy for the events of a mediocre life remains intact in the proletarian writer, but he has smashed the instrument, and what he expresses is a caricature that is more insulting and more mendacious than any of the imaginings with which Restif de la Bretonne or Marmontel bestrewed the literature of rural life.

Charles-Louis Philippe's fidelity is that of a writer who accepts literature totally while also totally retaining a sense of his humanity as a common man; who through his art and his training has espoused culture harmoniously, and who at the same time is constantly looking back toward his original condition and his nature, and who, far from perceiving a divorce between the clog maker's son and the precious writer, has the solid conviction that the two persons are one, and accepts with an often tortured conscience the dual responsibility that they represent for him. He thus betrays no one. He feels at one with simple emotions, with the heart worn on the sleeve, and he is also complicit with an inventive and subtle rhetoric; he is both instinct and virtuosity, spontaneous feeling and calculated art; he devotes all of his skill to remaining a primitive. It is this vocation that his work traces out and, to a certain extent, fulfills, but it is also one that is prevented by his death from becoming illustrious through the creation of masterpieces. The work that expresses him best is his admirable *Charles Blanchard*, and all we have of it are fragments. However, it should not be thought that the life of such a writer is a simple one, and with a few details Guillaumin has drawn attention to the contradictory impulses that rent his heart. His fits of moral distress were violent and cruel, and they would sometimes adopt the most facile forms of revolt as a way of escape. It is at such times that he wants "to prepare the masses to make every last demand," or turns against culture, calling on the writer to be "a savage, a barbarian" (but immediately he adds that he must "know his language and be capable of art"). He also says: "As for me, if you want to know my basic feeling here it is: class has left its impression on me. The writers who came before me are all from the bourgeois class. The things that interest me are not their things." At the same time he declares: "Of course, when we think of Balzac or Dante or Claudel, it is without invoking any idea of class, for what they represent, what they convey, is the essential human spirit."

In fact, the division he suffers from is not caused by social disharmony, but rather it reminds him constantly of the wretched condition of the poor and the misery of class-bound servitude. His own distress is entirely within him. It originates at the most intimate levels of his sensibility where love sheds no light. It makes him write: "Suffering has become a sort of obsession with me. All lovely things, the wind in the leaves, the sky, the night, make me suffer even more. I have no love." Or else: "Dark developments, frantic despair . . . I have money, security, I am complimented on every side, people want to be my friend, and all that simply makes me feel more bitter." Or this, which is quite tragic: "My book has brought me some nice letters. . . . I fold them up again and say: what use are they! The one thing you really need you will never have! I think that if one day I have a bit of money, I shall try alcohol." These are the sufferings of a young man, and with age they will fade or no longer be expressed. But they played a part in giving him a sense of unhappiness at its most basic, in keeping alive his immense pity for the wretched life. If his career as a writer is almost illustrious, if it allows him to bridge the gap that separates him from the other classes, his deeper life, the life of his heart, keeps him close to his own kind, and each one of his affairs or passing fancies dispatches a humble messenger to him, be she flower girl or laundry woman, to remind him that he must only ever love little souls from among the people.

This is the life that his work expresses, and that is why, however refined it may be, however justifiably proud and even haughty, it cannot rid itself of a resigned and patient sadness, where emotion is sometimes too drenched in tears. There are few writers whose books are more exactly modeled on life; each of his novels is the expression of a memory and the echo of an experience. *Good Madeleine* is his elder sister, a combination of childhood memories and female presence who, through her death, reveals to him what sadness is. *Mother and Child* is his own melancholic story, in which his mother's affection is the dominant presence. *Old Partridge* is a portrait of the clog maker's neighbor, the crippled blacksmith who wallows in destitution. *Bubu of Montparnasse* is the story of his first affair. *Marie Donadieu* the story of another of his loves, *Croquignole* a study of his colleagues at the Town Hall. *Charles Blanchard* is a portrait of his father. Is this closeness between art and life, this need to express himself in order to relive the humble lives associated with his own, and in so doing bring them to life, a weakness that affects his work? In any case it is the essence of his vocation, the one that allowed him to give artistic form to a humble, hidden world from which art seemed until then to be excluded. Perhaps he derived from his affection a sense of the world in which there is more resignation and wounded gentleness than tragic force. But exaltation is no stranger to his nature, and if he contributed with his books to the impression that the true sources of his inspiration were illness, wretchedness, and misery, it should also be remembered that when misfortune and ill health finally struck with a mortal blow, it was to a radiant world that he sought to bear witness. Guillaumin tells us that during his last moments, he sat up on his bed, took his eyeglasses from the table beside him, leaned on his elbow, and, with his face turned toward the window, stared out for a long time before murmuring: "Isn't it beautiful! My God, isn't it beautiful!" In his work there is hope for that light, for the sun that shines on supreme misfortune and that, for him, rose on the last day.

—February 17, 1943

Novels of the Land

There are numerous novels of the land at the moment, and not all of them are excellent. Even leaving aside those writers who choose the theme because it is fashionable, it is plain to see why a novel that is defined entirely by its subject carries within it the seeds of more than one type of failure. If a novel is a novel of the land, this means that its importance lies in a plot set in the country, in characters who are men of the soil or descriptions that convey a certain sense of nature. In other words, it has every chance of being an atmospheric novel, a realist novel, a psychological novel, in short, a novel governed by convention. What is more, the conventions associated with the novel of the land are among the most false and tenacious that there are. Country folk, whether in Maupassant, Zola, or George Sand, make up the most artificial portrait gallery that the art of the novel can produce. And the causes of this artifice are not always to be found in the excessively literary character bestowed on beings who are by definition quite foreign to literature. Country folk appear fabricated because in order to portray them, literature must become separated from itself, because it borrows from reality a raw material that it transforms insufficiently, and because it imitates what it ought to recreate using its own resources. They are false because they seek to burst onto the literary scene with their nonliterary "truth," into art with their "nature" in what makes it opposed to art, and into the regular forms of style with their simplicity that quickly descends into vulgarity. Hence, the novels that are most faithful to them are generally those in which literary inventions are the most numerous. For example, Jean Giono's novels are often insufferable when they attempt to reproduce certain verbal habits or typical ways of being, but they become natural when they yield to the admirable authenticity of lyricism. It is then that they seize hold of both land and people through images, metaphors, and the innovations that rhetoric can bring.

Similarly, nothing is less simple than Ramuz's art. Everything about it is out of the ordinary, and everything is contrived to give an impression of the extraordinary. The ingenuousness and simplicity that we associate with his name exist in parallel with obscurity and studied reflection. In him, thought dallies with the elemental. Tragic values are concealed behind immediate impressions. Candor, clarity, and spontaneity of expression erect insurmountable barriers around people, around the mystery of mankind. Each character, and in particular those who are most heavily charged with meaning, displays the least incomprehensible instincts, customs, and behavior. When they act, their actions are incontrovertible. When they think, they use ordinary words. They are accessible to the least discerning gaze. But from this simplicity the strange, the unforeseeable, sometimes even the absurd will soon arise. Opacity will feed on the transparency of the simplest substance.

Aimé Pache, a Painter from the Vaudois has a special place in Ramuz's work.[1] That is because this book, which is by now far from new, can be seen as a novel about its author. It is the story of a crisis whose outcome all of his books seek to confirm. It represents a drama that is the drama of his own creative endeavor. Why does a man born into a family of country folk, and who resembles them in his love of the soil, follow a different career and instead of working the land like them aim to excel as an artist? Does he betray those who have made him what he is? Is he prey to a deluded pride? Will he find in the quest for his vocation the same authentic values that were immediately available to him through the natural contact with things? It is easy to imagine that Ramuz actually experienced this drama, then overcame it, but was only able to endure the deep pain it caused him by reliving it in a fiction. Before becoming an artist, he felt the need to express the paradox according to which someone becomes an artist in order to be faithful to himself, but sacrifices something of himself by being faithful in this way.

Aimé Pache's story is quite simple. Seen from the angle that a summary can provide, it is conventional and moral. A boy from the Vaudois region whose family farms its own land—his father is a justice of the peace—has a talent for drawing, and his old teacher encourages him to develop it. Drawing lessons bore him, but he must respect his gift, and while pursuing his studies in primary school, secondary school, and then at university, he becomes more and more committed to what amounts to a single-minded vocation: the wish to be a painter. Circumstances allow him to come to Paris. He withdraws into solitude. For several years, he struggles against the difficulties of his art and the nostalgia he feels for his mother, whom he has left alone, and for the village he has left behind. He feels that what he is doing is not what he wishes he were doing. He persists patiently and obstinately. He shuns the lure of the town. One day, however, the candor and innocence of a young model touch him. Yes, he wants to live, live, and this temptation takes hold of him. He decides not to spend his holidays with his mother as he usually does; when she calls out to him, anxious and ill, he does not even respond. She dies. At her funeral, he merely puts in an appearance. A thirst for life consumes him. Alas, a few weeks later disappointment overtakes him, paving the way for remorse. He goes back to his village, which seems closed to him forever. What has he become? What will he do? Has he not betrayed his own kind? The outcome seems destined to be rather a cruel one. Confident in his own experience, Ramuz restores Aimé Pache to the land to which he has always been faithful. He rediscovers the source of what he has loved and served. He renews his acquaintance with his compatriots. He is reconciled with his ghosts. He is once again the person he was, without ceasing to be the one he has become. He will be a countryman and he will be a painter, "a painter from the Vaudois."

Despite appearances, this is not the story of a return to the land. What is serious and profound about it comes from the question that plagues the young man when he feels within himself the power of his vocation. Why is he a painter? Why did he develop such a passion? Why must he be different from those close to him when he considers himself to be just like them, and do something that no one has ever done either in his family or in his village? Strictly speaking, it is not the change in his social standing associated with this new pursuit that triggers the drama. The Pache family is rich, and it is natural that one of their sons should get an education. There is more than one way of being faithful to the land. Were he to become a pastor, for example, his family would be delighted. But the artist's vocation is an exceptional one. It requires whoever follows it to sacrifice every other value. Aimé Pache's inner drama is not that the man from the Vaudois is in conflict with the painter he is seeking to become, or that he is torn between these two instincts and cannot make up his mind; on the contrary, he feels in his heart that he is a painter out of a deeper attachment to his kind, and that to express what his kinsmen once were is to resemble them in what made them authentic. "Speak," he says, "the way they did, a genuine language, though they did so without knowing it. Paint the way they painted on barn doors, the way they painted on old boxes, oh! how they loved little sprays of flowers." There is thus no conflict between his faith in his origins and his instinct for his art; the same forces that find expression in others through the traditional life of the countryman lead him to express that tradition using the exceptional resources of art. Yet art is not just instinct. It is creation and culture, a power that, once received, is a power the artist makes his own. It is governed solely by its own laws. It is faithful only to itself. Aimé Pache wants to paint a great canvas representing his mother, the servants, the house, the trees, and the dog. But this canvas never quite works. He wastes years of effort on it. What is natural about his wish becomes artificial and unmotivated in his work.

Like all of Ramuz's characters, this young painter, plagued by an impossible dream, is in search of something authentic. An obscure malaise drives him away from the common path. What any of his compatriots can do unknowingly, he must know about in order to do it. He wants to become what he is; between his nature and his will he needs to place the potential for expression, which is a filter that must allow only what is essential to get through. This is a daunting ambition. Even during his apprenticeship as a painter, he obeys nothing but his own powers. He works alone. He experiments, makes mistakes, loses his bearings, and listens only to his own advice. In his moments of discouragement he consoles himself by writing: "I will have had no other master but myself, with my eyes, my heart." This effort leads to a crisis, and the crisis is followed by a resolution. But this happy outcome is based on a misunderstanding. The story of the young model to whom he sacrifices his mother, who leaves him after a few weeks and who allows him through remorse to rediscover his simple love for his family, explains the conclusion but makes it seems contrived. It is tacked onto the drama and holds up its development. Is it possible that once back at Les Bornes, Aimé Pache's artistic scruples could just subside? Is it likely that the canvas he paints—a curious painting that depicts one of his compatriots in the uniform of a dragoon, riding a mare that is rearing up on its hind legs—can for the first time fully satisfy him? Does everything really sort itself out in the end? There is little doubt that if the land has reasserted its hold over the young painter, he is now probably lost to art. On the other hand, we may imagine that the abatement will not last, and that disquiet will once again transform into a seeker the happy man who thinks he has found what he is looking for once and for all.

Paule Lavergne's novel *The Master* has the grace not to promise anything more than what it is, but it keeps its promise faithfully by combining subtlety of form with a story whose message is not without charm.[2] Having married a handsome fellow who is also unfaithful, lazy, and violent, and what is more abandons her after a few months of marriage, why does this young woman go on loving him and hoping for his return even though he has plunged her into despair? This is just a minor mystery, but Paule Lavergne turns it into a very fruitful one. The young woman is rich, and her husband is just a charming ne'er-do-well who passed himself off as the friend of a count but is in fact merely his gamekeeper. She has a noble spirit and a pure heart, and he has done everything to humiliate her. She is loving and sincere; he is vulgar and cruel. What is the secret of her attachment to him? We do not know the answer but we can guess what it is. He loves life, he cannot abide being tied down, and even when he is bad-tempered, violent, and vain he has the nobility to want always to be free and to be a master by nature, even though his condition has condemned him to be in chains. Paule Lavergne's subject could hardly be slighter, but the story by means of which she interests us in its twists and turns could not be more skillfully handled. A twofold dream introduces us to this man of mystery whom those who detest him cannot help liking. At one moment the old servant woman rehearses her grievances against the absconder, and despite all her bitterness hints at the wonderful memory she has of him. At another, the young woman goes back over the story that has ended so badly in search of the reasons for a calamity that she can understand, in order to convey more clearly to us how much incomprehensible happiness she still retains. So we are led from one dream to another, from a story of regret to a story of hope, and through this gentle movement we yield to the charm of an adventure that never loses its simplicity despite the subtlety of its outlines. Landscape has its role to play in this novel of the landed bourgeoisie. We delight in the brief descriptions that wreath the unaffected dialogue in coolness and mist. Admittedly, Paule Lavergne is capable of writing sentences such as, "In summer the land was laden with languor." But she spares us the false simplicities of peasant language, and the rather glib elegance of her style is not as ponderous as the contrived imitations of a style that displays no elegance.

These imitations are lavishly on offer in C.-F. Landry's book *Spring Mist* and Charles Exbrayat's *Jules Matrat*.[3] These two novels are made almost impenetrable by their mannered vulgarity and their ostentatious candor. What could be less simple than this search for a simple language, what a lot of conventions when the claim is that convention has been abandoned! And the inverse preciosity that gives itself the illusion of being truth itself turns feelings that one would wish to consider authentic into ridiculous fictions. Exbrayat's story has all that is required for it to be a touching one. Landry's is skillful enough to draw in the reader. But emotional simplicity and narrative talent are stifled beneath the dishonesty of a realism that is packed with contrivances. Neither drama nor anecdote is possible when an author manages to make us hate what is natural through his abuse of artlessness.

—February 24, 1943

Tocqueville's *Recollections*

To read a few pages from Tocqueville is to enjoy one of the most refined pleasures that the nineteenth century affords us, as we encounter the spirit of discernment in an era when what prevails is blind genius; a purely intellectual passion for knowledge and freedom from deception at a time when enthusiasm is corrupting everything, even politics; and along with magnificent flights of language, an expressive talent made up of a command of language and of clarity in the realm of ideas. Even though Sainte-Beuve, with the instinctive injustice that he displayed exclusively at the expense of his contemporaries, described him as a second-rate writer, it is alongside him and those who were his kindred spirits that the author of *Democracy in America* may be ranked, having revived along with the inferiority that is his lot in a sublimely perverse century the calm judgment and luminous style that were epitomized a century earlier by Montesquieu.

Tocqueville's *Recollections*, including several unpublished fragments, have just been brought out in a new edition by Luc

Monnier.[1] They are not among his best-known works, but through the vigor of their passion and the harshness of their language, the image they provide of a mind so worthy of observation is almost new. As we know, Tocqueville wrote his memoirs solely for himself. They were meant neither for his contemporaries nor for history. His sole aim was to entertain himself, by going over in his mind the turbulent events he had just witnessed and examining their peculiarities. He was ill at the time, and he sought to forget his anxieties about the present (we are in 1850 and 1851) by coming to a just and sincere verdict on the past. Their eventual publication, authorized by him late in his life and undertaken by his great-nephew a mere fifty years ago, was delayed so as to respect the sensibilities of a number of survivors whom the author had assessed uncharitably. Luc Monnier's project aims to restore the original and bolder text, with all due precaution.

These *Recollections* do not go back further than the 1848 revolution, and they extend only to Tocqueville's participation in the government of 1849. Through the nature of their testimony, Tocqueville's quality as a witness, and their narrative impartiality, they constitute a historical document of the first order. They provide history with an interpretation and with facts, and exceptionally, they both refuse to allow interpretation to alter the description of facts, and rid their concern with facts of any excess that might cloud this interpretation. The impressions are those of a memoirist, but the account and the search for causes are those of a historian. Of further interest in these *Recollections*, and of no less significance is their ability to alert us, by means of the self-portrait that the author indirectly traces, to certain features of the liberalism of which he has left us more of an example than a definition. In the public life to which his entire life would have been devoted, had he not been ousted by events of December 2, Tocqueville feels an unease that is due no less to the nature of politics[2] than to the originality of his talent. On his own side, he finds that there are certain weaknesses. He is not as brilliant an orator as he is a fine writer, and perhaps all the less eloquent for bringing to the rostrum those qualities of refinement and ingenuity that he displays in his books. He is as uneasy about manipulating people in the course of day-to-day contacts as he is about whipping up their feelings by speaking on great occasions. He is reserved and sensitive. He is reluctant to debate matters that are important to him, and he refuses to debate those that do not interest him. He pays no attention to mediocre people, and exceptional individuals often lack that rare and refined quantity without which he feels ill at ease. And he is too well bred to have much self-confidence. When he becomes minister of foreign affairs in Odilon Barrot's cabinet, he is just as afraid of the lack of trust he feels toward himself as of the number and scale of the problems he is called on to solve, and if his time at the ministry confirms his sense of his own skills, and so allows him to believe for the first time that he is not unworthy of occupying high office, it also marks the end of his public life, from which in short he finds himself excluded just when he is learning that he can excel therein.

More apt at understanding events than at driving them forward, in the final parliaments of the monarchy and the first parliaments of the Second Republic he comes up against a version of parliamentary government whose defects inspire in him not just suspicion but loathing. When he entered parliament in 1830 he had hoped to get to the heart of politics, but all he finds is a closed, inert world where there is no contact with the outside, a world that is entirely given over to the cultivation of self-interest, ambition for power, or the pursuit of even less noble passions. Tocqueville's verdict on the mediocrity of the July Monarchy is very harsh, but the strength of his condemnation of the practices in which the parliamentary world indulges would appear excessive if it did not always set out its reasons. The brilliant and varied talents to be found so abundantly in the parliament of the time cannot prevent the debates from being tedious and lackluster. These great orators feel only boredom when listening to each other, and in its turn, the entire nation is bored when it listens to them. The parties look around in vain for any serious subjects about which to disagree. They can find only trivial ones when they appeal to principles, and when they turn to self-interest, while they constantly discover very real examples of this, their entire effort is devoted to concealing them hypocritically behind a veil of ideas. For a man such as Tocqueville, whose remoteness from all dishonest ambition, because of its vulgarity, is as great as his disdain for devious thinking, this world where there is agitation but no action, and heated words but no passion, annoys him and drives him to despair by, as he puts it, dragging him down beneath his natural level. Nothing he sees there has any worth, and he expends the greater part of his energy in plotting, condemning this yet unable to avoid it. This reflects one side of his character. His inclination and his qualities make him avoid action. His task is to think about politics not take part in it. Though brilliant and even profound as a writer, as the leader of a party he can only feel embarrassment at his successes and annoyance at his failures. Yet he devotes himself to this life that he does not like and that is beneath him. He sacrifices his projects as a historian to it. He allows it to jeopardize his health. In order to live it, he gives up being fully what he ought to be.

For Tocqueville made politics into a moral obligation. He saw in it a duty imposed on him by his origins, and an inevitable consequence of his convictions. He had an unconcealed passion for it that was nurtured and enlightened in the course of his studies, and rereading the passage in which he confides this, one can only be touched by its simplicity: "I had spent the best years of my youth in the midst of a society that seemed to be becoming prosperous and great once again after regaining its freedom; it was there that I formed the idea of a moderate, regulated freedom, held in check by beliefs, customs and laws; the charms of that freedom had touched me; it had become the passion of my entire life; I felt that I could never be consoled for its loss." He feels attached to this aspiration as much by what threatens it as by what makes it worthwhile. No mind is more clear-sighted than his, and none is therefore more somber. He sees freedom compromised by those who defend it and by those who attack it. Each time an attempt is made to make it more secure, he sees it being further undermined. He witnessed those successive revolutions that only succeeded by destroying their own reason for existing, and that came to an end only in order to begin again in another one. What can a man do in the midst of such uncertainty, as all that he wishes to see stable begins to slide? Should he withdraw into himself and silently worship a pure ideal? But a mind like Tocqueville's is destined to use political means to guarantee the values he holds dear.

His liberalism has a moral aspect and an intellectual aspect. It would be an exaggeration to link it to something that would have to be called virtue, and to make it inseparable from a rigorous ethic. Liberalism does not presuppose saintliness, but it does require a certain degree of moral decency, a preference for aristocratic sentiment, a commitment to the sort of honesty that was widespread in the seventeenth century. Ambition is not to be shunned because it is immoral, but because it is vulgar; intrigue where propriety perishes and pettiness is triumphant must be avoided; the opportunism that flourishes on an incredible scale in troubled times appears monstrous to a true liberal, who no doubt has no desire to quit this life but intends to make his escape with a heart filled with faith and with never a nod to the executioner. From an intellectual point of view, liberalism of the Tocqueville variety is perhaps more striking for its method than for its content. Its primary feature is a horror of systems: To make events dependent on great first causes is to use rigor as a veil for the inadequacy of one's observations, to pander to minds that like to understand with a minimum of effort, and to eliminate humanity from the history of the human race. All of the dreaming that is so widespread in the nineteenth century comes from an excessive talent for deriving from one or two general causes the complex workings of a society that is no less influenced by secondary causes. But this disdain for systems should not go so far as to ignore laws; politicians who make events happen without understanding their nature willingly believe that everything can be reduced to minor everyday facts. And the little levers they manipulate seem to them to provide a complete description of the greatest things. That is another illusion. When Guizot, Molé, or Thiers consider the February revolution to be a pure accident, they attribute total power to chance in order to make it carry all the responsibility, and they ignore the lengthy preparations without which spontaneity does not occur.

Though it has no sympathy for the intolerance that dogmatism gives rise to, and embraces facts so as to understand them rather than to put them on a pedestal, if liberalism is content with neither theoretical certainties nor practical convictions, it nonetheless does not descend to offering a remote and hesitant view of events. No doubt there is an element of indecision in minds that are inhibited by so many scruples, and Tocqueville laments the uncertainty in which he was obliged to live, unable as he was to ever identify what was true and what was false in parliamentary battles. But this makes him all the more severe in his condemnation of dilettantism, and what he calls the literary spirit in politics, a spirit that looks for ingenious solutions rather than just ones, or admires the talent of the actors rather than thinking about the consequences of the play, is in his eyes one of the most regrettable faults of the French people, who are all too inclined to arrive at political judgments the way a man of letters would. On the other hand, this wish to test impression against reason and reason against facts leads the mind toward a melancholy objectivity and a gloomy attitude to the future. When he sees revolutions that call into question not only the constitution of governments but also the laws that seem to him to constitute society, Tocqueville wonders dubitatively about those principles that can be said to be immutable and those that will in due course be destroyed. His origins and also certain aspects of his thinking lead him often to believe that everything he has known and loved will not change, but his experience obliges him to conclude that when it comes to the constitution of a society, the range of possibilities is much vaster than the people who live in each separate society can ever imagine.

Leafing through these *Recollections*, one comes across a wealth of choice formulations and exquisite portraits (those of Louis-Philippe and Louis-Napoleon are well known, but the pages devoted to Lamartine, Ampère, Blanqui, Barbès, and Bedeau are no less memorable). They do not only give the mind the pleasure of encountering honest, firm judgment, they also affect it through a series of images that provide the most delicate depictions of the feelings of a tender heart. If we read the page he devotes to his visit to Tocqueville after the February days, and follow him through the empty halls of his old chateau, the damp and dusty rooms where everything seems dead; and if, before the spectacle of these places that time has already abandoned we revive the memory of long-gone days that present themselves to memory as days of delightful peace, we will understand much better than through even the most harrowing accounts the bitter taste of political upheaval and the ruinous power of history.

—March 3, 1942

Symbolism and the Poets of Today

In the little book he has written on the subject of Symbolist literature, Albert-Marie Schmidt, though struck by the diversity of viewpoints between which Symbolism is torn, has nonetheless discovered the common features in which Symbolist authors resemble each other.[1] They have, he says, a predilection for inner experience. They have a liking for technical innovation. They wish to take back from music what is theirs. They have a cult of literature. And these features are indeed represented and even reconciled in the greatest Symbolist master, and in one or two of his successors who were otherwise often mediocre. But Mallarmé himself is only defined by these features to the extent that, being contradictory, they represent him in the impossible demands of his ambition; and the spirit in which the others conform to them is lax enough for them not to feel restricted by the contradictions they encounter there. As a literary school, Symbolism is already difficult to grasp because the great poets who founded saw it themselves as an enigma; but this difficulty is augmented by another more awkward one, as soon as Symbolism is considered as something other than a historical movement, and once its presence is detected in the most ancient examples of poetry.

In this respect, the attempt to demonstrate the influence of Symbolism on young poetry today is not very meaningful, or else its meaning simply leads to a further level of mystery. There is doubtless not a single poet today who can avoid being the heir to Symbolism. But is this because Symbolism has absorbed all poetry, or because all poetry is symbolic? It has to be said that problems such as this vex the mind to no effect, and it would be tempting to dismiss them once and for all, were it not that, however severely they are rejected, they constantly reappear, and in so many guises that this covert survival is even more of a nuisance than the solution that they call for. It is thus quite fatuous to say of recent works such as those of Robert Ganzo or Jean Tardieu that they are symbolic; to say it is simply to acknowledge that their value is a poetic one. At the same time, the poetic intention in each different case consists in using the properties of language in the service of pure, rigorous expression, evoking something inexpressible using a precise system of words, and furthermore establishing analogical relations between forms, external images, and a reality that can only be known from within. Rigor of expression, the wish to link the inexpressible to what is expressed in a manner that is not vague but has its own necessity, and last of all the pursuit of analogy, these are three ambitions in which Symbolism is clearly recognizable.

The *Poems* that Robert Ganzo has recently brought out are well known to poetry lovers.[2] *Orinoco*, *River*, *Lespugue*, and *Domain*, all written over the last five years and previously published in various editions, have made his name as a poet and associated it with the idea of a profound and flawless art. These four poems are similar in the scope of their inspiration, the regularity of their prosody and perhaps also the way they combine their themes. Always expansive, developing through numerous stanzas, they are free of any oratorical developments and make each series of lines into the bearer of an entire universe of transformation and metamorphosis. Tightly clustered around each stanza, they appear confined by it to a fully formed world, and yet they flow from one stanza to the other as though, constantly challenged by desire, they may only come to fruition by going from one state of completion to another. Their form finds perfection in regularity. It shuns illicit beauties. It watches over the laws that it wins over to itself. It wants them to be simple so that its suppleness should be visible in their rigor. This traditional mode of expression is not excessively obscure. Sometimes it is limpid, its sole mystery being its absolute transparency. But there is nothing in this transparency to weaken the intensity of its resonances or curb their duration. What is clear is grafted onto what is clear to form a crystal that light traverses on a path that the eye cannot follow. The density of this magnificent crystalline verse provides the uniqueness and the honor of such poetry.

The subjects of Ganzo's poems are less traditional than their form. They bear no relation to ancient myth. They ask nothing of poems from the past. They are composed from the memory of an external spectacle or the evocation of sense impressions that, as they deepen, draw the mind into its most intimate recesses. The exotic images in *Orinoco*, or the wholly familiar ones in *River*, are directly borrowed from the world outside. They translate a reality it was once possible to see. They make it recognizable again. But in the same movement there is also the evocation of a more inward life, of a world that is nothing but an ideal, a reality in which the mind is revealed. The themes of inside and outside echo and recall each other, provoke and combine with each other so intimately that they seem to have always been inseparable. We sense that they were once distinct from each other, but once mingled, they proclaim their indissoluble unity. They lead us to the point where, as the fancy takes us, we can perceive the two realms in what divides them or in what blends them together. It is in these terms that *Domain* can be read. At one moment we recognize the medusa that becomes what illuminates it and is transformed into its outer manifestations:

This power is one that a water god assumes.
A sorceress, I light up
in the distant blue of a light.
Thus it was in my original torpor,
when with my blood still free of the grains
found on the thresholds of sunsets
I offered to the glinting of the sea
the crystal of my tentacles.

At another moment, what we perceive is the power of consciousness for which mimicry is creation, and to which fable gives its definitive form:

But I, a vapor, formed from snow,
breath of the self exhausted,
shall I break the spell
of my vain mobility?
I was blind—I am delivered—
deaf—I discover my voice—
my eyes, for the first time,
know the flight of a drunken insect.

The echo that reduplicates each of Robert Ganzo's poems, giving them to us twice, allowing us to hear them at different levels while leaving their words undisturbed, is like the wondrous passage from cosmic consciousness to the consciousness of the inspired poet that is the basic ambition of all symbolism.

Jean Tardieu's symbolism—to go on using that approximate term—allows him to evoke the disquieting nature of our destiny. The themes that are familiar to a poet as reticent and expressive as Jean Tardieu are those that vainly haunt the world, themes from which the world turns away in a frantic search for words of salvation, but that one or two exceptional writers repeat back to it with the harsh implacability of a threat. It would seem that a man in whom anguish awakens finds himself caught between two forms of torment. On the one hand, the world of things is cramped, it is stifling there and impossible to find any space inside it; everywhere, matter proliferates, there are no gaps, and it is all too accurately represented by the division of space into "lodgings." The soul protects itself against this torment by retreating into an entirely inward space, where there is nothing, where things have disappeared, where in the limitless confusion it no longer knows what it is, or where it is going, or what it is capable of; having first proved its salvation, this liberation eventually becomes inimical to it; perhaps this is because it can never accept salvation, even in the frightening guise of the void; but also because in this pure and icy space there awakens a nostalgia for palpable space, for things as they appear and for forms in their steadfastness, that brings it back to earth where once again everything divides it and grinds it into dust. So man lives on from one torment to the next. He suffocates in the midst of things and becomes lost in himself. He is exposed to a threat that he does not understand. He perceives a power that he cannot name. He obeys a voice that speaks to him without identifying itself. It is imperious and vague; it gives orders and conceals them. Yes, such is our fate. We do not have the right to remain at rest. A will is imposed on us, but we do not know what that will is. We are expected to swear an unknown oath. We are shackled to an impenetrable decision. We are under surveillance by the "invisible witness."

We should have been less willing to emphasize the tendency of the recently published collection to which he has given this title, had Jean Tardieu himself not given direct expression to these themes.[3] The anguished nature of his poems is not affected by this approach. What is specific about their images and sinuous about their rhythm, the harmonious pleasure that the ear encounters there along with the abyss that they open up for the mind, the precise contours and the absence that such precision reflects, all give the poetic work an elusive truth that provides an image of our restless fate. In this collection that is so perfectly attuned to poetry, several pieces express in our view what makes poetry endure beyond the ruin to which it aspires. They contain lines that are worthy of those whose recall has seared the memory of successive generations, and that these generations call to mind by yielding anxiously to their rhythmic incantations:

When I listen and do not hear,
when I look without seeing,
when I walk without taking a step,
when my sun goes black,
I disappear without dying,
I live without movement.
No hope, no memory
in the forges of the moment.
Be melted down? Yes, but to be reborn!
To finish so as to begin again!
The world can be recognized
on the faded paths.

The form of Jean Tardieu's poems is not always as regular as this, but it is always just as precise. Some of them replace syllabic rhythms with accentuated rhythms, according to the rules of tonic rhythm that he has tested out in an admirable translation of Hölderlin's "The Archipelago."[4] Others shun rhyme and yield to the power of a music without echo. But all of them are close to silence, interrupting it without transforming it, as if to summon us to it:

A road remembers
all the vanished steps.
But it waits and nothing yet
has really appeared.

Such hankering after silence is also part of the Symbolist heritage.

Michel Fardoulis-Lagrange's *Sebastian, the Child and the Orange* appears to be this writer's first book.[5] It is all the more worthy of mention for the way it eschews easy readability and has been published in a modest edition. The book is a work of prose, but the prose leads to a world of ambiguous relations, a universe of significant images and a succession of those symbols that the mind seeks to encounter in poetry. One or two of its external features link it to Surrealist traditions, but it differs from these through its wish to link words and figures not through the gift of chance, but through a deliberate and premeditated necessity. That is one if its most remarkable qualities. Between images displaying little or no connection with each other there moves a powerful spirit of harmony that attracts them to each other. They remember that they are part of a single whole. They slowly cleave to this reminiscence and are drawn together by it. This book could well be compared to one of William Faulkner's masterpieces, *The Sound and the Fury*, which contains the inner monologue of an idiot. Sebastian, too, is mentally handicapped, and the myth that the book seeks to bring to light toys with the possibility that madness offers to man, perhaps at the very moment when it takes it away from him. Unlike Faulkner's novel, Michel Fardoulis-Lagrange's book does not call on images to convey the real impressions of a madman or to evoke his disordered sensibility; it seeks rather to go beyond images in order to extract their symbolic truth, and it is through these glimpses of symbol that it seeks to convey to us the significance of delirium. The resulting pages are sometimes overloaded with abstraction, their significance diminished by an excess of meaning, but most of them derive from language an imaginary form of thinking that seems to set us back at one remove from reason.

—March 17, 1943

On Montherlant's Play

In the letter that forms the preface to *Queen After Death*,[1] a play that, as readers will know, is currently being staged at the Comédie Française, Henri de Montherlant expresses surprise at his own readiness to accept a subject that was not the result of an inner choice. He appears satisfied but also astonished to have in effect written the play to order. Here he is writing works at the behest of someone who is not him, and what is more, drawing inspiration from previous works in the same genre in order to write his own. What for previous centuries was the norm appears extraordinary enough today to require an apology, or at least an explanation—yet further proof that originality remains this century's idol.

However, the law of imitation is sometimes still observed in the theater. Jean Giraudoux tells the story of Electra. But novelists will not even toy with the idea of composing a novel that is the repetition of another novel, the way some of Racine's plays repeated those of Euripides. The most they will allow themselves is to borrow their subject from reality, to find a pretext for their work in everyday events (the way Goethe did with *Werther* for example, or Stendhal with *The Red and the Black*), but they would shudder at the thought of deriving a new literary work from any existing literature. Are they infatuated with novelty? They also have an incurable penchant for realism. They claim to obey reality more than themselves. They are afraid of being caught red-handed imitating something that is not nature. They have no time for a model that would cast doubt on their sincerity.

Montherlant thus did not invent the subject of *Queen After Death*, since it was Jean-Louis Vaudoyer who brought it to his attention; and it is not his subject, for it belongs to Luis Velez de Guevara, who wrote a play three centuries ago that closely resembles it while remaining quite different, *To Reign After Death* (*Reinar despues de morir*, 1652). The French writer seems to be afraid that people will underestimate his talent for invention, so in the same volume he publishes his own play and that of his precursor, to allow people to judge, he says, "whether there has been any adaptation." Again we find the same desire to be original. But in this case these scruples are quite unnecessary. The public being appealed to is perfectly capable of judging whether it is watching a work that is totally new and worthy of the best its author has produced, and it will obligingly examine how, starting from the older work, a mind that is so intensely curious about itself has succeeded in composing a new work in which it represents only itself.

In terms of anecdote the two plays are very close to each other. They have the same subject: A prince's secret decision to marry conflicts with his father's plans, for these dictate that a wife should be chosen for him in accordance with royal protocol. They also have the same outcome: The king has the prince's wife executed a few moments before he himself dies. Last, they have the same motives for action: His counselors drive the king to crime; the king hesitates because of the young woman's beauty and the fact that he is well-disposed toward her; the infanta, once rejected, feels her thirst for vengeance turn to pity. Beneath this identical material the two plays are entirely different: in tone, intention, and the human reality they portray. Guevara's play is often extremely clumsy, yet it has a number of qualities. It is a play about love in which the role of sentiment is to be conquered but not humiliated by power, and finally crowned with glory beyond the grave. There is an often surprising and sometimes effective contrast between the delicacy of the heart's dreams, whose expression is constantly renewed by preciosity, and the harshness of the decisions and the candor of the behavior. People insult each other roundly and kill each other recklessly. The king himself comes to inform the young woman that her fate is sealed, and he takes away her children in a cruelly offhand manner. The main character is the secret wife, the consecrated victim, whose astounding beauty dumbfounds the king, overcomes jealousy, vies with grandeur through its radiance, and suffers defeat only to reign resplendent for all eternity.

The main character in *Queen After Death* is King Ferrante. However reluctant one may be to impoverish a work by immobilizing it around a single figure, it must be recognized that the drama is that of the king. The king rules over everything with his solitary majesty. He rules over his son, Don Pedro, whom he subjects to the crushing power of his judgments and who, compared to him, appears mediocre, vacuous, and incapable, rather like a figure that has been rubbed out with an eraser. He rules over his daughter-in law, Inès, who indubitably does have grandeur, natural power, and a proud allure of her own, but who is so entirely under his sway that she sometimes seems to forget the man she loves. And if he does not rule over the infanta of Navarre, the princess he has chosen but who is refused, it is because she is his equal, and like him she carries within her, though with more pride and less responsibility, an awareness of inalienable sovereignty. In *Queen After Death*, love gives rise to scenes whose form lends them charm, though they lack the deeper significance of the scenes in which royalty is the theme. It is as if their author has written them with all of his talent, but without believing they are fully necessary.

Although the subject and the development of the play, along with the particular way in which tragedy is structured, have obliged him to make them ring true, they interest him only for their externals. He will not involve himself in them.

It is tempting to see in the fundamental drama of the king the drama of sovereign responsibility. The king is above everything. He gives human feelings their due. He sees what makes things trivial and what makes them important. He even partakes of what he is not. Within him he has limitless possibilities for experience, as though he could be present in all of the lives he commands and in all of the realities he sustains. And yet his will remains intact. He judges and decides with supreme authority. He is capable of embracing everything, and nothing hinders the sweep of his gaze and the diversity of its viewpoints. He is all things, but in order to act he must reject all things. Explicable motives that are of necessity particular ones are not the cause of his decisions. No counsel is definitive. In the course of his inner deliberations he listens to voices from without, he sometimes even invites them to speak, he discusses and argues with them; but when it is time to act, he makes up his mind according to personal criteria that take no account of everyday reason, and are the voice of omnipotence in him. That is why the king can follow neither his advisors, who urge him to kill on political grounds that are in fact partly impure, nor his feelings, as they seek to dissuade him from an act that is abhorrent and very likely bodes ill. He is alone before his ministers, those representatives of governmental guile, those technicians of authority, and alone before his children, in whom the pursuit of happiness has silenced every other voice, who think only of living for themselves, and are the heroes of a life of domestic bliss.

However, it would significantly alter the meaning of a play such as this to see in it nothing but an assertion of royal responsibility. Its tragic truth and power lie elsewhere. The drama of *Queen After Death* is the drama of the death of a king. Ferrante is the king in whom death has suddenly revealed itself. At the height of his powers, his death agony begins. His power is at its apogee, as are his intelligence and his vigor it would seem, and yet he is he is already absent from himself. He reigns over everything and everything is slipping away from him. He is a man of infinite greatness who has gone into decline, and far from dimming his greatness, his decline illuminates it as it detaches him from it. Ennui, the burden of ennui, makes everything weigh heavy on him. He has no patience with a future that is merely a recurrence. He broods over the vanity of what can still be done. He grows indifferent to what he loves. He who has shaped the world in his hands now sees the world scarcely brush against him. He has courage and he has strength but he no longer has faith. Among his entourage few are those who see the mark of death on his face; they would need to be of the same breed, like the infanta, to discern in his majesty the foul breath of the tomb. "Have you seen how green his face is?" asks Doña Bianca. "He looks like someone who has forgotten to have himself buried." Death toys with him, and he toys with death as if it were just a dangerous idea.

The truth behind the action of a play such as this remains almost invisible, but it is no less compelling. Why does Ferrante have the beautiful woman whom his son has married killed? For reasons of state? But the king sees only what is futile and pernicious about his deed. Will he let hate possess him? He has such a preference for his victim that he tells her his greatest secrets. Is he making her pay for the weakness he showed in her presence? He sees clearly that he did not demean himself by confiding in her, but rather succeeded in surpassing himself. In fact there is a mystery here that escapes him ("Why am I going to kill her?" he asks. "No doubt there is a reason, but I cannot see what it is"), and it is the mystery of his death. He has Doña Inès killed because he himself is going to die. And in bringing this innocent life to an end it is his own life that he is ending. Such is the tragedy of a noble destiny. The death of kings is never without its effects. When they succumb, someone else must also die, someone whose survival neither purity nor everyday morality can guarantee. What is royal about the decision that condemns a woman who is free of crime to be murdered is not the political value of the judgment or the rigor of sovereign resolve; it is the light cast upon it by the king's own death, a fatality that requires that the episodes of his life and his death should have an admirable and terrible sequel.

This light serves to reveal all of the tragic value of a denouement that the stage itself can perhaps only insufficiently reveal. Throughout the final act, Ferrante discloses to his victim all of the plots that are being hatched against her, the external interventions that seek to destroy her, the increasingly insistent pressure from outside. The discussion seems to center on Doña Inès's chances of survival, and it is around her that fate's cruel dilly-dallying seems to occur. But in fact, the debate goes deeper. The king is dependent on another sovereign, namely anguish. Anguish has usurped the throne; it occupies the palace, speaks with its implacable voice. When it speaks quietly, it inclines Ferrante to be merciful, makes him appreciate the beauty of the young woman, even distracts him from thoughts of justice; but when it grows more terrible, it fills him with the ponderous spite of a lion and inspires in him an urge to kill that, beneath its royal guise, is merely a desire for death. The murmur of this tragedy can be heard behind the ambiguous explanations of the king. That the king should be no more than a dying man in the grip of fate; that his resounding words should be those of death itself, death on a grand scale, death that inspires terror in the courtiers as they skulk in the dark corners of the room; that all of the ministers who enter and call for the death of a woman should in fact be unwittingly calling for the death of the king; and that the action should no longer develop according to visible motives but to the designs of an ambiguous fate, that is the inner truth of the drama, a truth that shines and is then extinguished without ever revealing itself.

Montherlant would seem to have preferred not to choose between the different possibilities that his play contains. During the first two acts, it seeks its balance in the tragedy of sovereignty, of responsibility in its struggle with the rightful demands of personal happiness. But in the third act, it establishes itself at another level and bases itself on the mystery of a majestic soul. From now on we cease to be interested in the petty hopes of these lovers as they yearn for tranquility; Doña Inès herself is no more than a lovely moth, doomed to burn with the flame so that it should appear more pure, and from now on it is not her death that is the issue but the suffocating, terrifying, solitary death of the sovereign who, by deciding the fate of another, unwittingly seals his own. The denouement only partly rids us of these uncertainties. In Guevara's play the prince proclaimed his dead wife queen and crowned her with gold: "Behold, Inès is crowned! I give you the unfortunate queen who deserved to reign over Portugal after her death! Behold the dead queen!" Montherlant's play dispenses with this external apotheosis and merely uses it to justify its title. It is with another piece of stage action that it comes to an end. As the murdered young woman is born on a litter to be greeted by the fervent grieving of all who are present, the body of the king simply lies there with no one in attendance, abandoned by the young page boy who was guarding it, alone as befits a king whom death renders more solitary than any other.

—March 31, 1943

The Romance of Marie Dorval and Vigny

While the romance of Marie Dorval and Vigny is one of the most celebrated of its kind in the Romantic era, it is far from being among the clearest. Whereas celebrated couples such as George Sand and Alfred de Musset, or Juliette Drouet and Victor Hugo, have enjoyed all the posthumous light for whose sake they were often more sincere, faithful, or inconstant than they would have naturally wished to be, the couple formed by the actress and the "pure spirit" immediately acquired a legendary form that has since proved an obstacle to any more objective study. A predilection for antithesis has presented the proud, chaste, and silent poet face-to-face with an image of such indecency and vulgarity that it remains only to wonder what power of bewitchment could have induced the dark Seraph to debase himself for seven years for the sake of a woman so exultantly shameless and deceitful.

By publishing Marie Dorval's *Letters to Alfred de Vigny*,[1] René Gaudier has sought to turn this situation around and not only rehabilitate the young woman but also let the poet share some of the discredit that he brought on her. In a short preface, using documents in the collection of his father, Charles Gaudier, he paints a portrait of Vigny that does not show him in an attractive light. He reveals a pessimist who quarrels with all of his friends, is discontented with fate for having made him neither famous enough nor rich enough, and is envious of any success that is not his own. More vain than aloof, his stoicism a sham; less cheated by fate than misled by his illusions, he appears as a man of insufferable character who drives those close to him to despair. His complaints against fate are unjust. If he rails against poverty ("To be born without a fortune is the worst of all ills. You can never escape it in this money-driven society"), he forgets that he lives very comfortably, shielded from the petty worries that oblige Lamartine, Balzac, or Gautier to take on work that exhausts them. When he complains that the soldier's calling brings only servitude without the compensations of glory, he omits to mention his lukewarm enthusiasm for the calling and how immoderately he takes leave. And if he can blame his ill health and that of his mother for the indolence from which he suffers, he nonetheless leads an active life in which there are as many trivial enticements as pleasures of the sort usually to be had in fashionable society.

René Gaudier criticizes Vigny for having been jealous and tyrannical toward Marie Dorval, as well as unjustly suspicious and guilty of the very deceptions of which he falsely accuses her. He lists the poet's relationships, for example with Mme Ancelot, Marceline Desbordes-Valmore, and perhaps Augusta Holmès, and finds proof in the poet's notebooks that he was neither faithful nor chaste (he calls him an erotomaniac). In contrast, Marie Dorval remained constantly close to him through all the vagaries of his difficult life; she lacked neither refinement nor kindness, and their parting caused her to suffer in a way that proves the value of her love and the delicacy of her feelings. On one side there is more constancy, nobility, and devotion than has been claimed; on the other, less decency and less sincerity. So it is that two figures whom legend had depicted in the least harmonious fashion come to resemble each other for good and for ill.

What do we learn from the collected letters themselves? Until now, only a few letters of Vigny's were known, and these were brutal, solemn, yet moving and profound in their solemnity. ("What remains of all that in my soul . . . is unhappiness, mortal dejection. For the first time in my life I feel there is a secret shame inside me. Do not pursue your offending beyond where my love and my kindness can stretch. I can still feel them inside of me, watching over you, but in fact I am reaching the point where I no longer know how to appeal to them, so reproachful are you and so tired am I of this constant battle.") The hundred letters from Marie Dorval that have just been published for the first time, and that take us from the end of 1832—almost a year after their first meeting—to their separation in 1838, contain just what is required to make René Gaudier's case against Vigny appear plausible. They are without any real literary value, but they do have spontaneity, cheerfulness, and a naturally sensitive tone that, despite some instances of Romantic extravagance, is entirely different from the vulgar, even "foul-mouthed" language that Dumas refers to. Most of them were written while she was on tour in the provinces. They describe the successes and sometimes the drudgery of these tours. They show us the glory of Romanticism gradually spreading to small towns, where plays like *Antony* and *Chatterton* receive more plaudits and greater acclaim than in the finest Paris theaters, thanks to the grace of an impassioned tragedienne.

These tours take Marie Dorval away from Vigny for months and sometimes years at a time. From one town to the next, she follows her wandering star. In the larger towns like Bordeaux or Toulouse she will spend several weeks, but in Chalon, Bourg, or Avignon she is no more than a visitor, hastily chalking up triumphs before moving on yet further, under the anxious impulse that keeps her constantly on the move. Why does she not return sooner to Paris, where her contract at the Comédie

Française is in jeopardy? With an apologist's zeal, René Gaudier believes it is her need for money that explains these long absences. That is what she herself said, and it is also what she believes. She has debts, her husband is tolerant but far from frugal, her daughters lead a wild life, and she herself has a passion for glittering performances where she sometimes loses more than she earns. But is that the whole truth? Hardly. There is something about her aimless traveling that appeals to her nature; as the daughter of actors, born and brought up on the road, it brings back the wonderful unpredictability of her youth. In a life where everything passes, where nothing happens because everything repeats itself, in which difficulties, solutions, failures, and triumphs are all the fruit of chance, she may never truly find enjoyment because she is aware of how empty it is; but she remains attached to it, and unable to break free. It is her folly and her passion. It is the counterpart to her deep restlessness. She will never sacrifice it in order to go and see the lover whose disaffection she fears. On the contrary, she fixes up new arrangements, one town calls to her after the next, and the years go by until finally she can no longer retrieve what she once loved.

This travel correspondence suggests that it is absence that allowed Marie Dorval to understand what was authentic and durable about her affection most thoroughly. In these circumstances, she lets herself yield to a passion that delights her feelings and sustains her soul; she is proud of these sentiments without which she feels she would be lost ("If my ill fortune decrees that I should lose a man like you, I am lost"); she embraces the affection of a heart that she admires and whose qualities she never misjudges. There is nothing base about her confidences or even about her jealousy. Never once does she say anything that could cast doubt on the honor she derives from this magnificent relationship. But this is also because being far away, she is spared its less fortunate aspects. She can escape the terrible suspicion of a lover who takes offense at the least thing, and demands a level of constancy she is incapable of. She can yield with a clear conscience on a passing whim to amorous dalliances that mean nothing to her. She lives a chaste life with an ideal she adores, and that her fleeting fantasies leave unsullied.

By nature, Marie Dorval is violent and overbearing ("Oh what a wretched woman I am, I complained to the doctor only this morning about my bad temper"). When she is living in Paris, Vigny's rows make her want to be guilty of what she is unjustly accused of. She takes revenge. Anger makes her say things that are beneath her. She reverts to being vulgar and base. She cries out horribly ("When I hurt you, that wasn't me. When anger forced me to say awful things, that wasn't me," and later, "No, my heart did not say the words that came out of my mouth"). She confides in people carelessly and unforgivably (for example, she tells Fontenay in 1832 that her lover "bullies her and bores her"). She becomes what legend has accused her of being, what Vigny, after a separation that he found deeply wounding, will henceforth see all women as being, and what she herself admits to being with a humble honesty that is simply infamy redoubled: a degrading creature ("Yet again, he is degrading himself through staying by my side, I must go away from him").

Vigny's behavior is definitely not as straightforward as Gaudier's severe remarks would wish us to believe. He chides him for his superior airs, the preening attitude with which he observes the woman he loves, the way he reminds her of his superiority and his largesse ("I knew the sort of attacks I would be exposed to by trying to save you," "Everything about me is devotion"). However, this flaw of pride is not only the failing of a character that is more vain than noble. It also signifies what Gaudier too easily forgets: the disappointment of the Romantic poet who sought to turn a young woman who was his opposite into the sister of Eloa, Emma, or Kitty Bell, a creature whom pity would restore to her divine origin, who would be pure thanks to a rehabilitation of which she must henceforth remain worthy. It is that dream that the actress destroys with her volleys of insults and transforms into a ridiculous parody. Where she sees just a momentary misdeed, the poet sees a catastrophe for his work; his mind and his heart are betrayed simultaneously; the failure he suffers deprives him of the only positive attitudes that his Romanticism, already much more negative than any other, still allowed him to have hope in.

The burning jealousy that fills the poet, and that distance renders less dangerous but does not allay, exposes him to humiliations that he suffers as though they were a further assault on his destiny. If Marie Dorval, through her easy approach to life, makes the hope he places in the redemption of fallen humanity seem ridiculous, she offends even more cruelly against the proud and haughty principles within which his morality is confined. How degrading to let suspicion plunge him into such obsessive anxiety! How shameful the torments are that he endures! He blenches if anyone approaches the actress ("But what terrible things are going on in you to make you turn so deathly white," she writes to him). He demands that she justify every letter she receives. He quizzes her relentlessly and in minute detail. He drives her to extremes that provide him with proof of what he fears, whereas she sees merely the consequences of his injustice. All of that skews the outlook of a soul that refuses to feel that it is base, but suffers from being unfaithful to itself even to the extent of being forced to utter bitter accusations of inconstancy.

From the earliest years, the romance amassed every possible drama and every sort of episode. Things were in place for a denouement to occur. Yet it is delayed for six further years. The actress goes on tour. She writes. She cannot put what she has abandoned behind her. On the contrary, she appears quite genuinely to want the passion that has taken over her life to survive. Unfortunately, she has also accustomed Vigny to her absence; when she returns, he who often writes a new name in his notebook, "Julia," is less willing to put up with quarrels that appear more loathsome now that his attachment is less exclusive. The break takes a few more days to happen. On August 17, 1838, he announces it in his diary in letters of triumph. On

August 18, he writes "Julia," and underneath that: "feeling the emptiness of my life." And on August 29: "I dreamed last night that I was devouring Marie's skeleton."

The actress's last years are like the negative imprint of the feelings that she helped to ruin without becoming unworthy of them. In the presence of Sandeau, who mocks her for it, she tries to kill herself with a stage weapon, in a reflection of what remained true even in her pretenses. She will no longer enjoy fortune or love. Her fame as an artist is on the wane. After losing her daughters, she loses her grandson. She dies a premature death, well and truly raving, and so fulfills the bitter prophesy of the poet: "You will never be happy." It can even be said that she was unhappy even after her death, since legend has given her the role of a base, perfidious evil genius, one that she never wanted to play. What was calculating about her always went hand in hand with a natural impulsiveness, and her ability to express everything did not debase the truth in her heart. Is it Vigny's fault that such a shadow hangs over her memory? Is it not also her fault, for having made the unfairest judgments seem justified through much of what she appeared to be? Trying to divide responsibility in this way makes little sense. If she deserves some sort of rehabilitation today, it is for having lived a Romantic drama with a simple heart if not a pure one, and with a rather naïve love for life that, all told, was far removed from the audacities and the superstitions with which the theater, where she reigned supreme, taught her to overload every sentiment.

—April 8, 1943

Novels

Novelists who are still young sometimes allow themselves to be tempted by an idea that seems so powerful and so important to them that they omit to give it sustenance, and believe they can derive a major book from it almost mechanically. There are those on the other hand who are more interested in the inner resources of literature, and can make do with next to nothing. An impression suffices, even something less than an impression: The state of trembling it causes in the person who perceives it, the hope that it thwarts, the intangible movement that, between two circumstances, expresses the story in all of its reality. With his *Child of Plauquet Woods*, Pierre Van der Meulen corresponds fairly accurately to the type of author who has discovered a sublime ambition and is fully satisfied by it.[1] With *The Tutor*, by contrast, Henri Thomas descends to that level of modesty where the thought behind a book is compatible with only a modicum of material, with literary resources that are almost invisible, with a truth that does its utmost to appear only in its own absence.[2]

Henri Thomas is a young writer who is already in full control of his talent, whose collection of poems, *Blind Labors*,[3] is one of the most successful to have appeared in recent years, and who in addition to a first novel has produced a number of translations that are remarkable for the rare sense of language they reveal. *The Tutor* is a very subtle and agreeable work, rich for what it appears to lack, and much more interesting than many a more striking work. Its technique may appear artificial, but this is justified. Its core is made up of two stories with very little to link them externally. During the Christmas holidays, a young tutor breaks free of the web of restrictions within which his profession holds him captive. He books into a hotel, where he meets a girl and spends a few moments with her. His aim is to start something more serious, but during the night he overhears a secret that dashes his hopes, and he returns exhausted to the life that he thought he had escaped from. The second story concerns the tutor's childhood memories, and it is no more significant than the first. Initially, we can scarcely discern this child who has an epileptic friend and who, through his discovery of the illness, finds himself deviating from the straight and narrow path of the well-behaved, hardworking model pupil. Events carry little weight in the story, and the inner denouement is more an attempt to eliminate them than to let them stand out more expressively.

The two stories are held together by commentaries that turn them into a genuine novel. They exist inside a book that subjects them to a hidden design. The first story is written by the tutor himself, in order simultaneously to express and conceal the memory of an encounter in which his life seemed about to meet with exceptional good fortune. What actually happened during the encounter we do not find out. We know it only in the form into which the novel transposes it. At the heart of the literary construct there gleams a soul of reality, unknown and brilliant, whose energy we perceive without recognizing its form. In composing this story, the tutor experienced an enigmatic joy that protected him to some extent against the encroachments of his profession. He decides to write another one, and what he brings to light is a distant childhood memory. What does he hope to obtain from these fictions taken from his life? To find consolation for what is mediocre about that life? Or else a refuge from events that could harm him? He is also appealing to chance, attempting to entice the bliss that is to be found in things. In fact, reality has its own sense of what fortune is and defies all attempts to predict it. It must be sought out in those moments when it appears in all of its profusion. "Pleasures of the ear, pleasures of the eye, pleasures of touch are all pathways that converge on an uncertain center where everything decays."

It could be thought that with these two unrelated stories, Henri Thomas has composed a novel whose unity is a fragile one. That is the impression these discrete pages will leave on the sort of reader who needs stories with clearly defined outlines and precise features, and who considers all thinking or any burgeoning idea as alien to the authentic life of a novel. However, if the two tales in *The Tutor* both have their own individual value—if they resemble a series of images, seen from within and reflecting a mind that fears that the more it grasps them the more it is in danger of erasing them—they are really interesting only as episodes. They involve us in another plot where what is imaginary has to give way to what is real. They lead us toward a state where fiction loses all justification and asks to be discounted. The novel entitled *The Tutor* is the novel of a quest. By pure chance, a young man whose mind is dulled by habit glimpses what is authentic about reality through a tear in the fabric of the everyday. But no sooner has he caught sight of this spectacle than it disappears. He tries to restore it as a literary image. He hopes that way to encourage his vision, to prepare his gaze for a depiction that he will be able to retain more easily. He turns his humdrum writerly tasks into a lure that will attract the deeper life. He builds a bridge in order to reach out to things. To no avail: The bridge leads nowhere. Once again, it is chance that allows the young man to gain control of the reality he is seeking. He glimpses it therefore in the knowledge that he cannot have it for himself. He grasps its tangled, broken threads and makes no attempt to shape them into a figure. He is satisfied with the purity of which he has an inkling, one that is perpetually hidden from him by a veil but that his mind can discover in the close or distant regions of existence as its poetic truth.

The abstract framework within which these two tenuous stories are contained could well appear cumbersome and ill adapted to the chance intervention that it seeks to circumscribe. But the writer's modesty is a successful ploy. In just a few outlines, with delicate colors alternating with great blanks, his portrait comes into being before our eyes with the rigor and the expressive power we are able to lend it ourselves. It obeys us, and at the same time it leads us on. It helps us to become its accomplice. The vision it extracts from us is presented to us as incontrovertible. Anything but discreet, and as such providing a perfect contrast with *The Tutor*, Van der Meulen's novel *The Child of Plauquet Wood* impresses powerfully upon us what it seeks to be. Its subject provides almost everything it contains, but what a subject! This young writer has tried to rewrite the story of Faust. He has imagined that Mephistopheles, dissatisfied with his first wager, obtained God's permission to wager on the magician's son. This individual, known in Goethe's novel as Euphorion or perhaps as Marguerite's son, becomes in this novel the illegitimate son of a baron from Lyon. Raised in the woods, he has a remarkable and stupendous thirst for knowledge, and with much greater talent than Pascal, he astounds the local teacher by demolishing the Euclidian system of geometry. When he reaches adolescence he becomes a sort of angel who penetrates nature's secrets and in quick succession revolutionizes the natural sciences, learns how to split the atom, and perfects magnetic flight. But this universal knowledge and power leave him dissatisfied. He cannot decide whether to embrace the world or to dominate it. He discovers untruth and its origin. And like Euphorion, leaving the earth behind, he kills himself in the magnificent mountains of the Dauphiné.

If this work is assessed against the ambition it seeks to sustain, it appears distinctly disappointing. It is not enough to present a figure in a mythical light to give it mythical splendor. And here on the contrary, it collapses beneath the weight of this permanent attribution, the contrast totally nullifies it, and in seeking something sublime in such exceptional proximity, it primarily reflects the naivety of an author who has seen only the outside of the extraordinary and not what lies inside. The child of Plaquet Wood, with his camera for photographing the dead, brings discredit on the deity whose son he claims to be and on the devil whom he obeys. He dissuades us from wanting to believe in him. He yields to something ridiculous, and while it may not kill him, it prevents him from existing. Remarkably, however, this fundamental weakness does not make Van der Meulen's novel any less interesting. There is something robust and picturesque about this young author's way of writing that serves to transform a story drawn from myth into an unfettered portrait of provincial life. Incidental details allow the drama to regain its power and a degree of verisimilitude. The ecstatic feelings of those who have lived alongside the hero, the seemingly fantastic light that he leaves behind him, its reflection on the faces of one or two minor figures all restore our faith in the idea that a mystery is possible. The figure of the manservant who represents Mephistopheles has something bizarrely burlesque about it that helps us overcome our disbelief. This fallen devil, who is well and truly fallen, is so deeply ensconced in his servant's condition that he loses sight of his mission and no longer knows from whence he came. For a while he continues to entertain the hope of penetrating the secrets of creation with young Faust's help. But he sinks into a state of degradation, and human nature becomes for him a slumber from which he will never awaken.

Van der Meulen's novel is thus redeemed by qualities that are not quite appropriate for it, a sort of rural atmosphere, natural descriptions, and a free and easy humor that would need no more than a little animation and sparkle to allow the myth to prevail through laughter rather than through solemnity. Such irony is strangely lacking in Maria Le Hardouin's recent novel, *The Black Sail*.[4] A persistently oratorical tone, a development that resorts to tragic effect for page after page, a haughty mix of humiliated sentiment and arrogant pretention, all situate this novel in the vein of the classical confessional work. The young heroine who tells her story is an invalid whose illness has blighted her childhood, and who is frantically attempting to find a breakthrough that will lead her to life. There are very few precise episodes. The best pages from a literary point of view are those that portray the struggles between the young invalid and her mother. These are strangely violent scenes. The child tries to gain the advantage by pleading and weeping. But her prayers fall on deaf ears. So she fills the air with her screams, smashes things, repeating with uncontrollable rage: "I'll make you give in, I'll make you give in." Her mother, who is just as violent as her daughter, lets her own anger feed off this rage, and these two creatures between whom a sincere bond exists turn their day-to-day life with its cursing and screaming into an appalling nightmare.

This violence is what gives Marie Le Hardouin's book its significance. Something impetuous sweeps through the story, carrying it along on an endless surge. One feels that the forces that illness represses are jostling to find an outlet. They hurl themselves against the barrier that contains them. They employ everything: dreams, love, the urge to write, in an attempt to reach out to an inaccessible life, to become durable, to become visible to the world. To live, live: this is what these confidences repeat in every shape and form, in an eager fever that is without order or repose. When something so demanding takes the route of autobiographical expression it eventually parts company with literary creation. It uses language as if by accident. It has no time for the strict rules of art. It strings one sentence to another, and with no concern for how tiresome it becomes, it sinks beneath the monotony of abundance and the indigence that comes from perpetual excess.

—April 14, 1943

Machiavelli

Three years ago, circumstances were not wholly conducive to a celebration of Guicciardini's quatercentenary, and it went unnoticed. In the case of Machiavelli, by contrast, he who could be called Guicciardini's master—were it not that the latter's interest in positive history, the precision of his thought, and his skepticism all came entirely from within himself—has been the subject of studies and publications that needed no pretext in order to attract the most enduring sort of attention. Augustin Renaudin's book *Machiavelli* is the work of one of the most knowledgeable writers on humanism, and his work sheds definitive light on all of the questions that the mind can ask about a body of thought that the centuries have not made any less enigmatic.[1] As for the edition of *The Prince* that we owe to Raymon Naves,[2] its only weakness is perhaps that it is followed by the *Anti-Machiavelli* by Frederick II, whose interest nowadays is merely that of a historical novelty.

In his mediocre preface to this essay Voltaire criticizes one of Machiavelli's translators for the inept way he lived his life. "A man," he writes brutally, "who has been first secretary of an embassy and yet cannot find a way to escape poverty has in my view no understanding of reasons of State." One of Machiavelli's contradictions is also to be found in the failure of his political career, and in how rarely he put own cautionary advice to good use. He was successful in neither his personal ambitions nor his patriotic hopes. He was just as mistaken in the way he managed his own affairs as in the way he managed those of his country. Though a republican, the author of a theory of republican institutions and then an exile because he was a republican, he forfeits the advantage that his opinions provide by joining forces with those who destroyed the republic, and he compromises himself in the eyes of his former friends without acquiring any real authority from his new masters. He earns enough favor to lose his influence, but too little to obtain powers that could replace that former preeminence. Hence, when the Ten of Liberty once again succeed the Medicis, he is shunned by his friends the way he was by his enemies fifteen years earlier, and he dies an embittered and solitary man.

In his political projects he is exposed to the same disappointments. His dream is to create a national state capable of defending Italy against foreign enemies. He talks up the talents of Cesare Borgia in the hope that one day, a providential figure cast in his image will achieve this dream. In the mediocre figures of the two young Medicis he thinks he can see the superior prince that his hopes call for. Against his better judgment, he puts his trust in the Holy See, which rules in those days by division and dispute, to promote this dream of union and strength. He relies on other Medicis to ensure the restoration of a free and enduring republic, though they are intent only on founding a dynasty. All of his dreams turn out to be illusions. The theorist of a politics of absolute realism is a man who, in his practical action and his behavior, is totally a dupe to his hopes. This calculator who relies exclusively on facts is constantly led astray by his own fancy. This pessimist with his uncompromising view of men puts his confidence in men who do not deserve it. His passions lead him astray; his hopes turn him into someone other than himself.

Augustin Renaudet brings out these contradictions and sees in them not merely an aspect of Machiavelli's character, but also a sign of the way he thinks. His political thinking requires two levels on which to express itself. As someone involved in affairs of state for fourteen years as the secretary of the Florentine Republic, he establishes a program of positive action, turns politics into an exact science with clear boundaries, and bases it on comparative and experimental historical method. His experience of affairs of state and his study of the Rome of the consuls and senators allow him to develop a theory of the republican state. His goal is the freedom of Florence. But at the same time he dreams of freedom for Italy, of national independence. He imagines a state created by tyranny in order to liberate the nation. He awaits the advent of a mythic lawgiver, a Lycurgus, Romulus, or Moses, who by imposing his conception of things will empower a government that has as yet to be formed. He entertains the dream of a dictator who will be not only strong enough to form the state but also selfless enough to disappear once his task is completed. There is thus in Machiavelli a rigorous mind that organizes the rules of human success into a precise system and banishes from it all superstition; but there is also a man of imagination who is no longer either a realist or a skeptic and who, like Dante and Petrarch, draws on myth and legend to construct a grandiose project that a reading of history ought to have discouraged.

It could be said that several of the themes in *The Prince* cease to be surprising when seen in the light of Machiavelli's dreams, but at the same time that the value and significance of Machiavellianism come from the silence that Machiavelli sometimes appears to maintain concerning his deeper motives. The major question that posterity has rendered classic by identifying a moral problem in his political doctrine is itself partly an expression of this ambiguity. Is Machiavelli immoral? Raymond Neves asks in his turn. If "moral" is understood in relation to the Christian notion of salvation, there is no doubt as to the answer; Machiavelli is one of those minds who see in Christianity a debilitating influence. He is not interested in the inner life and is blind to all spiritual ideals; the aestheticism of Rome offers not only the spectacle of corrupt power but also the scandal of a religion that, by accustoming men to humility through rewarding the weak, is responsible for the general state of indolence. Machiavelli's thought is immoral, too, if it is measured against the humanist ethic. The Hellenic ideal of intellectual nobility is as foreign to him as the Christian ideal. He is as indifferent to the salvation of the soul as he is to its splendor; neither Christianity nor humanity or the individual provides him with the rules according to which acts of human behavior can be organized. At the same time, this refusal does not lead him into doubt. On the contrary, he is strict when he commands. He demands rigorous submission from men. He offers them a law that will not bend. He prescribes an intransigent ideal. But this ideal is not an inner one; it is to be found neither in the soul nor in the mind. It lies in the state that offers a visible expression of national prestige.

Machiavelli's ethic takes as its principles those that presuppose the preservation or the creation of the state. It is linked in his mind to the project for a united Italy. Its secret justification is this noble task that must be fulfilled, and to which the will must sacrifice every other value. In Machiavelli's mind, the man who will reconstitute the Italian nation and drive out the barbarians will display exemplary moral behavior. To fulfill this duty, the Prince must impose on himself and demand of others the harshest possible existence, where nothing gives pleasure any longer, where everything is calculated and where crimes themselves are no more than the expression of a reasoning will. There is no way in which he can make government serve a particular sentiment, even if this sentiment is a virtuous one. He becomes virtuous by fulfilling his task, and citizens are virtuous by obeying him. When linked to a precise political task, such an idea no longer displays the surprising characteristics that it has when it is given universal form. *The Prince* is the manual of political technique that Machiavelli places at the disposal of the providential being who is charged with the task of founding the Italian state. It is the passion of the patriotic visionary that makes him identify national greatness as the supreme value. And it is the cold, calculating, realist mind that decides on the means of this conquest in the most objective possible way.

Machiavelli's patriotic opinions are expressed very clearly in *The Prince*. They form the beginning and the end of the work. But tradition soon ignored them, so that Frederick II's edition could simply eliminate them entirely from the text. As a result, Machiavelli's thought became more paradoxical. Indeed, it makes obedience to the state into the essence of the moral law, but at the same time it defines neither the state nor its role in human affairs. If this gap is less surprising when we recall that for Machiavelli, this state is inseparable from the values that typify the Roman past and the Italy of the future, it becomes quite remarkable if we give it a positive significance. We find ourselves thinking that the ideal being proposed by Machiavelli is one of submission to the state considered as having no specific nature in itself. The crowning value resides in a requirement that has no content, a de facto imperative, an order that is one of triumphant action. Morality becomes a technique for success. Its goal is to succeed, and the project is its principle. This is not the morality of an action that could find its justification outside of itself, as in the case of Italian renewal; it is the morality of the human act that, because it draws on the power of the practical mind, carries within it its own justification.

This technique, which permits the disciplined organization of men, brings with it its own assumptions. It is not satisfied with just any successful action. The success must also be the most reasonable and economical one possible. A superabundance of means that produces a mediocre outcome, a lucky break when careful calculation could have reined in chance, are failings that deserve blame and foretell future failures. Reason guided by observation and served by force can change the course of events. It is capable of effective decisions. It displays its own initiatives and its own effects. The first assumption of this morality is thus the primacy of reason and its capacity for action. The second is the value of individual effort. In a leader of men, Machiavelli believes that will should impose its law. At the origin of human societies there were legislators who framed constitutions and established durable disciplines. Behind every change there is a reformer who adapts fundamental precepts to existing circumstances. At the lowliest level, there is the citizen who obeys laws and takes up arms to defend them. All of these actions have a positive value, and hence a moral value.

Such action has its limits. First of all, there can be no question of setting man on the path of indefinite progress. In terms of what ideal could such progress be expressed? The ideal lies in the act itself, it is not a distant goal that men come ever closer to through their actions. All that can be offered is a system of axioms that will enable the creation of the state, delay its dissolution and give it as long a life and as much strength as possible. Mankind is trapped in a circle of instability in which things begin anew then reach their end in an inexorable cycle. Forms of government repeat themselves according to an unchanging order: As it becomes degenerate, each monarchy gives rise to an aristocratic regime that perishes in its turn as it becomes a democracy, while the corruption of democracy leads to dictatorships that once again turn into monarchies. In this eternal circle, human ingenuity arranges momentary pauses, but the influence of decadent forces always eventually overcomes the feeble powers that humanity possesses, and the precarious edifice collapses in accordance with the same law that once guaranteed its success.

Men cannot do everything: it is therefore their duty to learn what they can do, and not to act haphazardly but in accordance with the knowledge they possess, and by employing all of the means that their action presupposes. Such is the morality of the prince. He must act, that is to say found or sustain the state. If he acts unthinkingly, he will be a criminal, even if he does not always fail. If, in order to act, he appeals to an ideal that is not one of calculated action, he will be immoral, even if that ideal is the good in itself. And if the most accurate calculations and the most historically justified initiatives still leave him a victim of fortune, he will merit merely a little mild reproach and will still stand as an example, like Cesare Borgia, who failed but failed lucidly. What makes Machiavelli unique is that he vested moral value in a practical knowledge that draws on experience to anticipate success and seize opportunities. He saw in political action a total system to which all things are subordinate, but which is subordinate to nothing; that makes use of everything, virtue as well as vice, what is noble as well as what is base, and could only founder were it to acknowledge anything higher than itself. With admirable rigor he defined the requirements of a mode of action that, wherever it looks, sees only a means to an end, perceives only what can be put to use, and transforms mankind itself into a project. What is almost a thirst for human action and particularly for political action, this logical tyranny that obliges men to put themselves entirely in the service of action, even in what is most inalienably theirs, is Machiavelli's principal discovery. "If you wish to act in a reasonable manner, it will be necessary to sacrifice everything to action. Do not try to protect a particular moral outlook, a personal faith, a pure way of thinking. Action demands everything, it takes possession of everything." So speaks Machiavellianism, confronting the spirit of practical achievement for the first time with the full scope of its demands, and with the absurdity of all compromise.

—April 21, 1943

Eloquence and Literature

Charles Braibant has just created a collection that will contain texts that bear no relation to literature. There will be diplomatic briefings, explorers' tales, sailors' logs, and trustees' reports. To begin with, Father Martin Stanislas Gillet, the lawyer Maurice Garçon, and Anatole de Monzie propose three volumes, each devoted to a particular type of eloquence, and these different anthologies provide an excellent survey of the rich store of eloquence to be found in the sacred, legal, and political domains.[1] Where does literature begin and where does it end? To the Greeks and Romans, the inclusion of the major works of oratory in a nonliterary collection would have appeared incomprehensible. For them, eloquence was the supreme art. It ensured the greatest triumphs for whoever excelled at it. There was no one greater than an orator. Today, not only do we take a severe view of any success that is obtained through an immoderate use of the orator's talents, but we also readily exclude the best examples of oratory from the literary domain. The only discourse of that type that still merits literary study and attention belongs to the centuries we call classical.

This change has numerous causes. One of them relates to the equivalence that modernity has established between literature and the book. Only written texts have artistic value. For the ancients, the human voice formed the basis of literature. Someone had to speak and be heard for an art to take shape. The epic, the lyric, the theater, all presupposed this presence of a voice, without which there could be only an intellectual void. Eloquence was just one particular instance of the games that sound plays with the ear; or more precisely, it was their most general form, since it required of the voice all those resources that the other arts used selectively. This explains the development of the term *rhetoric*, which initially referred to the specific technique of the speechmaker, before being applied to the study and analysis of the main artistic practices. As we know, this original state of affairs continued after the advent of literature itself, and articulation, rhyme, and vocal effect went on being prerequisites even for those arts that had adapted most successfully to books. Poetry is the main survivor of this period when art was necessarily composed of speech and song.

Another cause of the discredit suffered by eloquence in literature's eyes is to be found in the ever-widening gap between the field of use-value and that of literature. Literature must serve no purpose: Such is the dogma that prevails in the modern era. Literature begins when the mind abandons the service relations that belong to practical existence and indulges in play, puts itself into play, and creates a work that is beyond the reach of the world of action. Eloquence on the contrary always has a goal that is relevant to active society. It must convince. It is part of an undertaking. Its perfection lies entirely in the success that it achieves. A fine speech is a speech that has obtained results. A speech without effect is a bad speech. Beauty of language, purity of style, and refinement of thought are simply means; they do not themselves make for an orator of distinction, and sometimes an orator has no need of them. What is required above all of a work of art is that it should be without purpose, and this is something that would never be required of a speech by learned counsel, a sermon, or a political address. On reading through the three anthologies in the Correâ collection, our first impression is that the eloquence that has the most influence on action in general, that has brought about the most significant historical changes and whose effects can still be felt in everyday events, is also the eloquence whose examples have the lowest literary value; not only does political eloquence not outlive the circumstances in which it triumphs, but it is also almost entirely absorbed into the extraordinary effects that it creates. (For example, the celebrated speech by Clemenceau entitled "I make war"[2] has lost all significance when it is read as a text, but part of its power is restored to it when we imagine its consequences and admire its results.) Sacred eloquence, on the other hand, seeks to affect people only internally, and its great names continue to provide a rich resource for literature. And texts delivered from the pulpit, designed as they are to transform men rather than serve them, and inspired by the most general and enduring of purposes, display even to the literary mind an interest that works written in defense of an individual or a cause have failed to retain. Like all classical works, the great sermons have managed to "cool down but not perish"[3] and change from efficacious words into abstract texts without decaying or losing their fire.

Of particular interest in the anthology of legal eloquence is the fact that Maurice Garçon, who is a consummate orator as well as an excellent writer, has organized the texts according to the way they relate to literature. This is a skillfully conducted study that carries its learning lightly. Orators, observes Maurice Garçon, do not create new forms; they are slaves to literary fashion; they adapt to their own purposes the principles that the written arts impose on tradition, and they make use of what is already tried and tested. For this reason, they form a small reactionary group in the world of literature and always seem to be behind the times. They are not innovators, and the only innovations they will accept are those that bear the seal of success. Hence, during most of the seventeenth century the wildest traditions of Renaissance erudition are preserved, and it is only in the eighteenth century that Aguesseau provides the lawyer's art with its models and its classical perfection. The Romantic school provides an exception to this rule. Lawyers snap up their innovations without waiting for time to validate them. Romanticism is so naturally oratorical that eloquence becomes Romantic simply by exaggerating its own tendencies. Speech, breath, and verbal intention give form to a literature in which the art of the orator simply identified what is most uniquely its own.

The first case dating from the sixteenth century to be cited is one that was pleaded by Claude d'Épilly. It is a remarkable example of the sort of pleading that can no longer be read, and that it must have never quite been possible to hear. This example is lengthy, bristling with quotations and laden with mythological embellishments. Everything in it is extraneous to it; its orator ventures down the strangest pathways of erudition. However, this sort of eloquence is not exceptional; it was a respected form for several centuries; it reigned supreme during the pure seventeenth century, and if Racine disdains it this is because it is still all-powerful. It may therefore be assumed not only that it did not appear tiresome, but also that it was not without its influence over the judges. It was persuasive because it appeared learned. It won their hearts with a show of erudition. A phenomenon such as this reveals the extraordinary value of rhetoric, of its figures even when they were badly deployed, and of images when they are given free rein. These quotations from Ovid, Macrobius, or the Prophets, these descriptions of Olympia, this welter of historical narrative bear no relation to the subject of the plea, and yet they make the court receptive to it. They contain no arguments capable of directly affecting the mind, but they influence it indirectly by recalling the rules to which the mind is attached, and by making it feel that it has only reached its conclusion after carefully examining everything.

While eloquence in this vagabond guise continues to reign supreme in the High Court, admirable lawyers such as Pasquier, Lemaistre, and Patru begin to appeal to intelligence with a clearer sense of its proprieties, and they seek to win it over through purity of expression rather than loquaciousness. For example, Antoine Lemaistre's language is very fine. It is brisk, rapid, and built upon hidden contrasts and developments that act imperceptibly on the listener. Patru is less natural, but his language is more strictly composed, and the constant decency of his arguments is to be admired. Maurice Garçon also mentions Omer and Denis Talon, who take their inspiration from the ancients and see them as models of simplicity, before coming to Aguesseau, who is the most reasonable, noble, and honest of orators. It must be acknowledged, however, that this classical model of eloquence has the disadvantage of coming thirty or forty years after Bossuet and Bourdaloue. It lacks the boldness and sublime familiarity that these sacred orators employed at a time when classicism signified youth. Whereas Bossuet's language, defying silence through the construction of a mighty edifice, developing around an idea that it sustains and finding its equipoise in a bold and complex system, is the liveliest of compositions, the most intensely animated series of operations and actions, Aguesseau's language achieves magnificence only through solemnity, and it remains perfect only thanks to the lifelessness of its organization. Already it is clear that maturity has been achieved, and that decline is making itself felt.

The eighteenth century sees considerable changes in the practice of oratory. With Cochin and Gerbier, eloquence becomes improvisation. With the likes of Gayot de Pitavel, it veers off into frivolous libertinage. With Loyseau de Mauléon (who defended Calas), Henrion de Pansey, or Target, it embraces morality and discusses philosophical problems. Improvisation leads to further changes. Even among the orators who know that improvisation is always calculated, and who bring off unexpected feats through long preparation and an intensified awareness of the rules, spontaneous expression gradually abandons form and becomes more natural and more dependent on pathos. Speeches grow longer, for since the improviser finds himself obliged to find the right words as he is speaking, he keeps on speaking until he has found them, going repeatedly back over the same idea until finally he can give it the precise expression that will make it striking and powerful. It is noteworthy that in the same period, sacred eloquence no longer calls on memory for assistance, and yields entirely to on-the-spot invention. If Father de La Rue calls for sermons to be read out rather than recited from memory, the celebrated Father Bridaine and the Abbé Poule prefer not to write theirs down and find their inspiration in the very process of giving them. Father Barutel prepares them inwardly through pious meditation, but he makes do with a few notes carved with a knife onto the back of his crozier. Finally, the sign of political eloquence is that it is prompted by circumstance but does not survive it. Danton is someone who does not write, does not think, and heeds only the genius of the moment, yet out of improvisation he produces the order, clarity, and power of his incomparable eloquence.

The first half of the nineteenth century is an auspicious time for legal eloquence. In exchange for a few contrivances, neoclassicism endows it with a pure and calculated means of expression; then Romanticism enriches it with its excesses. This is the heyday of the likes of Berryer and Chaix d'Est-Ange. Politics with Lamartine, Montalembert, and even Guizot, religion with the likes of Lacordaire, both successfully combine oratorical vigor, a penchant for style, and a striving after the sublime. This harmony is very soon shattered. With the Second Empire, the art of speaking changes along with society as it becomes less ceremonious. A lawyer must convince an audience that is persuaded when it is moved, and that it is moved by what is melodramatic. He abandons literary effect, since juries do not like it and he himself is often no longer capable of producing it. From politics he borrows procedures whose power over the crowd he has observed. He goes increasingly in search of effects, tears, and even moments of negligence in order to achieve success that is commensurate with his listeners. Maurice Garçon's book closes with a text by Henri Robert. This lawyer took the utilitarian principle to its furthest extreme. He slimmed down the legal argument, making it short and familiar, and without beating about the bush, with the greatest economy of means, he made eloquence into everything it can be when it is indistinguishable from action.

This ultimate transformation of the art of eloquence thus reveals that, having ceased for the first time to submit to literary influences, it either becomes dependent on politics or goes off in pursuit of its own ends. It is also the case that, for the first time, literature in which Symbolism is predominant considers eloquence to be its enemy. It rejects its ambitions and discredits its methods, even withdrawing from prose its capacity for practical action, and concerning itself solely with the deepest and almost incommunicable movements of the mind. How could eloquence draw benefit from an experience that tends merely to reduce it to nothing? The crisis that affects it is perhaps due to a moral decline, but it is due also to the unexpected purity of literature, that obliges eloquence to look for other influences, or else renew its awareness of its own laws.

—April 28, 1943

On Jouhandeau's Work

The latest books by Marcel Jouhandeau, in particular *My Own* and the *New Marital Chronicles* that have just appeared,[1] help us to comprehend the strange and indomitable character of his work thanks to what is most familiar about them. They seem to give us access to the very wellspring of the writer. To speak of oneself without recourse to fiction, to show us those who were closest to one, close during the creative process as well as in the secret heart of friendship is, for someone who has almost never written except in terms of himself, to invite the eye into the heart of the enigma of literary activity and to make us complicit with the transformations that have given words and actions in their immediate form an immutable value. "The lover of faces" leads us to the foot of the "tree of faces," leaving it up to us now to try and see those faces without the aid of vision, just as we would have seen them had he not obliged us to look at them eternally from an angle of his choosing.

In a certain sense, Jouhandeau's literary ambition resembles that of Gérard de Nerval. Nerval's self only entered the sphere of his work to the extent that the history of that self appeared to him to as the history of a myth, the concentrated image of a universal drama, and because in living, he believed that the life he was living was free of all contingency. In the same way, Jouhandeau's person only entered his work as the expression of a mythical reality; under the name Godeau, it took on the form of a destiny with which the fate of heaven and earth was bound up; under the name Théophile, it went in search of a meaning that would not just shed light on its history (or part of its history), but would make that history into an exemplary one, as befits what is eternal. Similarly, every being who ventures down Jouhandeau's path and is privileged enough to attract his attention, is carried along by the movement that renders him eternal, participating in his metamorphoses and ultimately becoming a satellite in orbit round the sun in whose exceptional light he sees himself in all his glory and all his shame. However exceptional Jouhandeau's literary career remains, and to satisfy those who can only appreciate a work if they can identify its antecedents, it is possible to link it to the tradition that was illustrated by German Romanticism, whose paradoxical heritage it represents without ever having undergone its influence.

In a few pages, *My Own* portrays the writer's parents and grandparents, and in particular his mother. It is a delightfully simple little book, full of such natural, profound sentiment that its passage through literature does not diminish its unique transparency. The different portraits that Jouhandeau has left us of his mother have a truth and purity that are rarely to be found elsewhere in French literature. Not only is filial feeling expressed with unyielding intensity, revealing itself completely with a modesty that is made firmer and nobler through being confessed, thereby resembling the reflection of a maternal love that itself never failed, and was never distracted or dulled; but this affection is also a light in which, instead of becoming more blurred, the features of the beloved face appear more distinctly, and acquire through sympathy all of the reality that usually only becomes visible through the eyes of a severe and suspicious observer.

The woman he called Agnes, though her family called her Marie, and who was baptized Alexandrine, appears to us as someone richly sensitive, with an ability to understand everything that came from her heart, not her education, someone proud, intrepid, and loyal to inner scruples that place her above any particular obligation by attaching her to what is essential and necessary. Courage, a tendency toward self-denial and risk-taking that is so to speak her outer emblem—and that of the whole family—, this capacity for spiritual violence are the herald and the presentiment of the proud rapture on which each of Jouhandeau's characters draws in turn so as to defy the abyss and, whether going from good to evil or from evil to good, confront what is grandest and most horrible without ever admitting defeat, and even less, feeling humiliated.

The *New Marital Chronicles* take us to the intimate heart of the writer's life by reworking and developing themes that a first book had already powerfully established. It is remarkable that Jouhandeau should feel the need to express in different forms the dramas that have moved him, to add to his initial transposition of them a second one that amplifies it or sometimes simply repeats it, scarcely changing its position in relation to a center that is always the same. Not only do the characters he has created follow him, but his subjects also require him to develop them several times, his stories ask to be carried over from one book to the next, the thoughts that are not satisfied with a first version of immortality beg for a new chance to survive, with the persistence of subterranean beings, breaking the surface of the earth in order to reach daylight. Such repetition emphasizes the predestined nature of the images that Jouhandeau extracts from the world, as well as the anxiety they arouse in him that they will fade if they cannot make contact once again with their cause. It is as if these imaginary beings that allow him better to understand the real beings who share his life needed constantly to measure up to the events of everyday life, as if mythical significance feared it might never exhaust a particular truth. Legend circles tirelessly around each story, and the more expressive value it has, the more it needs to go back to the reality it replaces.[2]

—May 19, 1943

The Thirteen Forms of a Novel

Roland Cailleux's novel *St Genès or The Brief Life* is made up of thirteen chapters, each of which is written using a different technique.[1] For example, one of them is the diary of a hero; another is a dialogue; a third, an inner monologue; a fourth, an exchange of letters. Each of these sections is very long, and each attempts to exhaust all of the means that its chosen form places at its disposal; it seeks to give the impression that everything has been said on the subject; it is a complete system of invention and information. Since Roland Cailleux proves highly skilled at overcoming difficulties, excelling in every genre and sometimes even overcoming the primary obstacle, which consists in not appearing to have instigated these difficulties solely for the pleasure of conquering them, his book is interesting in a way that wagers usually are not, and it is simpler, more natural, and less surprising than its outer appearance would lead us to believe.

The use of different techniques within the same work is nothing out of the ordinary after *Ulysses*. In Joyce's monumental novel there are stories, dialogues, inner monologues, and forms that correspond to no classical definition. There the novel appears with all its chances still open. It has been transformed into everything it is capable of being. A few years ago, some readers may also have come across a novel that set out to use every known novelistic procedure; over seven chapters, the plot was organized and varied using seven different techniques. These antics left no mark at all on the history of the novel.[2] The danger with an effort such as Roland Cailleux's is that it sometimes has the air of a virtuoso set piece; it suffers much too much from the skillfulness that it contrives; it is threatened by what is too brilliant about its achievement.

Why did the novelist choose this form? What made its choice seem necessary to him? In what way did his chosen subject impose this diversity of technique on him? Neither the critic nor the reader can avoid these questions, but they will not find it easy to answer them. At first sight it would appear that, having decided to write the life of a young poet named Genès, the author examined its key moments and described them using a form that can never be repeated. Every episode of this young life has a corresponding genre, which expresses it and then disappears along with it, becoming unusable for any other purpose. Just as every moment dies and never returns, so the form in which we encounter it cannot survive being put to use. It would appear therefore that the art of the novelist is an attempt to symbolize the movement of time, representing its inevitable passing through the variety if the novel's techniques, and expressing the unique character of each moment not through internal analysis but by employing a form that can only be made use of once.

In fact, however, the author has given his work a completely different meaning. Action itself has been eliminated from his novel. Not only has he denied himself the advantages of a story, he has rejected continuity of detail, the sequence of random accidents that give its substance to each day. Very little actually happens, and the tenuous plot is only revealed to us indirectly, reduced in its turn to its salient points. The young pupil at Bossuet School becomes an anxious student with an enquiring mind. He likes poetry, and his ambition is to be a writer. He meets and falls in love with a young actress, who dies leaving him with a daughter. He has two friends between whom he swings as if between the two tendencies in his nature; a shy and diffident father who conceals his affection; and a kind and domineering grandmother who displays hers without subtlety. He encounters the doubts that no well-brought-up young man can avoid, and ignorant of the future that awaits him, he disappears before reaching maturity into the obscurity of an incomprehensible end. There are no stories, we are never offered any anecdotes; the thirteen sections give us an intimate picture of a life at its principal moments, and through the allusions we find there, they help us to gain some idea of a story that deprives us of any picturesque exterior.

The novelist's determination to restrict himself to essentials is remarkable. The care with which he avoids the easy charms of the novel is no less worthy of interest. He excludes what is contingent and shuns what is pleasant. In this respect there is something exemplary about his effort. As in a classical work, he retains only the significant moments of the action that he wishes to present; he chooses them for the light they cast on the life that concerns him, and because they reveal it to us only in situations that deserve to be remembered. It is far from certain that everything that happens in a life is interesting; or else what matters, what attracts a novelist's attention is the fact that anything is interesting, and hence the project of describing the profound significance of life in a series of insignificant details, and deriving essential human value from what is considered worthless. Roland Cailleux's goal is quite different. In order to know his hero, all he needs is to imagine him as he adopts a range of poses. He makes him entirely accessible by describing him only partially. He says everything about him by summing him up. At the same time, if he makes do with these rare positive moments in order to provide an account of an entire life, he does not set about describing each moment using one or two features, but with the aid of thorough analysis and description that, by varying its approach, repeatedly presents his hero to us in a new dimension or from a new angle. This amounts to a sort of literary experiment: since in order to reveal the reality of a character it is not enough to change the circumstances in which it is allowed to exist, and since moreover Cailleux intentionally reduces such circumstances down to virtually nothing, he counterbalances monotony of situation with variety of method, and each time he enters the intimate world of the character he is observing it is by a new path, as he seeks to grasp him in his identity and his otherness in accordance with the revelatory mode that he assigns to him.

It could be said that Cailleux has not made as much of this project as might have been expected. Perhaps what was discreet and reserved about the portrait he wished to paint did not sit easily with the striking originality of this mode of depiction. But it would appear also that by putting his technique to a dual use, the novelist has made it unreliable. On the one hand, he varies the form in order to adapt it to the moment he is describing; he chooses it on grounds of psychological appropriateness, and sees it as tool for inner discovery. But on the other hand, he uses this diversity of form to introduce a source of interest into the structure of his book. This diversity replaces the pleasurable effects that are usually supplied by anecdote; it introduces a pleasing variety into the composition. In the first case, the form is chosen only because it befits the age that it has to reveal, because it is a mode of existence; in the second case, it becomes a mode of the story, a mere narrative trick. It is perfectly within the author's right to claim that these two requirements are not necessarily incompatible. But the fact remains that by using different techniques he arouses our curiosity more than he satisfies it, our attention encounters seduction rather than instruction, and his main concern is to achieve a charming variety of effects rather than explore the world that he promises to reveal to us.

Each part follows on from the next in a harmonious and convincing series. The novel begins with Saint-Genès's diary at a time when he is a pupil at a church school. All children write their memoirs, and it is plausible to equip a thirteen-year-old boy with a mode of expression through which his total innocence will be evident beneath a totally literary veneer. The first features of the young poet become visible: He is a dreamer, solemn, hesitant, and already curious about himself. When we meet him again a few years later, he is taking his baccalaureate. This being the age of interminable conversations, it is through dialogue that we learn about what he thinks, or what he believes he thinks, and about the brilliant, cynical friend to whom falls the task of being his interlocutor during his early life. The third chapter is a story narrated in the present tense, the mode of action and objectivity. Now he is a student, and the young man is seeking to come out of himself; he walks the streets, he reaches out to the world, he listens to people and discovers them, his apprenticeship has begun. After a lecture given by his father on the subject of family relations in classical theater, in which he discusses the eternal separation between parents and children, we reach the inner monologue that is reserved for torments of the soul, personal obsessions, and passion. Saint-Genès has met Marie-Anne. Alas, the happy "I" is soon replaced by a peremptory "you." The young woman has died; the voice that belongs to anguish speaks to him as if from within, to remind him of the episodes of his misfortune, the pointlessness of his grief, the second death of what he loved as she is gradually driven even from the memory provided by his dreams. After a long interval during which an old spinster's memories provide a picturesque portrait of his grandmother, we find ourselves in another mode: no longer one of effusion or moral accusation, but one of depersonalization, that supremely neutral mode, represented by the impersonal "you" (*on*): "You've had enough, you're fed up, you're exhausted and nothing changes." The young poet has risen to the challenge of becoming a writer. He has experienced his own cowardliness, his own idleness; he feels empty, and it is as a man who recognizes himself only in what is ordinary and commonplace, in the dreadful vulgarity of the crowd, that he lives henceforth in a state of self-loathing. Then comes a charming fairytale written for the poet's daughter, letters between Saint-Genès and his friends that confirm the main lines of his thought, one or two of his poems, before the novel finally embarks on the soul-searching with which it ends, something like the monologue of a dying man, of the final moments, the ultimate words of a soul already lost in the night, unaware of where it is, of whether it is dying or already dead, and turning its bewilderment into a source of supreme lucidity.

The common feature of all of these pieces is the perfection they display. They are such brilliantly written pages that it is tempting to see them as examples of rhetoric, bravura pieces for which, once their virtuosity has been congratulated, eulogy becomes pure praise. After these ten or fifteen tableaus, the figure of Saint-Genès no doubt emerges in what makes it both singular and general, a symbol of the hesitations of youth, an image of itself and all others; there is no doubt either that the world whose center Saint-Genès provides is composed before our eyes, and they clearly perceive its reality. But it must be acknowledged that the meaning of all these lives is inferior to the revelation we are given of them; we are less interested in what they are than in the manner in which they appear. More precisely, we are surprised that such a diverse, insistent, and skillful enquiry into a single soul has not allowed it to reveal a deeper truth, and our surprise makes us reflect that the types of expression that Cailleux employs are perhaps less varied than he would have us believe, that beneath their apparent variation it is always the same form that is playing with words. Cailleux goes from monologue to dialogue, from "I" to "you," from the story to the tale, but the structure of his sentences remains the same, the stylistic embellishments never change, the vision presupposed by the choice of certain images, the habitual use of certain words is in no way modified. It seems to us that the experiment he has attempted would have required a more radical transformation. To go from language in which metaphor is predominant to a language of pure abstraction, from a form that strictly adheres to meaning to a form in which it is words that have the initiative; to replace an impressionistic style with a dialectical one, is (merely to cite simple examples) to introduce into a work a more fundamental and fertile level of variety than can ever be achieved even using all the resources of the novel. At this level metaphor becomes total, and beneath the mysterious rays of a changing language, plunged first into darkness then into light, into the truth of dream then into that of waking, we behold the startling features of a world that is created solely so that we can know it, or else experience what is unknowable about its reality.

—May 26, 1943

From Praise to Sovereignty

The investigations of Georges Dumézil, whose work we have already had occasion to examine, have brought to light a number of traces of Indo-European society among the Indian, Latin, and Celtic peoples. They have also shed light on the first kings of Rome, especially Romulus and Numa, by distinguishing in the more or less fabulous aspects of their history the functions that they both initiated and represented. In a new book devoted to Servius, *Servius and Fortune*,[1] Dumézil now applies the same explanatory principles to a study of the king who no longer incarnates simply sovereignty, but rather a certain type of access to sovereign power, and who is considered to be the inventor of a social practice whose origins no doubt go back to the Indo-European era. This book provides an essential examination of the role played by poets in ancient societies: Poetry has never divested itself of the mysterious power that was exerted in those times by speech, a power so great that it could make or break empires and kings.

The first kings of Rome illustrate those aspects of sovereignty for which Vedic India possesses the exact counterpart in the way it conceives of its gods and its dynasties. Like the kings Varuna and Pururavas, Romulus expresses power in what makes it violent and magical; his reign is linked to terrible forces that are bestial rather than superhuman (the Luperci). Numa, on the contrary, like the god Mitra and the king Manu, represents sovereignty in its relation to the law; he is a legislator who controls relations with the gods and whose reign is one of piety and benevolence. The two sovereigns who succeed them maintain the same alternation between violence and wisdom: Tullus Hostilius derives his prestige from excess; he resembles Romulus in his love and his readiness for action, and he has his place in the tradition that will culminate with Caesar; but Ancus Martius restores sacrifices, is a respecter of institutions and a precursor to the calm and solemn authority of Augustus. They represent the two sides to power in Rome. The feature that these four kings have in common is that they bore the burden of sovereignty without having sought it; if, with the exception of Romulus, they are elected, as Roman ideology required, they are elected freely and fairly, and it is only with Tarquin the Elder and Servius Tullius that scheming, rivalry, and everything that goes with being an official candidate make their appearance. Dumézil focuses in particular on Servius's reign because, as the typical candidate, as the perfect example of the prince who is singled out by fortune and consecrated by praise, this sovereign is also the creator of the "census," a system that is as it were the consequence, the other side of the principle to which he owes his own election.

Servius, who was born a slave in the royal palace, is an upstart whose fate is predestined by divine choice and whose merits are of the sort that such grace brings with it. He is of service to the state and proves a generous benefactor to the people. This is recognized by an assembly that turns into a veritable symposium of praise and names him king in memory of his kindness. He thus becomes sovereign by virtue of his deeds and their official approval, and he earns acclaim for his victories and the distribution of food; he is elevated to royal status by public praise as a reward for his worth. Then once he is king, he introduces a classificatory system into society that is a reflection of his own experience. The "census" involves not only counting the number of Roman citizens, but also, while preserving the traditional framework as well as taking account of birth, classifying them according to the praise or the blame that their achievements and their services attract. Censorship is a form of praise that defines a citizen, a judgment that gives him his place in the social hierarchy. It is a system of rules for assessing and promoting all those who through their luck and their labors appear to be favored by Fortune, in the sense in which Servius, too, enjoyed her favors. It is clear that Servius's creation is merely the transposition of his own path to the throne, and that both reign and candidature are merely an exchange of appraisal between the king and the people, a form of reciprocal praise. As a candidate for sovereignty he derives from praise the technique that is required to win power; as sovereign, he bases the relations between classes and citizens on praise. In other words, he makes the system that allowed him to gain power valid for all, and he makes qualificatory assessment—the assessment of the king by his subjects and of the subjects by their king—the universal social instrument.

Alerted by lexical parallels and faithful to the comparative method that he judiciously applies, Dumézil has looked for traces of a comparable institution in Indian mythology. In the legend of Prthu he has discovered features that his argument links to the history of Servius. This king, who is born from the corpse of a renegade leader, is neither a hereditary king nor an elected one; singled out by the gods, recognized by the sages, he must be consecrated in order to reign, and this consecration presupposes the participation of official lauders who make known what he has done or what he will do, thus ensuring the immediate adhesion of all the powers in the universe. After this ceremony, the king lavishes his abundant generosity on his subjects; his gifts are not distributed haphazardly, but adapted in both their type and their value to the hierarchy of the classes, whose duties and rights are thereby confirmed. To a certain extent, these distributions are the consequence of praise. It is through praise that the king attains full possession of his power, and as soon as he is praised, he gives; he gives first if all to those who have praised him, then to all his subjects and all people; he gives out of gratitude and royal munificence. Made king thanks to favorable opinion, he derives the certainty of his power from the public voice, but it is thanks to the power that he owes to speech that he is able to be generous and rich, to reward men according to the social castes into which they are divided. Dumézil pays close attention to the differences that exist between this institution as it exists in ancient Vedic society and in early Rome. Roughly speaking, in India qualificatory praise (expressed by the root form *çama*, which can be compared to the Latin root form *cena*) primarily has a role in the consecration of the king; it is represented by an official personage, the sūta, bard, or panegyrist, whose role is not only to bear witness to the virtues of the prince but also to increase them by providing a model for them. In Rome, on the contrary, qualificatory praise is primarily directed at its subjects; its representative is the *censor*, who periodically establishes and revises each person's social status. Whereas in India the appraisal of the people by the king is restricted to the restoration of the natural social and cosmic order, or else to gifts in kind, in Roman society, which is not made up of immutable castes, and where individual advancement remains a possibility, the *censor* has the power to promote, sustain, or downgrade every citizen. By contrast, whereas praise merely plays a lowly, political role in the election of the Roman king, confined as it is to electoral debate and voting, and without an organ to express itself or any procedure that derives from it, in the consecration of the Indian sovereign it has a magical efficacy, making the king dependent on a sort of officiating presence, that of a specialized evaluator whose praise makes him into what he must be. It is reasonable to conclude from these observations that India and the Roman state retained and adapted for their own use elements drawn from the institution of praising that in Indo-European society must have comprised a twofold mechanism: the installation of the king through the praise of his subjects, the installation of the subjects through the appraisal of the king.

This power of praise is the power of speech. It reveals the sovereign role played by language in the governance of men. The poet, who is one of the pillars of royal power along with the magus and the priest, is the originator of a certain type of sovereignty. In "royalties of election" he plays the role held by Brahmans and magicians in "royalties of right." First of all, he foretells the future king; he is the first to recognize the one whom fortune has designated; he has an intimate relation with chance that allows him to see the chosen one whom she has crowned before anyone else does, and he presents him to the masses by revealing his entitlement, by making him so to speak visible. Then he educates the king; his praise is more than a certification, it is an inner preferment; it links the sovereign to the praise he must become worthy of, it parades his future greatness before his eyes, it makes him the prisoner of the worth it attributes to him; in Dumézil's words, as much and indeed more than *noblesse*, *louange oblige*. This power of praise finds exemplary confirmation in Indian mythology. When Indra, king of the gods, slays the demon Vrtra he is almost destroyed by his victory, and reduced to the size of an atom, he disappears into the heart of a lotus blossom. Agni, the god of fire, is given the task of finding him, but he searches the earth and the heavens in vain; as for water, he cannot enter this element without perishing. So the priest-god incants his praise, and made more powerful than he is by this eulogy, Agni hurls himself into the ocean where he discovers the retreat of the diminished god. And now, how can Indra be saved? Through praise. The priest-god reminds him of his former exploits, extols him with his compliments, and, says the poet, "thus showered with praise, Indra began gradually to grow."

This magical growth is the privilege of the language of praise. It is linked to acclaim, which, in the ancient rituals for the inauguration of kings, determined the mission of the sovereign by giving him the means to carry it out. The expression *vox populi, vox dei* derives from this original power. Favorable opinion makes kings by associating them with the gods, and "praise of men" is a divinity under whose patronage the sovereign who is chosen by the public voice exists. A king such as Prthu is called the master of wild beasts and the master of words; in order to be truly a prince he must possess lordship over speech and dominion over language. Because it is partly dependent on language, his royal power is only real through his mastery of words, a mastery that he maintains through the intermediary of the poets, or more precisely those official praisers of whom court poets are merely the degenerate descendants. The power of praise has as its counterpart the power of blame. In Ireland, the legend of King Bres illustrates the sort of authority that is exerted by words of insult. In opposition to the avaricious and grasping king stands the *file*, the poet, who transforms popular discontent into magical expulsion and precipitates the ruin of the prince simply by assessing his misdeeds. "Before the *file*," says Fergus, "lakes and rivers sink from sight when he censors, and rise into the air when he praises!" That is an echo of the all-powerful action of satire, to which peoples who were jealous of their rights, like the Celts, the Gauls, and the Irish, resorted in order to keep the tyranny of centralized power in check. Through the cursing of the *censor*, society rejects the oppression inflicted on it by a sovereignty that has become deranged.

It is remarkable that sovereignty of speech should be associated in both Rome and India with Fortune. There is a natural link between praise and success that depends as much on opportunity as on worth. Fortuna favors Servius from birth; she becomes his deity of choice, and he raises numerous temples to her. This Roman Fortune does not display the effrontery of the blind fate that rewards the foolish and betrays the wise. It is a recompense for personal merits that would be powerless without it, but that it cannot replace. It is like the divine face of all the varieties of quality—courage, wealth, skill, strength, cunning—that are necessary for success. With the aid of fortune, men manage their store of talent so as to acquire merit, and through praise such merit earns public recognition and is in effect increased. Praise is the counterpart among men of the esteem that fortune presupposes between the gods. It is not purely gratuitous because it records real services, just as chance is not purely fortuitous because it makes real virtues auspicious. But praise is also an act of faith in the future, and it has a power of its own from which all those who receive it benefit, just as through chance occasions, fortune increases to the highest degree the powers that it favors. Between fortune, praise, and sovereignty there are an infinite number of relations whose various meanings we can catch a glimpse of in Dumézil's work. It would appear that each of these three concepts is an instance of the gift: Fortune is a gift that the merits of the receiver are not enough to justify, and that makes him into more than he is. Praise is a gift that corresponds to this exceptional gift; it is also an appeal for royal largesse or a recompense for past retributions, but it is also implicated in the future, granting and giving the virtues that it extols; last, sovereignty, which is a product of the twofold gift of gods and men, is exercised and can be recognized through the abundant gifts that it lavishes. The main characteristic of the king is to be a giver, to give out of gratitude and out of generosity and goodwill, and to organize individuals according to the chance bestowal of this bounty. This conception of the gift is to be found in societies of the sacred type, and it contrasts with the notion of exchange that characterizes modern societies, according to which every value is consumed in order to produce an equivalent value that replaces it. This notion forbids any consumption that is simply pure waste, any unusable production, and it bases human exchange on relations of strict practical equivalence. We may note, however, that even when poetry fulfills a social role in religious societies, it continues to be a power that exceeds all forms of exchange. It is supremely what is given, what reveals the gift of the gods while lending credit to men.

—June 2, 1943

Religious Poetry

Dominique Aury, thanks to whom our knowledge of French poetry has been much improved and many a magnificent text brought to light, has recently compiled a new selection of the finest examples of religious poetry in France.[1] This work is composed with such simplicity that it is only after reading it that we become aware of how much knowledge it presupposes. It brings together works in which poetry is inspired by traditional religious sentiment, from Rutebeuf down to Péguy. Some of these poems are famous. Many deserve to become so, now that this publication has brought them to light. Almost of all of them reconcile poetry with religion, so that the collection does not present us with the sort of texts that are imposed on literature, to its astonishment, by excessive complacency toward what is touching about faith. It is poetry first and foremost that has been Dominique Aury's concern in making her selection. The works she offers our sentiments are worthy of the language without which religious inspiration would amount to nothing, and often they are even superior to the silence that is in fact the only extreme at which poetry may be sacrificed to a movement that transcends it.

Perhaps it is fortunate that this anthology has put aside those doubts that might naively be thought to arise when considering religious poetry. By religious poetry what is meant quite simply is Christian poetry; the great poets of our country adhere for the most part to traditional beliefs, and whether Catholic or Protestant, they have extended the invention of a language to embrace subjects they could not have found within themselves. Their faith is totally familiar. It is faithful solely to established texts or simple dogmas. It transforms into an extraordinary poetic force the emotions that any believer can experience in the normal course of a liturgical life. It reveals nothing that it has not already received. Any outlandish tone is immediately stifled. These bold creators who, through the power of image alone, invent new worlds, transform passions, and make mankind different from what it is, appear perfectly docile and submissive when they turn toward the source of all creation and all metamorphosis. It seems to them that they have achieved something entirely new when they rediscover in themselves what is most ancient. They become nothing but memory in order to encounter feeling at its most personal. If they speak of God, they become almost invisible as they share what they have in common with everyone.

Dominique Aury's collection wisely leaves aside those poems whose source lies in a purely personal meditation. This is not out of any concern for orthodoxy, but out of respect for the separation of genres. Between religious poetry that marries poetic fortune with a regular religious tradition, and poetry in which the mind invents sacrifices and temples for itself alone, there is merely the analogy of an equally disciplined language that has been raised to a higher level. It would be possible, for Dominique Aury more than anyone, to put together as a counterpart to a collection of Catholic and Protestant poetry another collection, no less rich and no less fine, containing texts inspired by an obscurer spiritual quest, and free of any adherence to dogma. The path leading from Maurice Scève to Rimbaud is marked by works that are religious by virtue of the inner experience they seek to convey, but whose nature also is that they escape religion. These works are less a case of deistic or philosophical reverie than texts in which the poet, putting into words the illumination that he has received or initiated, becomes his own high priest and penetrates to the heart of secrets that only have meaning in poetry itself. The classic example of such poems, which are religious through their deep sense of the ruin of words, is Gérard de Nerval's "Artémis."

The compliancy of inspiration to be found in Catholic or Protestant poets is not just one of the features of their faith; it is also linked to poetic truth. The finest religious poems have renounced all intrinsic meaning from the outset. They signify nothing in themselves. They lay claim to no intellectual value. They provide religious intelligence with nothing that it has not already learned with greater subtlety and profundity from the sacred texts themselves. What is more, they are often content to be the exact translation of these liturgical texts. From the psalms, the canticles, and the prose scriptures they take thoughts and even images and combine them according to the rules of their art. They transpose the language of ancient piety entirely into a new language that differs from it only in its words. This humility is highly significant. It is as if these great poets find in their submission to a meaning over which they have no control a way of distracting attention from it, of neutralizing it and reducing it to naught. Their poetry is not addressed to understanding, since understanding need merely consult the first book of piety it comes across to be entirely satisfied. On the contrary, it uses the borrowing it carries out in order to abolish everything that is still prosaic about a text that is understood. It is nothing henceforth but rhythm, accent, pace of voice. It is entirely contained within the invocatory reality of language, and it allows apparent meaning to give way to the new meaning that comes from the musical intensity of the lines and the vocal harmony of the words. In other words, these religious poems, whose total clarity of meaning belongs entirely to tradition, are the equivalent of highly obscure poems for which no other combination of words can substitute an analogous meaning. Each of them causes attention to fade before ideas and has importance only for the sounds, the figurative values, and the physical effects that it deploys. Making self-evident in the form of a translation what is in effect external to them, the poems themselves become untranslatable, and they exist only to the extent that they offer nothing new to understand, that they are incomprehensible.

If an attempt were made to classify by tendency and by category the varying forms that religious poetry has taken over seven centuries, it would be clear that they are few in number and can be arranged (rather arbitrarily of course) in four or five different genres. The most important, or at least the most classic of these is the translation of psalms or liturgical works. This translation is generally meticulous and faithful. There are paraphrases, but they count for less than the regular transposition of biblical poetry, verse by verse. Such precision goes no further than the literal sense. It is indifferent to the spirit of the text. The "poetry" of the Old Testament is neither translated nor imitated, because it would be impossible to do so; in its place there comes the incomparable poetry of the translator. Religious poems that express personal emotion are rare. The lyricism of Rutebeuf and Villon, with its starting point in a sentiment whose power can still be recognized today, finds no more than a perfidious echo in certain nineteenth-century works; the emotion of Rutebeuf in "The Nine Joys of Notre-Dame" is religious, that of Lamartine in "The Crucifix" profane. The works that are most readily inspired by religious feeling deal with the uncertainties of fate, fear of death, or the anxieties of a wasted life, all of which are ambiguous themes since they introduce sentiments that religion colors but does not create. The fine canticle to the Blessed Virgin Mary by du Perron, or those of Bertaut and Godeau on the birth of Our Lord, are a more direct expression of an emotion that would be inexplicable outside of the religious life, or indeed the religious experience. They are a response to a sort of spiritual turmoil. At the same time, it cannot be said they have any revelatory value. There is no mystical poetry strictly speaking in Catholic or Protestant poetry. The true mystical poems in our language, those born of an inner discovery, a ravishing or a revelatory anguish, were composed independently of religious traditions.

Two other genres have poetic invention in common. Those whom Dominique Aury rightly calls the visionaries derive a new vision of the world from sacred meditation. They imagine the universe in the form that dogma dictates to faith. They make creation visible behind nature, the tragedy of salvation behind history and the end of time behind death. D'Aubigné rends the veil of natural realities and imposes the presence of another world. By means of image, he takes us into an all-powerful system that is closer to us than our everyday life. He will not let us go until we are permanently confined inside his dream, damned with the sinners, saved with the chosen. In contrast to this poetry of the imagination there is the poetry that must be termed symbolic or more precisely, allegorical. The deeper religious life calls upon figures that explicit meaning can never entirely reveal. Language fills with metaphors that are alien to profane thinking; it is enriched with words that have a fourfold articulation. It opens up in so many ways that the usual syntactical links are replaced by more important relations that belong to allegorical meaning. This is not a matter of myth in the true sense of the term. The *Theorems* of La Ceppède, along with the allegorical sonnets of Drelincourt, possess in principle a key that the knowledge and practice of religion places in our hands. They provide a translation of the universe through parables, in the same way that D'Aubigné's *Tragiques* provides an imaginative expression of it. They attempt to contain the entire wealth of things, the entire system of truths within a few figures whose total interpretation would be the equivalent of a new creation of the world.

D'Aubigné and Corneille appear to be the two poets who put the most faith into their works, and thanks to whom poetry is permitted to be religious with a plenitude that would be unimaginable without them. Corneille's psalms, the humble fruit of his labors, conform entirely to their model but derive from their supreme use of language that sense of glory that is one of the rarest of religious sentiments. D'Aubigné is probably the only poet who, without imitating biblical poetry strictly, stands as a rival to it. From his admirable poems there arises a voice that is as disturbing, fantastic, and imperious as that of the great prophets. It is, precisely, excessive. It speaks brilliantly of wretchedness and of splendor with simplicity. It challenges God as if it were another voice of God. It has the despair that comes from certainty and the pride of those that tremble. It is gentle and human. There is nothing more worthy of admiration in any sublime poetry. In the inexhaustible poetic riches of the sixteenth and seventeenth centuries, Dominique Aury has found new forms of beauty that were little known or even unknown to almost everyone. The solemn, somewhat arid works of Protestants like des Masures or de La Jessée, the great poems of du Perron, superb for their eloquence yet at the same time lit from within by a gentle light, the sonnets of Desportes, the canticles of Bertaut, keep company with the admirable poems of Sponde, Gombauld, Malleville, and Godeau, whose finest verse is now familiar to us thanks to earlier volumes by Dominique Aury and Thierry Maulnier.[2] But La Ceppède, Martial de Brives, and Drelincourt above all are the three names that remain powerfully present in the memory of those who did not know them, or only had memories of them that were deceptive. In La Ceppède's *Theorems*, religious sonnets to which the poet adds long theological commentaries, there is a rare sense of abstract decoration, an extraordinary symbolic opulence, an almost barbarous predilection for rich spiritual ornamentation, but also a muted, secret sound that can be heard in the pure words of Sonnet 88:

Often have I tried to follow you, my life
Along familiar paths your mercy shows
But always, but always your several foes
Have seized me by the sheet, my strength borne off.

Now that I hear your spiritual call
To mark your footsteps with these measured feet
This world, this charmer, this foe is a cheat
Clutching me by the cloak, threatening my will.

By a thousand vanities I am possessed,
So much, so long besotted, I am pressed
For time to follow you to Calvary:

Henceforth, lord, grant that learning by your favor
From the young man who slipped his captors, I
May leave these habits to the world forever.[3]

And have Drelincourt's Christian sonnets ever been granted their rightful place? A near contemporary of Corneille's, this obscure poet is capable of writing verse whose brilliance is double-edged: the visible brilliance of golden words, the purely intellectual brilliance of inner visions, as for example in this sonnet on precious stones:

What, can so much fire and radiance and light
Emerge from such a cold, crude, dark element?
And do so many Stars, born of these dark Quarries,
Make of the earth another Firmament?

Brilliant minerals, earthly Lights
With which the heads of Kings superbly shine,
I see you merely as vulgar things,
And for me your brilliance is just a feeble ornament.

Invisible sun, who gave being to the World,
Come fill my heart through your fecund power
With the heavenly jewels of Hope and Faith.
And let me, when I cease one day to hope and to believe,

Obtain in your heaven and possess with You
The priceless Crown of radiant Glory.[4]

Even less well-known is Father Martial de Brives, whose *Paraphrase on the Canticle of the Three Children* of 1660 admirably combines the abstract value of words with their evocative power, and employs an unexpected idea as a metaphoric *trouvaille*:

Heavens, fearful Machines
Of azure, all hanging vaults,
Where God with outstretched arm
Revealed his divine power:
Glittering tabernacles,

Circles of Land and Wave,
Brazen bodies, massive and prepared,
Bless the Judge of the world
Who in motion placed your rest.[5]

These fine works emerge totally fresh from the oblivion that has preserved them for us. Having remained in their absence as if outside of time, they are young thanks to our ignorance and brilliant thanks to our curiosity.

—June 9, 1943

Novels

"When criticism takes the form of a *judgment*," wrote Paul Valéry, "this entails comparing what an author intended to do with what he actually did."[1] And indeed, Maxence Van der Meersch's novel *Bodies and Souls* does require us to relate it to its author's intentions.[2] Otherwise it would be difficult and pointless to talk about it. All that could be said of it—that it is the fruit of much labor, that it required a great deal of observation and study, or that it offers an opinion on serious ideas—would scarcely conceal the scant interest it offers as far as the art of the novel is concerned. And it is true to say that as a novel, it is of almost no interest in literary terms.

What was Van der Meersch trying to do? He appears to have dreamed a lot about illness and suffering. He has observed the struggles of doctors and patients. In the former, he identifies a type of truth that generally goes unremarked by the latter. He has looked into whether the art of medicine, which is fragmentary, materialistic, and has no inkling of human destiny, does not ignore those who are ill when it treats their illnesses.

Ultimately, he has taken sides against classical medicine and enthusiastically promoted the thinking that places greatest emphasis on diet. On that basis, his book develops as a long series of episodes that portray a young doctor who, devoted to sickness and suffering, returns to the straight and narrow path of the healer's art, and even to the love of God, while university professors and celebrated surgeons end up in dishonesty or despair.

There are no hidden messages in Van der Meersch's novel, and that is what guarantees its honesty. There is nothing ambiguous about its project. He has given himself the role of convincing the public. He uses fiction to persuade it of real problems. He openly mixes truth and falsehood in order to make the truth more striking. What does it matter to him if he is told that a novel can prove nothing? It is, precisely, the novel that he has chosen to use as his mode of exposition, not to say as a means of demonstrating a point. And he has aimed to derive from a lie enough that is entertaining and persuasive to win us over to a harsh and difficult truth. He ought not therefore to be accused of writing a thesis novel, because that is what he set out to do; he has generously shouldered the risks associated with a disparaged genre that is almost impossible to defend.

Perhaps Maxence Van der Meersch's error comes from his ambition, which has led him not only to express his ideas on the art of medicine and on faith, but also to portray scenes from everyday life and to depict what he judges. His method as a novelist is that of traditional realism; and there is no doubt about what happens to realism when it is applied to the world of medicine, to descriptions of hospitals and to scenes involving students. Van der Meersch has spared us nothing: abortions and caesareans by the dozen, asylums and sanatoria, morgues and amphitheaters, and he has made unbridled use of the violent situations and horrible circumstances that many a novelist before him has made available to the lover of curiosities. It is impossible to know what the author hoped to achieve through the repetition of almost identical scenes. There is nothing more monotonous than these opened-up abdomens, these rotten organs, this prodigality of blood and germs. It is as if, having consciously collected together a large amount of learned knowledge, he felt reluctant to deprive us of it, and expanded his book until it acquired the dimensions of his documentation, so becoming, without him realizing, a sort of catalogue of rare diseases and complicated operations. What is excessive about such learning makes it in fact rather flimsy. It encumbers us with its indiscretion and it is too apparent not to appear suspect to us.

It is to be feared that success will eliminate the book that Van der Meersch dreamed of. His arguments will please some people, his descriptions even more, and the vulgarity of detail will mask the spiritual concerns that were meant to illuminate the work as a whole. It cannot even be said that a novel like this provides too complacent a portrait of the ponderous, soulless world whose downfall it foretells. The portrayal of this materialistic milieu is picturesque. In no way does it convey the sense of a restricted life or an impossible fate. It consists of gaudy imagery that corresponds exactly from without to a set of theoretical views.

The impression of a closed world allowing neither hope nor escape that Van der Meersch has vainly tried to convey to us through his immense effort at realism, can be forcibly felt in Alice Rivaz's little novel *Clouds in the Hand*, and with a simplicity that fully deserves to be mentioned.[3] This first novel, which has a preface by Edmond Jaloux, does have its laborious moments, and it can be clumsy and irritatingly derivative; it is often written in a strange fashion, and local expressions sit alongside unfortunate lapses of style. But even with all of these ultimately superficial flaws, it still exerts a rare power of suggestion that owes nothing to the plot and almost nothing to anything the author has contrived. Rivaz takes us by way of a brief story into a suffocating world in which she confines us once and for all along with her heroes, leaving us no hope of any sort of change later on. For a few hours, her characters struggle to free themselves before our eyes. One of them, burdened with a humdrum office job, dreams of handing in his notice and becoming a solid peasant in the south; the other, who works in the same office, betrays his fiancée for a woman who loves and desires him. Throughout the day we see these two characters come and go with their accomplices, before the gate whose threshold they wish to cross. To what end? The first of them does not hand in his notice and will never do so; the second yields fruitlessly to his desire and is left with neither memories nor wounds. Their dreams are merely "clouds in the hand."

One of Alice Rivaz's qualities is to have successfully contained the entire curve of two lives within a very brief timespan. What will happen the following day is of no importance. Whether there is a fresh urge to escape enslavement, a total renunciation or a muted rebellion, it all comes to the same, interchangeably; events no longer have meaning for these feeble beings who have been unable to overcome their condition. We have the devastating feeling that for two men, and perhaps for everyone, history considered as the possibility of an inner and an outer renewal has just come to an end. No hope lies in the future because there is no future; time has really stopped. Another feature of this novel is the entirely inward—and yet insurmountable—nature of the fate to which it condemns us. The men do not succumb to the hostility of extraordinary twists of fate; destiny inhabits them in the form of a lack of willpower, a desire that is too feeble and does not survive once it is satisfied, a deceptive dreaming in which all hope of true action is exhausted and finds no substance. Saintagne and Lorenzo are not just pathetic nihilists who conveniently salvage from their downfall a determination to bemoan it; everything is weak, everything is faded about the fate they give themselves, and even the wake they leave behind them, the "what does it matter" or "what's the use" that provide the significance of their failed endeavors vanish without laying claim to the least importance, as useless as the sham humanity whose defeat they represent.

André Dhôtel's novel *The Pathetic Village* takes us further and further away from a realism with which, nonetheless, he cannot quite manage to make a clean break.[4] This is the book of a writer who is still young, who has a rare talent, who heeds only himself and who effortlessly[5] produces a sparse, enigmatic and almost identical sound from language. The first impression we have of his heroes is that they are transparent. Dhôtel speaks of them in short, simple, direct sentences; he describes what they do, he accompanies them in their adventures, he says what they think: for us they are like pure crystal. However, there is also a certain laziness about a mode of description that is never complete enough to capture what is essential. Seemingly distracted, the author forgets a number of facts without which we can know nothing; dreamily, he omits to reveal secrets that would require too much thought and that continue to escape language. This produces a peculiar feeling in the reader. If in his view he can see through these characters so clearly, if his gaze passes through them without undergoing the least refraction, it is because they are nothing but clarity and purity, and this transparency is precisely the property of what cannot be seen, of what possesses enough simplicity, discretion and absence not to detain vision; it is the mystery of daylight itself; it is the gracious incognito of light. Dhôtel's heroes thus possess a truth that preserves them from shadow and depth; they are like two-dimensional beings on whom tricks of relief and perspective bestow no false mystery. At the same time, they must also integrate with the world, they must live, participate in collective behavior, and that is when the problems start. In *The Pathetic Village*, Odile and Julien stop off in an Ardennes village, and their presence disrupts the lives of its inhabitants. These young newlyweds have immediately begun thinking about a divorce, because they are too alike to live in harmony but too close to part forever. But they make the mistake of ignoring their true nature; one of them, who is a poet deep down, persists in wanting to become a mechanic; the other, who is strikingly beautiful, is astonished by the dramas she unwittingly provokes. Soon catastrophe strikes, unfortunate experiences come thick and fast. It is not that the undertaking that these young people have in mind is totally unreasonable; on the contrary, there is common sense, application, and seriousness in their behavior, but this seriousness drives common humanity to behave extravagantly, and they are held responsible for the follies of others. Finally, after several twists and turns, the novel ends with hope for a reconciliation. Odile and Julien stop quarrelling, and the pathetic village promises them peace.

In one sense, the subject of the book is this: How can novel heroes gain a foothold in reality? How can they become farmers, find an occupation, engage in practical work without creating an imbalance? It cannot be denied that this question has created a problem for art itself in Dhôtel's case. The amalgam between reality and his characters is imperfect; despite the various walk-on characters he introduces, the village seems like a fantasy; it is hard to take it seriously, and its dramas seem stripped of their consequences because of the fragility we assume in their protagonists. The book's true charm lies in the mixture of lucidity and torpor, precision and insouciance that characterizes its main figures. It is as if the most alert among the men, the most industrious among the young women live with a slumbering double who from time to time becomes involved in their actions. Everything that is strange about existence stems from the interventions of these unexpected sleepwalkers.

We conclude this survey of recent novels with a note about the first book by Dominique Brejon de Lavergne, *The Anachronistic Heart.*[6] This book tells the story of a young lover who is so timid and so filled with prejudice that because he has not been formally introduced to the woman he loves, and who appears to love him in return, he allows her to become engaged to someone else. The absurdity of this situation is developed by means of analyses that reveal its inevitability. Imprisoned within itself, a prey to its own diffidence, the most intense form of passion is unable to overcome the proprieties with which it surrounds itself, and we witness the unhappy young man during a brief stay in a spa town, circling vainly round a woman he is free to make his conquest, meeting her fruitlessly twenty times a day and finally losing her because she does not know him, and politeness prevents him from speaking to her. A sort of high-flown humor gives charm to this little book, that could well have been yet another commentary on an absurd world, but is merely the dismal image of an anachronistic heart.

—June 14–15, 1943

French Suite

Too many books on the subject of France, to many studies of her genius, too many books of all kinds in which zealous minds act like mirrors of an eternal truth have made it almost impossible to tolerate all of the pages that try to pass for an explanation of France, and seek to add to the enigma that it is natural that she should be, the clarity that results from entirely superficial analysis. It is too easy to claim that this need for self-definition is itself an element of the French spirit, that no nation has sought with more passion and rigor to formulate what it once was, that such a search is part of her history and has participated in her history, so that to deter her from her predilection for self-representation is to deprive her of one of her best means of action by depriving her of the image of the riches that she holds in store. Such excuses can merely increase our suspicion. For since the refusal to speak about France, the decision to reject all such self-examination as too vague, indiscreet or inevitably foreign to the unique mystery of a people, may itself also be considered as a characteristic feature of our spirit, as the secret voice of opposition and contestation that is inseparable from every word spoken in France, it is clear that one runs the constant risk of being caught up in spite of oneself, and even through one's silence, in a controversy where yes and no have equal value, and one feels bitterly angry with all those lovers of talk who attribute meaning to the fact that someone says nothing, and turn even the decision to be silent into words.

Discretion is without a doubt the noblest quality of Claude Roy's book *French Suite*.[1] Since an inner need has led him to talk of France, he has done so in an undertone, as if a murmur appeared to him as the most decorous mode in which to formulate his precepts and his definitions; he who is by nature so lively and spontaneous, so wedded to the light of the visible, has devoted all of his brilliance to making himself indistinct, turned all his color into nuance and all his dynamism into hesitation; there is nothing excessive in what he says. His critique of what is measured is itself extremely measured, he reminds us of principles and forms in a tone of confidence, and he speaks in accents of the deepest sensitivity when he touches on what is most intimately personal to him, and what for all of us is more intimate and personal than ourselves. He neither lingers nor hastens by. He illuminates without dispelling shadow. His analysis is a sort of incantation. And he borrows the voices of many celebrated commentators, as if to conceal his own voice from us even though it is the only one we are interested in, and it is beneath the mask of all those he cherishes, Marivaux, Vauvenargues, or Supervielle, that we must seek those features most apt to show us what he is and what it is about French reality that he wishes to portray.

It may be that the numerous authors, be they modern or older, who have set themselves the task of thinking about France have finally succeeded in grasping what makes her truly herself. It is even beyond doubt that their almost constant accord makes the authenticity of the observations they share highly probable. In any case, when French observers are concerned they bring to the fore if not the deep-rooted nature of the physical and political persona that constitutes a nation, at least the unchanging manner in which the French see and define the nature of their country. If this way of seeing things invariably entails an illusion, such untruth is part of the truth it contributes to concealing; it is that truth as it is always perceived, distorted, and falsified by those whom it concerns most intimately; it therefore expresses through its imprecision the precise relations that bind people of a given nationality to their nation, the necessary laws according to which they reflect, in an unreal manner, what it really is. However, this first level of approximation is still highly insufficient. It is not a matter of France as she sees herself, or of the French as they reveal themselves in their theory of France. For the French people who are concerned by this national meditation, be they historians, moralists, or politicians, not only constitute a tiny number who may or may not betray the thinking or the instincts of the group, but they also belong to the bizarre elite constituted by writers, that category of men who feel a special sensitivity to words, and for whom all problems can ultimately be reduced to a certain type of expression. It is perfectly possible to imagine, therefore, that what their observations express is not the views of the French about France, but what an analysis of language and a reasoned or unconscious familiarity with style allow them to glimpse of the French spirit as it is embodied in language.

Yet more must be said. Writers who have written about France have studied her through her history. Even if they have called upon objective disciplines such as geology, geography, and every sort of science, they have of necessity enquired into her past, and it is from the fruits of her duration, the military and political events, the writings and the monuments that they believe they can extract information about her current situation. There is a difficulty here that can only be overcome by an act of faith. However serious the analyses, however precise the enquiries or general the conclusions, all the definitions that can be given of a people are historical. They concern what it was, account for what it has done, shed light on what it sought to be, but they take no account of the present moment for which they were written and quite arbitrarily extend the truths of bygone centuries to the new field on which the centuries have come to die along with their truths. This remark does not venture to question the enduring value of history. It is simply based on what is self-evident: Nations change. They belong to a cycle that is greater than they are. They become what they are not only by virtue of their nature, but also as a result of universal changes that alter the face of the world. What can we learn from such conscientious observers who, in analyzing the historical diversity of a people, also claim to have grasped the nature of what brought it into being? They tell us this, if only we are willing to hear it: Here is what this people was, and that is what it will never be again.

In fact, the present of a nation as it is expressed by the writer who deduces it from the past is all the more contentious for simultaneously displaying that writer's reaction to the past and his sensitivity to recent circumstances. It may be that he considers his own feelings to be authentic, since they are after all those of a child born and bred in that country, and an exceptionally enlightened and sensitive one at that. If he observes that the nation he belongs to is slower-moving than it was, less generous with its resources and less confident about its fundamental choices, if he feels that it is instinctively attached to routine and anxious about the innovations that destiny brings, he turns toward himself and toward the past, where he discovers a whole range of examples that mount a protest against this impoverishment, that explain it and even derive from it the hope for great riches in the future. In one of his best chapters, Claude Roy observes that for centuries, the French people conveyed an impression of enthusiasm and fickleness; in reaction to the dangers associated with that temperament, its elites succeeded in imposing the opposite qualities, so that finally seriousness, clarity, and sparseness became the prerogative of the ordinary French person, while the aristocracy went in search of the frivolity and folly whose charms they had initially rejected. This "there-and-back" movement is perhaps just wishful thinking. It at least provides an excellent illustration of what often happens in the mind of the historian. If he seeks so intently today to include in his definition of France not restraint but excess, not order and clarity but the riches that come from violent traditions, and instead of the virtues of day a nocturnal sense of the infinite, it is perhaps because as a representative of the elite, he feels an inner yearning for those tendencies that are so cruelly lacking in the majority, and because he feels it necessary to revive a relish for them by linking them to a distant heritage.

It is in any case a fact that in recent times, the main lines of our spirit have changed (according to the essayists, at least). Some have replaced common sense with a capacity for paradox; others have replaced the need for certainty and peace with passionate strife and a thirst for adventure; yet others have eliminated the hills and valleys of our spiritual landscape, representing it merely as a twisted chain of peaks and chasms. Finally there are those for whom what characterizes the French spirit is an ability to be reasonable in the midst of delirium, impatient in forbearance, in control yet full of ardor, constantly thirsting for what opposes it and constantly seeking to strike a balance by making irreconcilable contrasts coexist. That is the drift of the study by Aragon that recently appeared in the *Cahiers du Rhône* under the title "Controversy on the Genius of France."[2] In our tradition, the conjunction "and" has acquired a use whose significance is peculiar. It falls to the will of the French to join together things that for other peoples are mutually exclusive; either simultaneously, in a quest for profound harmony, or successively, out of a singular liking for vicissitudes, to posit forms that are so different as to be near opposites; to be at once a Christian and a materialist, a classic and a rebel, both critical and original, a traditionalist and passionately committed to what is new. Everything that takes shape through contradiction, is linked by dissimilarity or is mutual within discord; what is both pride and discouragement, resignation and ardor, insouciance and fidelity, nonchalance and seriousness, is all part of the French character and explains why France, so ordered and so drawn to a life without ups and downs, exists solely within a time scale that is racked by explosions, and whether grand or laid low, in the ascendant or in decline, scattered or converging on itself, she displays a diverse series of superimposed figures that make up the recognizable and even perfectly harmonious face that is hers. It should be added that despite this use of the conjunction "and," French genius does not appear dialectical. Its oscillations do not obey a law of deepening development. They are unforeseen rather than logical, and at the same time more stable and more regular than a continuous process of self-contestation might lead one to presuppose. It is in relation to a balanced, almost unshifting unity, driven by an urge to put to the test the plenitude of its powers and the elasticity of its genius, that French history combines together the greatest variety of relations and obstinately reduces the diversity of its details to its overall harmony. "Variety and continuity," wrote Paul Valéry, "these are fairly regular, remarkably rapid oscillations around certain forms of equilibrium, be they a return to some ideal or a return to experience, an alternation between the need for novelty and the need for the authority of tradition: those seem to me to be the most obvious and consistent features of what France has provided, taken as a whole."[3]

What value can this assertion have today? Is it the result of analysis or the lesson provided by an ideal? Is it a hypothesis that the writer has discovered in himself in order to transform his doubts about the present, or does it represent an approximation provided by historical observation and literary tradition? There is no answer to these questions. It can merely be observed that a mind like Paul Valéry's, so wary of history, has no hesitation in deriving from the countless facts about what has been, from that ocean of events, decisions, works, attitudes, and people that can be related to what we assume to be the reality of France, a perfectly clear and simple definition such as the one we have just quoted, that can be applied to all ages, even to today. This surprising abuse of concepts would be inexplicable, were it not possible to see it as the effort of an artist to think about himself in the form of a history to which he feels intimately bound. When Paul Valéry defines France, he does not do so after studying everything that may be attributed to her. His definition is an amplification of one or two precise ideas that have been suggested to him by French poetry and by lengthy reflections on his own poetic works. "After what I have said," he writes, "it will be not be surprising to hear that I consider France itself as a *form*, and that it appears to me to be like a *work*."[4] This therefore brings us back to language and, more vaguely, to the knowledge of a nation provided by its literature. It must be admitted that everything we know about a people comes from the modicum of general truths that we gain from the frequentation of its great writers, and that are confirmed by one or two concepts borrowed from its history and its geography. No doubt this is sufficient to sustain political faith and a confidence in destiny, as Claude Roy has done. But it is not enough to make silence something to be condemned.

—June 23, 1943

Hoffmann's Fantastic

Albert Béguin has recently presented us with an exemplary version of *Tomcat Murr* in a first complete translation.[1] Hoffmann is the most popular of the German Romantics, but he is not the best known, and the breadth of his reputation, based as it is on what is simplest about his art, has given rise to an image of him that betrays his true figure. What his name brings to mind before all else is the horrible with its rather crude stratagems, the world of ghosts and the strange realm of nocturnal obsessions, and it is thus that a perfectly amiable writer has been made to pay for the mistake of responding to fame by writing works that fame required. His blackest tales incur the reproach that he himself, speaking as Kreisler, directs at a magician: "You prepare marvels the way a cook does, with the aid of strong spices, and you think that men whose imaginations are jaded like the stomachs of bon vivants will be tickled by such extravagances."

In contrast, works such as *Tomcat Murr*, *Princess Brambilla*, or the *Golden Pot* are fantastic without being dark, and however extraordinary they may be, they affect our sensibilities with enigmas that are more profound than the images that reveal them. Nothing could be more lighthearted than the caprice of *Princess Brambilla*. The people in it are involved in a shadow play, they come and go as their appearance metamorphoses, and the harmony of their movements has broken free of the world's gravitational pull while still respecting its laws. It is joy rather than the episodes of a baroque plot that opens up imaginary vistas in the story; such transparent, lively sentiment cannot fail to lead us into realms that are inaccessible to humdrum existence, and we recognize the presence of a hidden power there much more confidently than we would in elfin or spectral apparitions. This gaiety is a fiction in itself: It does not arise from a natural encounter with events; it presupposes the actions of a conjuror who momentarily rigs reality, and uses his lies to win our minds over to the truth of an inner fairytale. But having first been a chimera crafted by a skillful magician, this absurd joy survives the false conditions that produced it to become the marvelous truth to which no other can henceforth be preferred.

One aspect of Hoffmann's originality is that he sought out and represented authentic reality in the guise of a dual contradictory figure. On one side, fright and darkness, hereditary curses and the fantasies of the insane; on the other, the transfiguration of dream, the blessing of beauty, the self-evidence of poetry. These two series of images help us in equal measure to go beyond the simple world. They have the same value and the same meaning in so far as they both give us an inkling of the unknown that surrounds us. To be cursed or blessed is to experience with equal force the strangeness and incomprehensibility of fate, and be bathed in the light of the true sun, be it black or white. Between these two situations there is moreover a great affinity. Both are accompanied by anguish, a harrowing, tragic anguish when the unknown appears in the form of an abyss; or a gentle, overwhelming anguish when the inconceivable enraptures us and takes us away from ourselves. The drama of joy is as difficult to endure as the drama of suffering. For each of them brings us into contact with an original, absurd reality that is incompatible with the basic conditions of our lives; an all-powerful reality that is totally astonishing and contains no end principle, no exit, no limit.

Another feature of Hoffmann's originality is that he preserved the mystery of that mystery by refusing to link it to anything known. What are these depths that reveal themselves to human nature in the rapture of fright? Is it evil, is it good? Is it God, is it the reverse side of things? As Albert Béguin has shown in his excellent study *The Romantic Soul and the Dream*,[2] Hoffmann uses religious images solely as symbols and refrains from insisting on their content. He avoids pronouncing the name of God. Unlike many other Romantics, he does not even accept the belief in a lost paradise, or a golden age that we could restore through a desire for harmony or a fidelity to myth. That makes him a very different writer from Tieck or even Novalis. The anguish of a storyteller such as Tieck is the sort that attaches itself to vanished visions of childhood, to the search for those earliest figures that suddenly rise up from the depths of our memories and lead us off into a labyrinth where we eventually become lost without finding anything. What could be more captivating than a story like *The Elves*! In it, visions are pure, fantastic apparitions reveal only pleasures and beauties to us; but over this perfect world there hangs the curse of what is ephemeral; the moment comes when man's desire for knowledge destroys the magic of childhood, and the result is misery, death, and night. For Tieck, the unknown is thus inseparable from our earliest childhood years. Hoffmann on the contrary has no wish to clarify the unknown in which the roots of Hoffmannian being are immersed, and if he gives it a name, sometimes calling it "prince of the spirit," sometimes "soul of the world," he spares it any qualification, as if he knew that what is strange dulls every attempt at clarity by which we seek to grasp it.

However, this hidden power that shows itself to men in various ways, in the ravings of madness and in the inspiration of dream, and that we can basically only know by refusing to apply the conventions of our fragmentary knowledge to it, is not a matter of pure indifference or arbitrary whim. Certain beings who are willing to be faithful to it, and especially those who pursue it in the realm of art, are tasked with exceptional duties, with an existence that, however impassioned it may be, must never confine its passion within appearances, nor seek to possess it or enjoy it once and for all in images drawn from reality. It is in this guise that the essential myth of Hoffmann is revealed. Indeed, all of his significant works reproduce an identical theme that provides the symbolic expression of his life, namely the theme of the artist or of the artist's love. In *Tomcat Murr* the character of the artist is incarnated in the figure of the Kapellmeister Johannes Kreisler, who is the writer's superior double and the image of what he would have liked to be. This highly complex figure is far removed from the one that facile Romanticism contrasts with the traditional dullard or philistine. It combines the two tendencies of the Hoffmannian universe: on the one hand, a sensitivity to dark forebodings and the disharmony of earthly desires, but on the other, an ability to live in harmony with the mysterious truth of nature and to reflect it in art. Anxiety accompanies Kreisler's every action. It is anxiety that sometimes transforms him into a parodic character, and it drives him to extravagances whose artificial nature he finds unbearable. The same anxiety allows him never to betray his enigmatic dream amidst all of life's complications, and to follow his inspiration when the moment calls for it. When the illusion of the ideal appears to the artist in the guise of a real person, it is anxiety once again that restrains him from trying to grasp it completely, from treating it as the goal of his aspirations. "The love of the artist" is in Hoffmann's eyes the crucial ordeal. He was in love with his young pupil, Julia Marc. He was tempted to sacrifice his vocation to her, and was finally pleased, "on behalf of his art," to see her marry some ordinary bourgeois. Throughout his life he searched for the meaning of this drama, which for him could not be considered an accidental event; he felt that something worse than stagnation lay in wait for artists who try to possess their dream, and he described their fate by portraying that of the painter Etlinger, who, having gone mad, tried to paint the model he was smitten with in blood.

Tomcat Murr focuses on a character who also appears in other works by Hoffmann, and who represents one facet of the fantastic for him. Master Abraham is a typical magician who, like the archivist Lindhorst in *The Golden Pot* and the charlatan Celionati in *The Princess Brambilla*, lives apart from the world whose workings he is familiar with and whose effects he controls. His gift does not allow him to apply supernatural powers or transform reality by summoning up forces that exceed it. He is more of a mechanic than a magician, a kind of superior illusionist, a humorist who changes the course of the visible without altering its nature. His favorite instruments are optical mirrors, pranksters' tricks, automata, and crystal balls. Everything he does remains within the bounds of reasonable entertainment, and in the end it can always be explained almost entirely without resorting to mystery. Yet, his interventions are enough to transform things. Though nothing but a hoaxer, he is all-powerful. He causes dramas to happen, he spins yarns as though people were merely shadows, their resemblance multiplied and erased in his mirror according to his whim. The fact is, the fantastic is to be found in reality itself, and it takes nothing at all, a passing similarity, an infantile hoax, to reveal to blind humanity the mysterious movements of its own behavior. In the highly involved plots of *Tomcat Murr* we find the same concern for the imaginary when it results from the most justified human actions. The characters are isolated from each other by secrets that come from natural but little-known situations: adultery, children switched at birth, unknown bloodlines give rise to a bogus mystery that is like the reagent that reveals a deeper mystery. What counts, what is truly strange, is not that the daughter of Duke Ireneus was the victim of a twofold switch at birth; it is the fact that, despite such incredible jiggery-pokery, what makes itself felt is the weight of heredity, and that despite all of the obstacles separating them, people continue to attract each other unfailingly and implacably, in accordance with their own past affinities. The great novel plots that were dramatized so incomparably by Jean-Paul (*Hesperus* appears to have inspired the laborious convolutions of Kreisler's story) are augmented in Hoffmann's work by the fact that neither the most outlandish combinations nor the most bogus assemblages of individuals can prevent hereditary complicities from being revealed, and that these fateful forces are more mysterious than all of the actions that seek to conceal them.

Those familiar with *Tomcat Murr* will know that the cat's memoirs are mixed in with the episodes of Kreisler's life, even though they bear no relation to them. This mode of composition is one of the most successful inventions of Romantic humor. Face to face with the exemplary artist whose torments and trials he describes, Hoffmann had the idea of presenting a caricature of it in the guise of a cat who is also a poet: The streak of seriousness and the Olympian satisfaction that the tomcat combines with its poetical ambition are enough to transform it into its opposite, and turn the actual creator into a boor whose experiences are farcical. Between Murr and Kreisler there is the same opposition as exists between the ageing Goethe and the young Romantic school. The cat's memoirs are a sort of Goethean autobiography in which the Sturm und Drang of adolescence is followed by the years of apprenticeship and then the serene wisdom of maturity. Indeed it would be wrong to believe that these farcical memories contain only satirical intentions, or that Hoffmann does not occasionally slip in ideas that he holds dear. One of the features of irony is to jest about what is dear to us in order to defend it from a hostile gaze. Some celebrated lines by Tieck state that humor should be treated solemnly, and solemnity with humor. In *Tomcat Murr* we find the whole gamut of Romantic irony, and this latter is one of the best ingredients of Hoffmann's fantastic. Not only are the adventures of the tomcat the mischievous counterpart to Kreisler's misfortunes, presenting their truth in a paradoxical light, Kreisler himself is the epitome of the humorous character, either when displaying his inner torment through sarcasm and greeting the seriousness of conventional life with grimaces, or when reconciling the hostile principles of nature in this interplay of emotion and intelligence. The magician represents the mystificatory side of irony, its mocking, wicked face, the urge to destroy the fragile harmony of things by discovering the discordant note on which it is bound to break. There is nothing less simple than a sentiment such as this, which played so significant a role in Romanticism. Hoffmann gave it one of its most captivating forms of expression, if not its purest, with his terse and ponderous style, all explosion or all languor, and composed so it seems of rare dreams and interminable reveries.

—June 30, 1943

On the *Song of Roland*

Émile Mireaux has just published a study of the *Song of Roland* that offers some entirely new conclusions and is based on an original critical method.[1] Without criticizing Joseph Bédier's work, he nonetheless challenges some of its results, and in particular he changes both the chronology of the manuscripts and the way they relate to each other. He does not believe that all our epic legends are religious in origin, and in his view the poets obeyed material and moral interests that were not always identical to those of the pilgrimages. He brings all of history, its political movements as well as its main spiritual trends, into relation with our *chansons de geste*, and this comparison provides him with precise indications that explain their origin and their success while also determining the precise date of their appearance. In Mireaux's view, it is wrong to separate literary history from general history. Stylistic, compositional, and structural considerations are not so valuable that they cannot leave room for a study of the events to which a work relates, and a work can be better understood by restoring the historical circumstances in which it took shape than through the abstract search for the features that characterize its internal order.

A few facts provide the starting point for these hypotheses. He acknowledges that the Oxford manuscript—known to be the oldest French version of the *Song of Roland*, indeed preeminently *The Song of Roland*—derives from a prior manuscript that the text alludes to when it mentions "the *geste*," "the ancient *geste*," and, in two passages, "the *Francor Geste*." This *Francor Geste* naturally brings to mind the *Gesta Francorum* that an anonymous knight brought into vogue when in 1099 he wrote the travel diary of the Crusade, the title of which was borrowed by Foucher de Chartres when he wrote a similar work a few years later. Mireaux thinks he sees resemblances between these texts and certain passages from the Oxford manuscript, and this allows him to conclude that the latter is an imitation. In particular, he offers an interpretation of the final line of *The Song of Roland* that dispels its obscurity: "So ends the tale which Turold hath conceived [*Ci falt la geste que Turoldus declinet*]" means "Here concludes the *geste* that Turoldus translated [*Ici finit la geste que traduit Turoldus*]." It must therefore be supposed that Turoldus had at his disposal if not the historical text concerning the Crusade, at least a story, written in Latin, whose content was legendary and whose form was historical, and that told of the imaginary exploits of Charlemagne in Spain and a number of the real exploits of the Crusaders in the East. The poet refers on three occasions to this story in connection with Archbishop Turpin, and he dedicates it to Saint Giles. It is probably earlier than the Chronicle of the Pseudo-Turpin and must have differed from it in a number of features that it is possible to reconstitute. The role of the archbishop in particular, which in the Chronicle is more in keeping with ecclesiastical dignity, remained that of a warlike and pugnacious cleric in whom the spirit of the Crusade was brilliantly revived. The Baligant episode (it will be recalled that in our *Song*, after the death of Roland, Charlemagne routs the immense army of the "admiral of Babylon," Baligant, which had made landfall not far from Saragossa) provided its most original element. Mireaux thinks that the *Gest Francor* was composed just prior to the Second Crusade in 1146 by a clerk of the Cistercian order in order to reawaken the zeal of the Crusaders, and that the Chronicle of Pseudo-Turpin that was written after the failure of this Crusade in 1149 by a monk from Cluny provides a sort of refutation of it.

Research has revealed that one of the sources of our *Song* was a Latin document from well into the Late Latin period, and the *Song* itself in its Oxford version is of much later origin than was generally believed. The date can be established by noting the role that the *Song* gives to one of Charlemagne's companions, Geffroi d'Anjou, "the king's gonfalonier." This role and this title can be linked to the ambitions of the house of Anjou, which toward the middle of the twelfth century reigns over England, holds power in France, and is in search of titles of nobility. It appears that by writing or rather revising the *Song of Roland* in 1158, Turold became the agent of Henry Plantagenet's ambitions, his propagandist, so that our finest *chanson de geste* was written at the behest of the king of England and to serve his cause. This Turold is thus apparently a clerk from the Loire region or from Normandy, whose exile in some Cistercian monastery in Great Britain made his evocation of *douce France*, the land of his fathers, the *Tere Major* more nostalgic.

As the final stage in a long development (leaving aside the Venice, Châteauroux, and Paris versions, which are less important), the Oxford text does not just presuppose the *Geste Francor*, which it follows quite faithfully while adding the sort of allusions that would satisfy Plantagenet pride, but a whole series of prior works. While proposing a date for Turold's *Song* that is later than that of most critics, Mireaux acknowledges the existence of an archetype to which he attributes an extremely ancient origin. Having gone gradually back in time, noting the rare traces left by the legend of Ronceveaux, the year 1000 is the date that he chooses for this first draft of our *chanson de geste*. The poet of this first *Roland* effectively dated his work himself. When he makes the Saracen say (in a text that is perfectly present in later versions):

> Said the Saracen: "I marvel much at
> Charlemagne, who is old and gray
> I understand he is over two hundred years old"

he is not so naïve as to believe and argue that Charlemagne reigned for two centuries, but he wishes to indicate that Charlemagne's dynasty lasted for two hundred years and that, at the time he is writing, this reign has just come to an end. Indeed, Mireaux believes that this first *Song* was written as a defense and illustration of the Carolingian dynasty toward the end of the tenth century, at a time when the grand dynastic drama that would drive the imperial line from the throne of France was reaching its close. In the main epic episodes he recognizes the dramatic plots and the tragedy of betrayal to which the last descendants of Charlemagne fell victim. In the noble figure of Turpin, the Archbishop of Rheims, he recognizes the antithesis, the satirical personification of the actual archbishop of Rheims, Adalbéron, who betrays his king and delivers him into the hands of Hugh Capet. Last, he sees in the lines full of pathos that present the death of Roland in such a strange light an expression of the anger and despair of a last-ditch supporter of the fallen dynasty. Such would be an explanation of how the entire Carolingian epic took shape. It came into being in those milieus that had remained loyal to the family of Charlemagne, to the court of the dukes of Aquitaine and to that of the counts of Vermandois and the metropolitan see of Sens. It arose out of a reaction that was both political and sentimental in nature, and which, after the fall of the Carolingians, made Charlemagne into a legendary hero and placed him at the center of almost all of our epic writing. The first author of *The Song of Roland* was probably a clerk who, living among the supporters of the old dynasty in the area of Troyes or Sens, set about giving voice to their regrets and their passion by writing a poem on the Roncevaux affair, whose traditional elements he discovered on a pilgrimage to Santiago de Compostela.

This original poem, which is perhaps preserved in its main lines in the version of the *Carmen de prodicione Guenonis* (Song of the Treachery of Ganelon), a sort of verse analysis to be used by scholars, probably contained the main themes of the *Song*, with the exception of the later Baligant episode of course, and also that of Blancandrin. Through his analysis of the latter episode (Blancandrin, it will be recalled, is the "pagan sage" who seeks out Charlemagne at the beginning of the *Song* to negotiate the surrender of King Marsile), Mireaux has discovered a number of allusions to the Mediterranean campaigns of the Normans. It appears to him to have been written around 1080 in Norman Italy, during the last years of Duke Robert Guiscard and Pope Gregory VII. It mentions the issue of the relations between Muslim princes and Christian princes, and it recommends intransigence of the sort that the Normans had so decisively abandoned, particularly in Sicily. It is thus quite possible to imagine that there was an Italo-Norman version of the *Song*, written toward the end of the eleventh century, and there are grounds for recognizing the text of it in the Norse version known by the name of *Karlamagnussaga* and written at the behest of King Haakon of Norway. The distant origins of this Italo-Norman *Song* should not surprise us, for in the Italy that had been colonized by the Normans of France there arose a vibrant center for epic poetry where other *chansons de geste* came into being, in particular *The Song of Otinel*, as well as those of *Apremont* and *Gaydon*. It is probably this text, adapted in Sicily, that was sung during the first Crusade, and served to arouse the enthusiasm of the Provençal army of Raymond de Saint-Gilles and the Norman troops of Bohémond and Tancred.

It is clearer now how Mireaux's study goes about reconstituting the history of *The Song of Roland*. Born around the year

1000 in Northern France, our oldest *chanson de geste* is first and foremost the work of a Carolingian loyalist. It rapidly becomes popular, and the *Carmen de prodicione Guenonis*, which provides an analysis of it in high-flown Latin, provides information about the sequence of its main episodes. Three-quarters of a century later there appears a first rewriting, whose author, a Norman troubadour from Italy or Sicily, invents the Blancandrin episode and probably alters the end of the poem. The Norse translation called the *Karlamagnussaga* is witness to this new version. The second revision is the *Geste Francor* of 1146, written in Latin just before the Second Crusade by a Cistercian monk who, to support the preaching of Saint Bernard, adds the Baligant episode that is designed to prove the usefulness of the expedition to the East for the liberation of Spain. Last, a third revision, in favor of the Plantagenets this time, gives rise in 1158 to the Oxford text, the first known textual version of *The Song of Roland*, that draws its inspiration from both the *Geste Francor* and the Italo-Norman version. Four different texts, three of which can only be assumed, four versions that from the year 1000 to 1158 lead us from northern France to Sicily and England and evoke the fall of the Carolingian dynasty, the Norman conquest in the Mediterranean, the First and Second Crusades—these mark the main stages in the development of our *chanson de geste*, with its close links over two centuries to the history of France and Europe.

It is not our place here to examine whether Mireaux's elegant erudition has reconciled hypothesis with fact. Our concern is to identify the characteristics of an explanation of this sort, to identify what it adds and what it takes away from traditional understanding. It is apparent from the outset that Mireaux does not contest the presence, at the birth of this epic creation, of a poet who no doubt found the material for his work in local legend, who collected the elements of it in the sanctuaries that line the road of the pilgrimage to Santiago de Compostela, but then transformed them in accordance with the rules of an art in which he was a master. There is therefore no question of going back to the old theories according to which epic poetry corresponded to a collective work that was imposed on the singer by popular inspiration. It must be acknowledged, however, that the theory of successive versions whose culmination is today's *Song of Roland* singularly devalues the *chanson de geste*, considered as a work of art organized according to the requirements of its inner unity. We are asked to believe that the work whose order and composition are of such delight is the result of repetitions, interpolations, and general patchwork carried out by adapters over more than a century and a half. Is that possible? We must at the very least assume that the most recent of those adapters was an extraordinary artist, who recreated the work as a whole, organized its episodes harmoniously, breathed the same spirit into them and out of the raw material of his predecessors crafted an original work. Is Mireaux inclined to grant such a role to the author of the Oxford version? It would appear not. On the contrary, he is particularly critical of this text whose preeminence, even though Bédier acknowledges it, seems to him highly questionable. Even granted that the Oxford manuscript is merely a bad copy of the true poem by Turold, the unavoidable conclusion is that the latter's work was mediocre, that he was content to add the Baligant episode translated from the *Geste Francor* to the Italo-Norman *Song*, and that in no respect can he be said to have written as a creator. Where then, in such a system, is the true author of our finest *chanson de geste*? Is he to be found at the beginning of its development, or in the middle, or at the end? The fact is, we look for him and he is nowhere to be found.

Mireaux's main task has consisted in showing that *The Song of Roland* was not necessarily born along the pilgrims' way, that it was not suggested to *jongleurs* by monks who wanted to attract pilgrims to their shrines, and that it bears the mark of political events as well as religious interests. The first *Song of Roland* was not addressed to pilgrims. It was written in praise of Carolingian glory and fidelity to the ancient dynasty. It is not ecclesiastical in origin. This conception, which complements Joseph Bédier's argument rather than contradicting it, would seem to leave part of the problem that the latter sought to clarify steeped in shadow. In Bédier's commentary it is clear who the public of the *chansons de geste* was, and it is visible why, having been written for pilgrims and shrines, they should have found success and a justification in the great movements of Christian faith that flourished in centers of worship. But in terms of Mireaux's interpretation, who were the first audience of the *chansons de geste*? Where were the regular popular gatherings during which the crowd was capable of being interested by a political poem? How could a work that evolved in quite a restricted milieu rapidly become the work of an entire kingdom and of all Christendom? The interest of Bédier's system is that it shows by what agency the art of the poets and the great popular movements came together, under what influences their collaboration emerged and why it proved durable. It does not seem that the history of our epic poems can easily do without such an explanatory model.

—July 7, 1943

Kierkegaard and Aesthetics

The translation of Kierkegaard's works is progressing in a more methodical fashion than was previously the case. Ferdinand Prior has completed his translation of the first great work by the Danish writer entitled *Either/Or*,[1] and it would appear that the work that follows it, *Stages on Life's Way*, will not be long in coming. These are writings that, on a monumental scale (the first contains more than six hundred pages of dense text), sketch out some of Kierkegaard's fundamental ideas as well as the movement of thought through which these ideas are revealed, expressed, and already superseded. The successive translations that have appeared in France over the past fifteen years have paid little heed to chronology. With a strange indifference to the order in which their author wrote them, they have made available works whose main significance often lies precisely in their order. Kierkegaard did not set out to present a definitive body of thought. The expression of his thought was also its cause. He himself was modified by it, while the circumstances of his life influenced its development in a different way.

His thinking developed in the process of expressing itself; it took shape in close proximity to life; it developed in accordance with its own intrinsic unity. These three developmental causes show how complex the movement of a work such as this one is, and they do not allow it to be studied in a haphazard fashion.

The book that Prior has entitled *Either/Or*—which is an exact translation—and that other commentators have chosen to call *Dilemmas* or *One Thing Or Another*, reveals that from the beginning of his literary activity Kierkegaard is in possession of the "philosophy of the stages of life" or "of the spheres of existence," and that two of the three stages he identifies already possess their full significance for him. In fact, however, he does not yet feel the need to specify this idea of "stages" formally. He studies the "aesthetic" state of mind and the "ethical" state of mind, without seeing them as two specific phases in life. It is to the characteristics of the aesthete, the man who lives in an aesthetic manner, and to those of the man who lives a moral life that his attention is powerfully drawn: the notion of stages will only come later. It seems clear that what preoccupies his mind in the first instance is the strange reality of the aesthetic (two years previously, he devoted his thesis, *The Concept of Irony*, to it), so that if he is so attracted to this state of mind, it is because he was able to observe it in himself throughout his youth. What is more, Romanticism makes a hero of the aesthetician; his poetry is a rapturous combination of imagination and reflection that takes us to the heart of the aesthetic. The writer who lived his life on the borders of Romanticism could not avoid seeking out its significance, so that "aesthetics" is in certain respects the tumult of Romanticism as Kierkegaard was able to grasp its effects on his own mind, from his twenty-third to his twenty-sixth years.

At an initial level, the aesthetician gives value only to successive sensations. He yields to the passing moment. He takes pleasure in the immediacy of what he is. Don Juan, on the subject of whom *Either/Or* provides a lengthy study, is the figure that seems initially to represent the aesthetic way of life most effectively. In Don Juan, all that matters is desire. Desire is a seducer. It seeks out an object; when it has found one, it seizes hold of it; when it is satisfied, it looks for another one, and so it goes on. Don Juan's primary characteristic is his spontaneity. He does not employ subtlety or cunning to make a conquest. He has no intellectual gifts. He is a man without skill. He lacks the gift of speech. In fact, Don Juan does not seduce, he desires, and this desire exerts a seductive power. It is the force of his passion that allows him to dominate the object of his passion. He triumphs without preliminaries or combat, in the immediacy of the instant; he needs neither a future in order to plan a project nor a past to allow him to look back with pleasure on his deed: he is immediately what he does. It is clear why music alone can express him; he escapes categorization by language; insofar as he is pure sensual spontaneity, he is entirely musical in nature.

Yet Don Juan as a type, however conducive it may be to a simple definition of the aesthetic (the aesthetic equals the immediate), already displays the contradictions that will enrich and then destroy it as a state of being. Don Juan does not desire what is exceptional, but what is totally common; he desires all women, and in each woman, femininity as a whole. Before his desire all specific differences disappear, everything becomes equally important and equally beautiful. Hence, his desire not only has the power to dominate the object it is in search of, but it also embellishes it, idealizes it; in short, it makes the very person it is seducing seductive. But along the way, the aesthete is clearly beginning to lose touch with reality. The object transfigured by passion counts less than the passion, and the passion imprisons within itself whoever makes it his law. We have left reality behind and entered the world of dream. Dream is the realm of the possible. The dreamer turns away from what is, lets realities dissolve into possibilities, and even rises above these possibilities, or else he makes only fleeting contact with them. Here we are as close as possible to the situation of the Romantic. Like the Romantic, the aesthetician has a life that is primarily an imaginary one. He seeks out every possible state of being, emotion or thought, good or evil, joy or sorrow, and he seeks it out without living it, so as to extract from it what interests him. He is a virtuoso who enjoys the reflection of enjoyment, the illusion he allows himself, the chance happenings he brings about. He seeks initiation into everything but will adapt himself to nothing. He finds pleasure in seeking, but refuses ever to find. His watchword is the one that Kierkegaard takes from his own *Diary*: "Pleasure does not lie in what gives us pleasure, but in the idea we form of it."

This description leads us to the image of the seducer, whose celebrated portrait is to be found in the *Diary of a Seducer*. Johannes the Seducer has nothing in common with Don Juan except a love of the erotic. This young man who becomes engaged to Cordelia in order to persuade her to break things off, whose only interest in seduction lies in the labyrinthine preparations and calculations it requires, who is besotted with the feminine only so as to invent "interesting" situations and who suffers from a sort of disease of method that makes him toy with the mere ghost of desire, is as remote as can possibly be from any spontaneous form of desire. There is no longer anything immediate in his way of doing things. It cannot even be said that he uses deception in order to find pleasure, because deception itself is his sole pleasure. He deceives others and he deceives himself, interminably substituting image for sensation, and image of image for image, until he is no more than a self-besotted, sterile reflection on instinct. The outcome of this orgy of abstraction is boredom and despair. By operating purely arbitrarily, the aesthetician changes every relation; he wants to be the most unhappy of men in order to be the happiest; having lost contact with the simplicity of the present, he constantly transports himself into the past or the future, finding nothing in the future but what has already been, and yearning in the past for what has not yet happened. He turns the void into which he is launched as if it were his natural element into the raw material of his experience. Nothing is what truly amuses him, and he knows that his amusement means less than nothing. Such a vertiginous drift is infinite. It is boredom to the second degree, boredom that seeks to seduce itself, is an infinite reflection of itself, and cannot even founder in its own insignificance. Melancholy, that reverie that finds seriousness in play, that seeks to save itself by drowning, allows the mind to find an escape from its dissipation and become transfigured; a personality that dissolves into an interminable series of appearances is trying to become conscious of itself in what gives it eternal validity. But the mind increasingly becomes the prisoner of its whim, and personality becomes increasingly lost as it goes in search of itself. The result is melancholy and eventually despair. Despair is the ultimate aesthetic conception of life, the life that forms a conception of its own nullity, but it is also the primary aesthetic punishment of the seducer; he is like a fox with several exits to his lair; anxiety keeps him alert; he wants to go outside; seeing a light, he thinks it is a glimmer of daylight and he prepares to flee, but it is not an exit but a new entrance, and so it will be forever. Prey to despair, he is always in search of an exit, and all he ever finds is an entrance through which he descends ever deeper into himself.

Most critics agree that Kierkegaard's aesthetic output as it relates to him is both the truth and a lie. Written beneath a mask of pseudonyms as if it concerned someone else, it is nonetheless a revelation of what he was, of what he could have been, of what he prevented himself from becoming by means of this revelation. It could be argued that one or two of the most general features of the aesthetician have their origin in Kierkegaard's character, and that the tendency to take pleasure in the possible rather than in the real was particularly strong in him. The viewpoint of the immediate was only accessible to him through a reflection on the immediate. "I gave myself an imitation of youth," he wrote. This reflection on existence was the way in which he existed, but it did not lead him to lose the sense of existence. On the contrary, it led him, in a state of often extraordinary tragic tension, to give pride of place to the fact of existing, to make thought and existence inseparable, so that he who was always tempted to poeticize life rather than to live it ultimately expressed the problems of existence with the greatest profundity. The tendency he became aware of in the process of describing the aesthetic stage was that he was a poet, that the poetic element both held him back from marrying and prevented him from becoming a Christian as he would have wished, and that instead of being the extraordinary, he only imagined the existence of the extraordinary. The aesthetician is first of all someone who lives poetically, and to be a poet is "to sing rather than be, to relate to the true and the good by means of fantasy rather than to strive existentially to be true and good." If Kierkegaard nevertheless went beyond the poetic viewpoint, if the relations he entertained with the idea of existence were so profound that his mission to be a "reflector" of this idea also modified his existence, he had first to discover that he was a poet, then that poetic existence was a contradiction (for to be a poet is to spend one's life singing of what one does not live; how could one possibly make one's life into a work of poetry therefore?), and finally that the consciousness of this contradiction allowed him to be something more than a poet, and all of that is latent in the description of the aesthetic stage, and in the debates with Romanticism that, precisely, deny this contradiction and lead the poet to confuse existence with song.

In the preface he writes for the translation of *Either/Or*, Frithjof Brandt seeks to show that Kierkegaard links his own case to the Ahasverus type, representing melancholy and despair, and not to the seducer type, representing pleasure. The story of Johannes the Seducer would thus be an idealization of the story of the Danish critic P. M. Møller, who was a fellow student at the university. In fact, this problem is probably not very important when it comes to understanding Kierkegaard. It can hardly be denied that a book like *Either/Or*, and also *The Diary of a Seducer* itself, relate to the life of the author in a twofold manner, first because they describe states that he actually experienced, or experienced by imagining that he could have experienced them; but above all because they are indirectly addressed to the woman who could have been his fiancée, Regine Olsen, with whom he had just broken up and whom he wished both to drive away from him by pretending to be dishonest, and perhaps to win back by expressing his despair. *The Diary of a Seducer* was written in order to reject her, as he wrote in his diary. "In order to wean the child, the mother blackens her breast." His book is thus a message, but a veiled message that cloaks itself in contradictions. Sometimes he wants to convey to Regine that her existence could have been that of Elvira, Marie de Beaumarchais, or Marguerite; at others, he praises marriage and reveals to her that he could have got married. Or else he alarms her by making her dread the woes of conscious suffering, or he shows her how much he loves her by saving her by means of this chivalrous disguise. In this way he reveals himself by wearing masks and conceals himself as though he wished to privilege the gaze that is capable of perceiving him. He writes in order to be misrecognized, to be recognized, to be his accuser and the accuser of his accuser. The endless twists and turns of this indirect communication also bear a relation to the movement of aesthetics.

It is hard not to think that while half of his book is devoted to describing the moral stage, to justifying marriage and presenting life as a task to be fulfilled, Kierkegaard appears less directly interested, at least in *Either/Or*, by the realm of ethics than by that of aesthetics. No doubt he is neither an aesthete nor a moralist, and his dream was to be a married man just as in his dreams he was a seducer. But this is precisely where the difference between the two attitudes lies. He could be a seducer, ideally: The dream of being a seducer is part of seduction. On the other hand, morality cannot tolerate being exclusively imaginary but requires a real choice and even an absolute choice; it is knowable only when one puts it into practice by getting married and fulfilling one's duties. There is thus a way of being unfaithful to aesthetics that provides the exact definition of aesthetics, but morality means unequivocal fidelity and undivided responsibility. It is perhaps possible to live a religious life poetically. It is impossible to live a moral life poetically.

—July 13, 1943

The Art of the Short Story

In a preface to a book by Jean Fougère,[1] Marcel Arland wonders why books of short stories are not more popular with the public. Is that true? It seems doubtful when one considers the writers who excel in that art, foremost among whom there is Arland himself. But if it is true that readers prefer novels, or at least see in them a more worthwhile genre, the fault lies with the humdrum mediocrity of those authors who use stories of a few pages as an outlet for their idleness, and prefer them because they look like an easy alternative.

Marcel Arland has no difficulty in proving that the short story makes far more demands than it reveals, that purity is its first law, that it calls for unfailing mastery and lays claim to a justification that obedience to rules alone cannot give it—in short, that it is required to be simultaneously exemplary and unjustifiable. Young authors would do well to heed such praise for a pure, precise, and natural art. Were one tempted to add something to it, one might say that they should try not to compensate by turning to the novel for an art that is undemanding, accommodates weaknesses, and reconciles perfection with what is negligent and free. The novel has almost ceased to be a literary genre, because it has abandoned what is arbitrary about formal rules in favor of the no less arbitrary imitation of "reality." Let us not forget that the popularity enjoyed by the novel brings discredit on it. It is easily accessible, it asks to be read, it discourages no one; it puts itself into any hands that care to open it. These are all signs of decadence.

One of the typical difficulties posed by the short story is that it is complete and perfect in itself, and yet it generally has its place in a collection whose unity must be genuine. This is not simply an artificial requirement. A book is a book. It is what it should be. If it is made up elements that accumulate according to a process of haphazard and extraneous growth, the least thing will make it fall apart, and it will always be less than the sum of what it is made up of. One of the perfections of Arland's short stories is that they are independent and yet form a series that cannot be broken. Each of them expresses the work as a whole; it is both itself and everything it will become by joining together with all the others. We hear its unique voice and sense the harmony it will create in an as yet absent choir. The echo appears to come before the original sound, its void calling that sound into being in a composed silence that is always on the point of bursting into music. This mysterious continuity between moments that appear to be separate is in our view one of the singular charms of a collection of short stories, and it is difficult for us to agree to its omission. There is nothing finer than this imitation of time in which the days of one set of people are added to the days of others, to create the secret of an existence that is both identical and entirely dissimilar.

If there is one thing to be regretted about Colette's book *The Képi*,[2] it is the discordant note that is introduced into it by the last of the four short stories that make it up. Instead of reaching a climax there, it is on a weak, alien note that the book ends. The final node that should have held the fabric together and given it its consistency is lacking. All of the stitches have not come undone, but the beauties of each section are isolated from each other and tend to break off relations and leave them unfinished. The first three stories have in common the fact that they are neither straight inventions nor pure memories, but a rare combination of truth and lies. This mixture could not be bolder. The savor and natural quality that Colette gives it are a source of great pleasure. If she allows herself a place in a story we assume to be imaginary, she either stays on the edge so that we see only her shadow, acting merely as the discreet ear that is receptive to the fiction of a voice, present through a silence that acts as a sounding board for what cannot make itself heard; or else she becomes one character among others, one whose features we recognize, whose actions we follow, who no doubt does not have the major role but who throws light on events through the sensuous relations she has with them; and on those occasions when Colette's *I* pervades the narrative so completely that any invention becomes unwarranted, the story, having lost its fictional center, attaches itself as best it can to the narrator and seems to emerge accidentally from her own story. That is more or less the way the three short stories of *The Kepi* are organized.

But in the fourth one Colette no longer appears. She is entirely hidden from the eye that searches for her and from the hope that she will appear. All that remain are two unremarkable heroes and a storyline that we find amusing in the very process of ceasing to remember it. Consequently, our frustrated attention turns back to the preceding stories and analyzes them unconsciously. On the one hand, it sees how slight the material of the storytelling is and how fragile are the circumstances that are offered for our interest; on the other, it discovers the incomparable skill with which the story is animated, and the fascinating process that leads us from one series of images that is genuine to another that is mere trickery, from truths that are confided to the fragile illusions of the novel. These conclusions make us wonder whether Colette is not either too close to her short stories or else too distant from them, whether she does not nullify all invention in them, either because she is so present that our sole duty is to think of her or because she withdraws from them and leaves them infinitely poorer for her absence. Perhaps Colette sticks too closely to the rules of traditional technique, which imposed a duty on the author always to tell a story, come what may. The story is always there in the narratives of *The Kepi*; it is complete, has a beginning and an end, and expresses a little drama that is well constructed and perfectly rounded off. But its relations with the narrator sometimes become arbitrary, even when she is its witness or its heroine. Why does the first tale, which gives its title to the work, beguile us with a sense of harmony that appears lacking in the others? Because the person who is at its center, the aging Marco who falls for a young officer and lives with him happily until one day, a practical joke reveals her for the age she is, is not totally indifferent to the young woman who tells the story; she takes an interest in her character but also feels a certain horror; she is distant enough from her to be able to follow her as if she were a stranger, through the twists and turns of an adventure that is partly hidden from us, but she is curious enough about her fate to look at her cruelly, portray her pitiably, understand her sincerely, and catch her in the network of implacable and compassionate sentiments that lies at the heart of her talent for observation. Thanks to this exchange, the story finds its true place; events become the substance from which the writer's language draws its nourishment, and anecdote combines naturally with memory to give rise to a world in which what happens acquires enduring and unchanging form.

There is no art that offers us more rewarding pleasure than that of Marcel Aymé, but also none for which any commentary could appear more superfluous. It is not that fantasy is generally speaking resistant to analysis, or that it is so transparent that the eye sees straight through it and cannot study its pleasure or recognize the source of its vision. It is the fact that in Marcel Aymé's work, the ingredients are perfectly visible;

entirely turned outward, they flaunt themselves like a lure for critics, and every tale announces: "This is what I am made of; it could not be easier to reduce me to my component parts; nothing could be less worthy of an enquiring mind than to be unable to find the secret of my inner workings; I am happy to repeat myself and I obey a sort of formula that allows me to reinvent myself indefinitely; all of that is within reach of any passing observer." In fact, if this is a trap, the only people who will fall into it are those who, on observing the back of a tapestry, would show no surprise if they found that it was exactly the same as the front. It is no doubt easy to say that, from an unlikely and unjustified starting point, Marcel Aymé's tales move to their close by way of a regular series of consequences that are not strictly logical but obey the logic that belongs to ordinary, average humanity; that extraordinary premises produce an extraordinary conclusion by following the most ordinary sentimental developments; that the baroque invention of the beginning succeeds both in exhausting all the potential of its peculiarity and in developing according to the resources of everyday reality; that this collaboration is only possible thanks to what is both bantering and ingenuous, affected and natural about the storyteller's interventions, as he seems idly to follow the gentle drift of his tale, and draws out of it on a golden thread everything precious, extravagant, and natural that it contains; and that finally, this mixture of realism and caprice, arbitrary invention and precise observation, results in a gentle charm that is simply an expression of profound human feeling. That analysis may well be true, but it must be said that it is of little interest. Its only merit is to make clear what it fails to address, to remind us that if the pattern of the tales is often rigorously ordered, this rigor makes us aware above all of the spontaneous nature of what flows through it; and to remind us that however visible the presence of mind that the author feigns, it is the idle play of his distraction that makes us appear like enchanted sleepers. Everything that seems to justify so precisely the tales in his most recent collection, *The Man Who Walked Through Walls*,[3] also reveals that it is unreasonable to assume that they have some purpose; our sole wish is to show consent, docility, and as when we are sleeping, a confident obedience toward images. In any case, rejecting the perfidious intentions of the author who makes public display of phrases designed to explain his art, we reap the pleasure it brings while refusing the bonus of believing that we understand it.

The unity of the ten tales that make up *The Man Who Walked Through Walls* is sufficient to give us the impression of a real world, which we enter through different doors and where we are reunited with ourselves, provided we are first of all capable of becoming unreservedly lost in it. That is the reward of a natural reading. In *Visit* by Jean Fougère, a collection that has a preface by Marcel Arland containing his reflections on the art of the short story, the continuity comes from the rapidity of the scenes, from the brief instant on which each story focuses, from this fleeting present that is recounted to us as something unique yet is nothing but a variation within the monotony of duration. Almost all of Fougère's stories describe a few moments in a life we know nothing of, and that is thus exposed entirely to our gaze, as though its entire history, with all of the episodes that explain it, were being made visible. Considerable tact is required in order to produce this degree of illusion, as well as considerable ease and a precise sense of how events can be condensed down. It was thus with much sympathy that we read this collection by a young writer who has gone straight to the heart of the difficulties posed by the genre, and been granted the power to overcome them.

Very little happens in those short stories. In the two stories by Marius Richard contained in *The Birth of Phaedra*,[4] on the other hand, the wealth of anecdote is considerable. The secret side of lives is expressed there through more events than the ordinary fabric of the days can support. But these rebounding circumstances, this froth of adventures, are perhaps designed only to conceal the simple emotion that the author was unwilling to betray. It is to this sentiment that we are attracted, as though to a wellspring that appears more precious to us than all the inventions that flow from it.

—July 21, 1943

The Religion of Rabelais

In a work that he has just published in the Bibliothèque de Synthèse Historique series, and that is the fruit of ten years' labor,[1] Lucien Febvre once again broaches the problem of the Renaissance. There is a myth of the Renaissance. In spite of studies that have made it impossible to deny the profound wisdom of the Middle Ages and its knowledge of ancient culture, scholars seem unable to resist the urge to explain the sixteenth century in terms of an effervescent humanism. It seems simple to assume that at the end of the fifteenth century men went feverishly in search of vanished treasures, and being better versed in true Latin and pure Greek, amassed the basic materials of erudition thanks to the invention of the printing press; that taking advantage of recent discoveries, they multiplied their increased learning in relation to time by extending the field of their knowledge in space, so that Copernicus is grafted onto Pythagoras just as Andreas Vesalius is onto Hippocrates; and that thanks to this encounter between profane experiences that presuppose an emancipation from religious faith, the sixteenth century marked the dawn of a rationalist and skeptical age. Lucien Febvre's conclusion is far removed from such a view. But what seems to count for him more than his conclusions, and to have provided the main reason for writing his book, are the considerations of method whose absence is the cause of many an error concerning the Renaissance. Roughly speaking, historians tend to apply notions and even terminology to past centuries that only have meaning in relation our own; they interpret historical realities in the light of what is possible today; they rethink in modern mode what can only be understood if we abandon our habits of thought; furthermore, they are easily tempted by simple, coherent explanations. Even today, therefore, anachronism and a lack of clarity are the main pitfalls for history.

The starting point for this study was provided by Abel Lefranc's thesis on Rabelais. As is well known, in his introduction to the critical edition of the *Works*, the great Rabelais specialist rejected the traditional view of a mocking and skeptical Rabelais, or of Rabelais as a timid supporter of the Reformation, and presented *Pantagruel* as the secret manual of rationalist faith, and Master Alcofribas as a bold innovator "who went further than all contemporary writers along the path of philosophical and religious opposition," a believer in disbelief, a freethinker whose goals, concealed by latent irony, display a degree of temerity that no one had dared even imagine for many a century. Febvre does not just believe this argument to be false; in his view it is also impossible. It does not fit with contemporary accounts, it conflicts with the texts, but even more it presupposes an unfeasible anticipation of times to come. For Rabelais to take his place at the top of the list of modern irreligious sprits, he would have had to discover, independently, a set of historical, scientific, and intellectual reasons that were absolutely unknown in his century, that no stretch of the imagination could ever have provided, because everything required for their discovery was lacking, even the words. His unbelief could only appear to us as a pure creation *ex nihilo*, a conviction without cause and conceived independently of all concrete conditions, a surrender to empty words. "Not to believe" is an expression devoid of meaning for as long as it is not grounded in a precise system of judgment. The problem that Lucien Febvre studies in painstaking detail with reference to Rabelais is why the sixteenth century could not "not believe."

The case of Rabelais is naturally very obscure. This is less because of there are few texts by him than because everything in the century is difficult for us to understand. There is no shortage of contemporary testimony. First of all there are the professional men of letters whom Febvre calls "academic Apollos," those Latin verse poets who thrive on ambition and quarreling, men like Visagier, Nicholas Bourbon, Macrin, and even Dolet and Scaliger. Do they accuse Rabelais of impiety? Louis Thusane and Abel Lefranc thought so, but Febvre proves that all established texts are favorable to the author of *Pantagruel*, that the epigrams that speak of atheism are aimed at Dolet or at unknown individuals, and that if some items do perhaps concern Rabelais, their target is made up merely of the legendary misdemeanors associated with him: drunkenness, debauchery, slander. In short, neither the jealousy nor the quarrelsome passion of these followers of sterile Muses could raise a single significant accusation against a writer of renown. After the "boon companions" come the theologians and the controversialists. Before 1550 there are four texts that provide flimsy evidence. First, in 1533, a letter from Calvin that does not denounce the impiety of *Pantagruel* as was thought, but on the contrary reports an accusation by the vicar of Saint-André-des Arts, Nicolas Le Clerc, in order to refute it. Then, ten years later, there is a text by Guillaume Postel in which Rabelais is accused of atheism, but alongside other evangelists and thus, says Febvre, in good Christian company. In the same year there is the condemnation by the Sorbonne that once again places Rabelais not among the ranks of the libertines but alongside the leaders of the Reformation. Last of all, in 1540 the violent attack by Puy-Herbault, "*l'enraigé Putherbe*," is driven by personal rancor, and it is in any case more an attack on Rabelais's morals than on his lack of religion.

The most important text and the only possibly decisive one dates from 1550, and it is by Calvin (in *De Scandalis*). There, Rabelais is presented along with Des Perriers and Gouveia as having initially been drawn to the Gospels before eventually becoming an atheist and a materialist under the influence of his sacrilegious laughter. This is a harsh and specific accusation; these men, writes Calvin, do not hesitate to say that "all religions were forged by human brains; that we believe there is some God because it suits us to believe it; that hope in eternal life is designed for the amusement of idiots; and that everything that is said about hell is designed simply to terrify little children." What are we to think of such a rigorous indictment? Febvre's examination of it is one of the best parts of his book. He does not limit himself to an analysis of the text or dwell on its lateness or on the reasons that could at that time have exposed Rabelais to reprisals on the part of Protestants. What is crucial for him is to ponder what it is to be accused of atheism in this half of the sixteenth century. What was in the mind of the controversialists when they accused their adversaries of being atheists? This grievance is much in fashion at the time. For Castellio, Rabelais has "faith neither in God nor in Christ," but for Henri Estienne, Castellio is a blasphemer; in his turn, having denounced the scandal of Pantagruel, Henri Estienne is called "the Pantagruel of Geneva and the prince of atheists." In his letter to Erasmus, Rabelais himself denounces Scaliger as a devil who is "as fully an atheist as it is possible to be." Atheist is thus reduced to being the supreme insult, a term of abuse that divided believers hurl at each other without giving it any precise meaning. You are always an atheist in someone's eyes. Ronsard calls the Huguenots atheists, but Antoine de La Roche-Chandieu retorts:

> Atheist is he who, mendaciously, supports the Papacy
> While mocking it and seeing its falsity.

In addition to this triviality of tone there is another mode of reasoning that must be noted. Viret, for example, the solemn Protestant from Lausanne, declares that to be an atheist is not only to deny all divinity, but it is also to acknowledge God while knowing nothing of Christ. Why is that? Because he condemns for its possible consequences a doctrine that in fact denies those consequences; because the very widespread use of deductive logic allows the atheist conclusion to be derived from the deist premise even though it is not explicitly contained in it. In the same way, Rabelais is accused of blasphemy because unbelief is a possible consequence of his Epicurean works. It is not his thought that his accusers have made available to us, but the syllogistic processes of the controversy over his thought.

From his analysis of Rabelais's writings Febvre draws a prudent but precise conclusion. Neither his burlesque japes nor his obscene familiarity call into question his religious belief; they are churchly mischief with its origin in the Middle Ages and can be explained by the habits of the time, like the ambiguous texts on the immortality of the soul or on miracles. As for the religion of the Giants, it appears close both to the Reformation and to the religion of Erasmus. The Reformation? The affinities are hard to deny. In *Pantagruel* in 1532, in *Gargantua* in 1534, on more than twenty occasions, the Christian religion appears indistinguishable from a religion of the Gospels, with no outer ceremony and no reference to the Virgin or the saints. The catalogue of the Library of Saint-Victor shows that Rabelais was interested in the affairs of Germany; Pantagruel's quietism is an echo of Luther's doctrine; furthermore, Calvin praised Rabelais for thinking himself an Evangelical while Postel reproached him for it. And Erasmus? The reverence of the young Rabelais for the author of the *Colloquia* is in no doubt; there are copious borrowings from Erasmus's catechism; most of what is daring in Rabelais is initially there in the boldness of Erasmus. And optimism, confidence in nature and profound humanity all link the Giants' credo to "the philosophy of Christ" more than to the Lutheran faith. Febvre thinks that when Rabelais abandoned the Reformation (as early as 1542, and definitively with the *Quart livre*), he remained faithful to the intellectual ideal of Erasmus, as to a youthful dream that was increasingly under threat from confessional intolerance and religious strife.

It is obviously possible to distance Rabelais from the evangelical and Erasmian faith that his texts allows us to attribute to Grandgousier, Gargantua, and Pantagruel and to see in numerous reassuring utterances the calculations of a libertine who is skilled at mixing the antidote with the poison. That is what certain critics have maintained, but Febvre makes it highly improbable, not just through his research into what Rabelais intended, but also through his examination of the general conditions of unbelief in the sixteenth century. The sixteenth century remains a century that wants to believe. Belief is as strong and as widespread then as it was in preceding centuries. Religion continues to govern all of life; it imbues every custom, informs all thinking, and gives its rhythm to time; it exists in habits and in minds; it even directs those who might be tempted to escape from it. Were someone to have yielded to irreligion, he would have found support neither in philosophy nor in the sciences. Far from seeking to break with religion, philosophy, which has only the language of scholasticism to call on, strives after a perpetual movement of exchange between Greek wisdom and Christian faith. If the sciences bear that name this is merely an anachronism. Scientists have no knowledge of precise instruments, accurate observation, or even concern for truth. There is not a single point of contact between bookish knowledge and practical knowledge. Cloistered geographers remain indifferent to mariners' tales. Fifty years after the voyages of Christopher Columbus, Jacques Signot's *Description of the World* makes no mention of America. Until 1512, the scholar Alessandro Achillini raises questions about the equatorial regions and answers them by citing Aristotle and Avicenna. Everything is unstable and imprecise; there is no world system, no law or any sense of law. Science is no more than a farrago of opinions that credulity accepts without any logical reservations whatsoever.

Febvre's conclusion is that a man who in Rabelais's time might have attempted to write a revolutionary anti-Christian work would have found no serious grounding in either philosophical speculation or scientific progress. The ground would have collapsed beneath him. His unbelief would have been an empty opinion, unrelated and insubstantial, and as far removed as could possibly be from what we call rationalism. "To wish to make the sixteenth century into a skeptical century, a free-thinking century and rationalist century, and to glorify it as such is the worst of all errors and delusions." He then adds, "All in all, the deep religiosity of the majority of those who created the modern world is a relevant notion in the case to Descartes; as I hope to have shown, it is also applicable a century earlier to Rabelais." To understand the full significance of these perfectly precise statements, it is enough to add that they raise the issue of precursors in a particular way. To some extent, the Renaissance appears to Febvre as an era of precursors, but the precursors themselves are men without descendants who engender nothing. One precursor is the unbeliever who in a wholly religious century calls out "I deny," but his denial is of no historical importance: It is of no more consequence than the sneers of a drunkard. Another precursor is Leonardo da Vinci, who has glimpsed the sciences of the future, but his ideas will come to life only centuries later and have as little effect in his own time as if they did not exist. Another precursor is Giordano Bruno, who after Nicolas of Cusa imagines the idea of the infinite multiplicity of worlds, but what use is this discovery if only Galileo's spyglass and Herschel's telescope will be able to turn it into the truth? This pessimistic view of the precursor that condemns him to a sort of incognito existence places emphasis on the demands of history. On the one hand, the historian who is sensitive to differences assumes a gap between epochs that means that all anticipation is imaginary; on the other hand, a study of societies and milieus encourages him to consider only men's actions, and these are always more or less consistent with the general goals of an era. In these conditions, what sense can the efforts of the precursor have? Too attached to his era to be recognized by future ages but incapable of having an effect on it, since his projects are ahead of his time and are incomprehensible to it, he does nonetheless serve a sort of purpose: that of obliging history, in spite of itself, to take account not just of what was done, but also of what was dreamed of, in vain.

—August 4, 1943

Women Novelists of Today

Is there an art of the novel that is specific to women? Do women novelists have qualities and defects that are peculiar to them? In discussing books written by women, we can solemnly swear that we have no intention of responding to problems of that sort, in which other critics sometimes find their amusement. All that can be said is that the number of women who like to write, and what is more write successfully, is always considerable. Of the five novels we have just read, two are written by already successful writers, Elsa Triolet and Germaine Beaumont, while the other three would appear to be first novels and have enough merit to dispel any qualms regarding those that are to follow.

Five observations do not make a statistic. It is tempting nonetheless to remark that out of the five novels that have appeared almost simultaneously, three have a family drama as their subject, and only one has as its heroine a woman in love who confides in us about her misadventures. Two of them are written in the first person, and one of them, the longest, is entirely devoted to the story of a young man, whose sentimental adventures attract numerous female figures toward him, each of whom however remains rather hazy, and seems to fade beneath the sheer number of them. These novels are often written without elegance. It is even tempting to believe that there is a willful sloppiness about them, so totally offhand does their form appear, even down to matters of simple correctness. *Agnes of Nothing* alone is written in a bright and nimble style, whose moments of effective brilliance appear subdued by night.[1]

In *Agnes of Nothing* the story is important—first and foremost because it is an interesting one. Yet despite the fact that it casts no shadow beyond itself, it is important, too, because it seeks to reveal something other than itself. That is the sign of a narrative in thrall to its own seductions. It contains a mystery that is revealed but not dispelled. Led on by the movement of the story as it is being told, its own movement continues even after the end of the story has brought everything to a halt. Germaine Beaumont's heroine finds herself one evening in a region that is unfamiliar to her, in a house she does not know, in a family for whom she is a stranger even though it is her husband's family. These initial pages are of the highest quality and amount to almost the entire book. Without them, the rest of the story would merely display an artificial realism. But any reader who has followed Agnès to the Fonts de Laumes, arrived there with her in the dark and the rain, and in that soft mist, gone past the ruins of the abandoned factory alongside which the rain falls with an empty sound, before finally entering the house where all is torpor and lies, will know that the young woman will never escape from this darkness. She does not come up against a precise secret. Something secret has impregnated nature, and it casts a veil over people's minds. She is condemned to struggle amid the questions it raises, and that transform the very people who approach it into mysteries.

This secret lies at the heart of the house. But is it really there? When Agnès discovers that her mother-in-law is a madwoman who gets up in the night to make cakes with cement, she has merely put one name to the misfortune into which she feels she is sliding. When, in a further descent into the dark heart of things, she discovers that she loves the man who greeted her with insults, and that this man lovers her also, she simply opens a further door onto the woebegone region to which her journey has led her. With every revelation a prop gives way, but the house remains invisible, and if the eye glimpses a brief figure, it becomes lost as it pursues vague images that appear then promptly vanish. In the end, all that remains is the frail, feeble almost extinguished soul of poor Agnes, whose ordeals are like an encounter between her dreams and herself, and who slowly, amid the confusions of her misery, becomes aware of something stable that will remain in her memory. Germaine Beaumont's characters are too caught up in their own stories to prevent her novel from adopting a conventional plotline. But Agnes and her sister-in-law, an untrustworthy and inscrutable woman who haughtily conceals herself behind a curtain of lies, display their own truth and are sufficiently real to appear mysterious for what they are rather than for what they do.

If the domain of Chaligny is inaccessible, it is because it is the refuge of a family, and families always close ranks against outsiders, be they daughters- or sons-in-law. In Gabrielle Cabrini's *The Resurrection of the Dead* there is another version of the solitude of the family.[2] A teenage boy and girl, Lazare and Stella Maris, live lives that are stifled and crushed by the affection lavished on them by their parents. They are trapped in the toils of the feelings they inspire. They are prisoners of the air, the sun, and everything that leaves them free to be loved so possessively. Cut off from the rest of the world, they are also cut off from each other by this relentless affection that disappointment has transformed into a colorless sentiment. Is it hate? Is it love? The children no longer even know the name of their prison, and they escape from it into dreams and fantasies that dally with imaginary friendships. Gabrielle Cabrini deals with three subjects in her novel. The first theme is that of adolescence. Lazare and Stella Maris represent the passion of youth when it feeds on dream and feels at home in fiction. Their imagination provides them with company. They are generous, callow, eager, and disillusioned. It takes nothing to fill them with delight, but then they become sullen or mortally offended. The second theme concerns the misunderstandings that accompany affection. These four beings who are crammed together devour each other abjectly. They are as close as it is possible to be, and remote from everything that allows them to live together. It is as if, in this isolated countryside, they had disappeared underground in order to repel the life that would separate them, and the slow death they encounter there fills them with a dismal and wretched anguish. It is from this death that Gabrielle Cabrini wants to save them, and this is her third theme. In fact, they are saved by catastrophe. By destroying the balance of their discord, a stranger fills them with a desire to be free. The girl falls in love with the newcomer. The young man embarks on a heroic adventure. At the end of the novel, everyone is dead except for Stella Maris, who, now reconciled with her family, looks on as they rise again and rediscover their love thanks to the tragedy that has rescued them from their morass.

In Gabrielle Cabrini's book, the story sits uneasily alongside the lyrical passages. When you live underground, nothing happens; imaginary events have no need of duration. But when you have to return to the world, the story becomes more demanding and adventures have to develop as best they can. After *Le Grand Meaulnes*, Dominique Rolin's *The Marshes*, and not forgetting Cocteau's *Holy Terrors*, it is Cabrini's turn to take hold of a theme that has received a generous airing in contemporary literature.[3] To her credit, she has paid no heed to extraneous influences, and she has introduced natural and sometimes authentic sentiment into a subject that has become distorted by artifice. Her way of writing is not without its impurities. Her style avoids what is tedious when ease becomes mechanical, but it is repetitive without ever managing to establish itself, and its images lack some of the power that a simpler and more concentrated form would provide.

Marguerite Duras's style is not without its defects either. But it has the good fortune to be curt, spare, and constrained, and such ill temper is perfectly suited to a subject that will tolerate neither pathos nor grace. The prison of the family is once again the subject in *The Shameless*.[4] However, whereas in *Resurrection of the Dead* it was violence and frenzy that created fate, here everything is degenerating into mediocrity, into the icy cold of feelings that have no future. What are these five individuals in search of, bound to each other by a pointless and cruel misunderstanding? Why, nothing. The two brothers who are callow, lazy, and malicious, lead mean lives made up of pleasures they are content with. Their father has gone into a sullen decline where he defends himself against scorn with his sarcasm. Their mother has a feeble love for her son, who dishonors her. This family group is coherent and indivisible. Each member lives surrounded by the cowardice that he or she acknowledges and is proud of, because it belongs to all of them. The shamelessness of these joyless beings lies in the way they have declined in all innocence, with a sort of disdain for the honorable world that does not form part of their family. There is nothing grand about their insolence, but they feel no shame about their baseness. Part of the book is devoted to the emancipation of the fifth character, Maud, the girl. She is in love with a young ne'er-do-well she happened to meet, and she has no qualms about causing a scandal by going to live with him. If this scandal liberates her, it does not do the same for the rest of the family. Shamelessness is too powerful a force within it. Rather than saving face, what matters is concealing one sort of dishonor beneath another more profitable one. Maud's love is as grim and dismal as the sentiments that are exemplified by her family. It is clear that the destiny that the girl has to overcome could not be more mediocre and pointless. She must shoulder the burden of her shamelessness. Will she succeed? Perhaps. It is not possible to know. That is the best part of the book.

Even more devoid of hope is Marion Delbo's novel *Mr. Durey*, a brief tale of unhappy passion.[5] A woman who is already no longer young sees the handsome fellow she is in love with abandon her out of love for another woman. She takes poison. Using the inner monologue form, the novel tells the story of the final moments of this life in which everything is lacking. It contains neither profound invention nor any boldness of technique. Yet neither does it contain any of those random developments to which a genre of this type so often resorts. Everything about it is simple, somewhat facile, somewhat vulgar; its understated character is its distinguishing feature. Marion Delbo's heroine calls to mind—the comparison is inevitable—the characters in Colette's novels. Ironic in the face of distress, helpless before her desire, overcome with passion at the memory of a body, like them she is bitter and ardent, but she lacks their cruel purity, and above all she is deprived of the resources of an art that would give enduring life to the shudder and confusion of the senses when they are driven to desperation.

Elsa Triolet's novel is a masterpiece of virtuoso art. Of all the novels discussed here it is the only one where ease is supreme, and it extends over more than five hundred pages without flagging. Its inventiveness piles on adventures, generates episodes, and unfolds events; scene follows hard on scene; only the inevitable outcome can interrupt this headlong course that in principle should never end. The hero of *The White Horse* is perfectly suited to the impulsive ease of this development. He himself is all ease and brilliance.[6] What is he? A sort of Gil Blas it is said, a free being who is marvelously gifted but vainly in search of a way of putting his liberty to valid use. Nothing ties him, nothing distracts him, but everything is a temptation. He travels from Paris to Berlin to New York. He goes from rags to riches, from prison to fame. A more agreeable life, a more attractive hero would be hard to imagine. Love seeks him out and he responds to it graciously.

The abundant nature such artistic ease has its drawbacks, but its advantage is that it gives a lightness to the symbols that tend to weigh down so many successful fictions. This Michel may resemble the postwar era in whose brilliant pleasures he indulges; he may bring to mind the loss of values that affects a civilization in which courage, generosity, and the finer sentiments no longer play a part; last, he may find himself fighting in the war and rewarded with the glory of a pointless death: These abstract intentions are swept along by a movement that takes no account of them and replaces them with the pleasure provided by reading what is utterly charming, and more than a match for boredom.

—August 25, 1943

Montesquieu's Travels

Our era shows a liking for Montesquieu that publishers are eager not to disappoint. Scarcely two years ago, a volume of unpublished *Notebooks* provided the wider public with a set of *Thoughts* to read.[1] More recently, Louis Émié invited us to reread *True History*,[2] a rather fragile little novel that the author had left lying among his papers. Today, Marcel Arland offers us a more significant work, *Montesquieu's Travels*, whose value he sets out in an excellent preface.[3]

These travel notes, written in an unaffected style and designed simply as an aide-memoire for their author, are generally quite remote from any thought of publication. Sometimes the presence or at least the shadow of a possible reader can be discerned, but more often than not the public is absent, and if in the course of his travels the writer is thinking of future works, in particular *The Spirit of Laws*, as he gathers material for them, he remains free to be himself, and glad not to be obliged to transform everything he sees into something that has literary value. What makes these pages so pleasant and almost noble to read is the fact that they are free of any readerly considerations, even though they were written by a man who was never loath to be read. Travel writing calls for an author who knows how not to travel as an author, or who discovers in the perfection of the natural world an attraction that allows him to forget himself. It calls for a Montaigne, a Montesquieu, or a Stendhal.

In certain respects, what is natural in Montesquieu can seem like the height of artifice and the pure product of careful application. If his ingenuity is visible like that of the Persian, it is merely a most elegant and polished expedient for showing astonishment at what is shocking. The mind feigns ignorance. It adopts an air of extreme simplicity. It is "candid" in order to reveal the mild stupidity of those who think they never are. Thanks to its highly contrived yet lively style, it constructs for itself a second then a third nature that are pure invention. The Montesquieu of the *Persian Letters* is so natural by virtue of fiction and careful practice that he seems only to be so at that price, and we readily admire the effects of this supreme mutation that is capable of passing itself off sincerely for what it is not.

Like the *Thoughts*, the *Travel Notes* show that what is natural in Montesquieu runs much deeper, that it is not merely a sham and that if the mind imitates it and provides it with an image, this is simply the imprint of the most authentic type of spontaneity. Among some eighteenth-century writers, even in Voltaire, there is nothing more remarkable than this natural quality, which appears entirely put on but in fact stems from a sincere nature. They appear detached, offhand, and sarcastic, and we feel they are at ease in the world because culture has provided them with all the means that such mastery requires. But we feel too that they are not cut off from themselves as was once thought, and that if they are natural, they owe it to their nature. That is the secret of this magnificent historical moment. There you could succeed in being the opposite of yourself while not ceasing to be yourself, and whether through artifice or truth, the two-faced Janus that each one is for others and for himself creates the same impression: that of being in perfect conformity with men and things.

What is natural in Montesquieu comes from an indefinable something that allows him to be content with everything without ever being contemptible, and to become what he is without having to force himself. The portrait he left of himself is the rarest expression of equilibrium and the instinct for living, and quoting certain passages from it can still astonish: "I wake in the morning with a secret joy. . . . I behold the light with a kind of rapture; and for the rest of the day I am happy." What is expressed here is remarkable because it points to a sort of mysterious sympathy with life that can only be poetic in nature, in a mind that is itself not poetic and indeed has no real gift for the arts. It is from a complicity with the sun, an intimacy with the day that he derives something that is almost beyond happiness: rapture or joy, and this joy is not directed outward, has no wish to become public or to be dissipated through being expressed, it is a secret joy that is tied to its cause by an understanding that cannot be sullied. Montesquieu's love of the light, in a life of marvelous composure that seems immune to any sort of thunderbolt, remains the guarantee of an instinct that is of a higher order than any commonplace wisdom. It is a moving profession of faith from a man who will grow older and risk losing his sight without ever cursing the light of day.

"My machine is so favorably constructed that I am struck sharply enough by every object for it to give me pleasure, but not enough for it to give me pain." Such temperate curiosity explains the pure cast of these travel notes. The way in which he takes an interest allows him to control the object of his curiosity. He is not quite an amateur, traveling aimlessly and taking a dilettante's pleasure in whatever turns up. We are spared the attitude of the futile traveler, haphazardly learning about things that he comes across, which is just as objectionable as that of the systematic traveler whose erudite concerns dictate his every step. Montesquieu's comings and goings involve serious thought in preparation for his works, but that preoccupation does not take him away from himself. He welcomes everything he encounters, takes pleasure in it as though his sole aim was to enjoy it, and yet never neglects for long what he is thoughtfully and confidently in search of.

This persistent seriousness, and even more so the moderation that makes him take a discreet interest in everything, prevent him from giving himself very much personal space in the journal. That too is quite delightful. The *I* of the traveler is neither impersonal nor abstract: it is lively and sensual, it sees, it hears, but it only shows itself for as long as is necessary. In what are merely notes, and moreover not intended for publication, anecdotal episodes are reduced to a minimum. In Germany, Montesquieu catches a fever, yet the only reason he mentions it is in order to speak of the Augsburg doctors who cure him without knowing of what exactly. In fact he has no desire to tell himself the story of his adventures. His notes are not the memento of a self that has a need for memories, or that seeks to understand itself with the aid of a mirror. He shows little astonishment at what happens to him, and as a result, very little does. In this respect, his diary is quite different from Montaigne's travel diary, in which the author not only dwells at length on his bouts of colic but also constantly derives knowledge and pleasure from a wealth of episodes. In Montesquieu there is nothing superfluous. If facts also play a role, and even if they are minor ones, his concision presents them to us bare, compressed by the meaning that illuminates them. Ellipsis transforms even stories that are told just for the pleasure of it into maxims. And these thoughts provide the reader with the pleasure to be found in a story that can be listened to without needing to be thought about. Here, for example, is an anecdote about Florence: "Italian families spend a lot of money on canonizations. The Corsini family in Florence spent more than 130,000 Roman crowns in order to have a saint Corsini canonized. Marquess Corsini the elder said, 'My children, be good, upstanding people, but do not be saints.'" Few rogues have cost their families more than that saint. Then there is this brief tale about Rome: "In Rome there is nothing more convenient than a church when it comes to praying to God or murdering someone. . . . An Olivetan monk who had been accused by his prior of stealing some corn went to him for confession, and shot him with a pistol and sought refuge in a church." And this thought on the subject of Genoa: "There is nothing more mendacious than their palaces. What you see is a superb house, but inside there is just an old servant at her spinning-wheel." We should not forget that Montesquieu traveled in Austria, Italy, Germany, and Holland, that he spent a long time in England, and that this writer who missed nothing and whose curiosity was indefatigable turned this substantial material into no more than a small book, discreetly reduced to its essentials.

Another pleasing feature of these notes is that they reveal the freest of minds, one least wary of what it discovers and least disconcerted by what is new to it. "When I traveled in foreign lands," he writes in the *Thoughts*, "I became attached to them as though they were my very own: I shared their good fortune, and would have wished them always to flourish." And in a phrase that deserves to be read with a pinch of irony, d'Alembert recalls his self-satisfied search for the best of all worlds: "According to his observations, Germany was designed to be traveled through, Italy to be stayed in, England to be thought in and France to be lived in." But whereas this sentiment would be distinctly unpleasant if it sacrificed clear-sightedness to a desire to take pleasure in everything, it has its value thanks to the severity that accurate observation constantly obliges him to show. Everywhere there are rogues, misers, poor countries made dishonest by poverty, rich ones corrupted by their wealth, enslaved peoples governed haphazardly by mediocre princes, free peoples who sell their freedom and become unworthy of what they are. In Prussia, he meets a crank of a prince who "inflicts a terrible tyranny on his people" and whose sole wish is to have great soldiers, because as a child he had a warrant officer as a tutor who talked of nothing but the details of regimental life. In Venice, a republic that loses a war "out of avarice and fear," without even drawing its sword. In England, a people that is no longer worthy of its freedom since it has sold it to the king; "and if the king gave it back, they would just sell it to him again." These observations do not disturb the traveler, nor make him lose interest in other countries, where he continues to encounter other men. "You have to take them," he says, "as they are: when I am in France I make friends with everyone; in England I make friends with no one; in Italy I pay everyone a compliment; in Germany I drink with everyone."

If he is interested in everything that deserves his attention, be it exploring the Harz mines in Hanover, collecting water from the fountains that produce copper in Hungary, in Venice examining an ancient machine for cleaning the canals, or contemplating the leaning tower in Pisa, Montesquieu is attentive above all, in keeping with his primary interest, to systems of government, the mentality of peoples, their decline or their prosperity. He needs not just to observe but to explain, and in the end to explain things in terms of simple causes. That is the counterpart to a curiosity that appears to be universal. It looks for reasons, and rarely does it find none. It is in search of general truths that will allow it to introduce some order into the disorderly spectacle of human actions. Its goal is to understand what it is not content just to observe. This gives rise to numerous remarks whose ingenuity now escapes us, and a number of others that seem to come down to us only because they are mistaken, as when he predicts the fall of the English monarchy or writes the following: "I do not know what will become of all the inhabitants who are sent from Europe and Africa to the West Indies, but I believe that if any nation is to be abandoned by its colonies, this will begin with the British nation." But such overhasty explanations are also the expression of an almost voluptuous passion for knowledge, a sort of rational libertinage that has no need to see things accurately to love truth, and on the contrary finds joy in truth even when it is passionately deceived by it.

Montesquieu is not indifferent to the arts, and churches, painting, and sculpture figure among his memories. What he says about them is disappointing. The pages he wrote on the Gothic manner or on drawing rather cruelly expose his limitations. There is something feeble about the docile manner in which he willingly contemplates and appreciates great works with the aid of the explanations he is given, and then makes his own without ever putting them to the test. Yet it would be foolish to reproach him for a way of discussing the arts that is not primarily his, but is traditional; he praises what is natural about Raphael, he likes his beauty, his harmony ("it is not painting," he says, "it is nature itself"); in Leonardo's *Last Supper* he sees life, movement, astonishment, all the passions and all the nuances of human sentiment; this is simply a traditional way of loving the arts—indeed, it corresponds to what Raphael and Leonardo themselves said—and it would be easy to forgive him for it by saying it is as good as any other when it comes to talking about inexpressible truth, were it possible to feel some genuine, spontaneous admiration behind it. But it is that sentiment that is lacking, it is that warmth of delight that we search for in vain in so many descriptions that say what they cannot quite manage to show. Perhaps the bogus passion that is all that the arts inspire in him reveals the lack from which Montesquieu's own art suffers, as though what is missing from the natural quality in him, where nature delightfully dallies with herself, is a little of the movement of a sensitive soul that will later on become the secret of Stendhal.

—September 8, 1943

A History of French Literature

Kléber Haedens has never had much time for the authors of literary manuals; he has criticized the most famous of them and raised suspicions about those that appear quite innocuous. His disapproval of official policy governing the teaching of literature in France has been so comprehensive and robust that it has acquired almost classic status. It would be trivial to repeat those strictures in one's turn, the effect of which on the limited readership of literary reviews has been considerable, whereas in schools and colleges its effect has been nonexistent. Now here he is today, the author of a manual in his turn. He has braved reprisals and laid himself open to becoming the victim of his own severity. Having been the arrow, he has become the target. Fortunately, his new book, *A History of French Literature*,[1] has no truck with the sort of petty concern for caution and cleverness to which young writers are not always immune.

His book was written for his own pleasure, and for ours. To appreciate it, it is necessary to be a little like its author, to like what is free and pure, to ignore what is superfluous, to have verve and wit, to be profound when required, but above all to have a sense of art and style. The form of his book is a source of intense delight for the reader. It is all ease and brilliance. Images illuminate it and rigor sustains it. Speed of expression carries it along. It is worthy of the great works that it evokes. That being the case, it would be ridiculous to linger over its faults. If some people do not like it, all the better; there are perhaps good grounds for objecting to the easy pleasures it provides. But this history of literature has one quality that sets it way above its critics: it is itself a literary work. Unlike the manuals that have so often annoyed Kléber Haedens, it is what it shows and is attuned to what it praises. It is a mirror that in no way debases the beauty of what is reflected in it.

There are countless ways of writing a history of literature. The way Kléber Haedens has chosen is neither very exceptional nor very profound. It has no time for literary problems or historical ones. That astonishing reality whose true nature is different from the elements of which it is the sum, in which causes act in ways that neither physical nor psychological determinism can even hint at, and that is constantly traversed by currents, waves, and surging wellsprings; the subtle matter that establishes relations between works and their authors that are simultaneously fixed and changing, that can only be discerned through them even though it is quite distinct from them; in short, the entire strange universe constituted by literature remains foreign to Kléber Haedens's study, for which books and the men who wrote them are all that exist. He is unconcerned by the "backworld" [*arrière-monde*] against which every important work stands out, any more than he is interested in history. He has all books at his fingertips: he either likes them or does not like them, and his feelings traverse dense layers of time without suffering any refraction, and eliminate any mark of age from the object they have chosen.

The word "history" could be understood in his book the way it is understood in narrative: to mean "story." Writers are characters and their works are events that a pen in search of effects singles out for a role in some future novel. The pleasure this gives us is of the sort that we find in a tale. Though we know these passing phantoms on whom no fantasy casts new light, we discover them as if they had emerged from the unknown, and we observe their depiction with a curiosity that feigns ignorance the better to find satisfaction. What will the young Du Bellay do? What is the meaning of Molière's comedies? What should we think of Laclos or Musset? We expect to get the descriptions we anticipate, and reading in a way that disrupts the episodes so as to get to the outcome, we are a step ahead of the ultimate judgment that brings the unending adventure of a masterpiece to its close. It is thus that from the outer darkness of literary possibility there arise, as if in a windowpane, fragments of faces or outlines of works. These sudden silhouettes are lit up by the gaze that alights on them. They are illuminated by the passion they arouse. They become admirably visible before vanishing inside the mind of the reader in a chaos of dreams. Everything gives them life and makes them endure, be it admiration when it singles them out or denigration when it nullifies them.

It is easy to recognize in Kléber Haedens's criticism the sort that is inspired by taste when it knows no law. Beauty is the beauty he likes, and what bores him is deadly. But if this impression no doubt has a basis in truth, it receives further development by its author, who prefers to impose his decisions rather than defend them. He sometimes proclaims his views with a promptness that requires no explanation: "D'Urfé has no talent whatsoever." "Gobineau, what a bore as a philosopher!" He sometimes also gives his reasons, but he presents them with a peremptory vigor that means they are not open to discussion and will alienate all those who cannot discern the well-meaning justifications beneath the authoritarian rigidity. Or else he resorts to images, and images affect only the sensibilities that are already attuned to them, illuminate only the imagination that is expecting them and repel minds that are not already intimate with them. The product of this system of provocation is an imperious sentiment that will delight some people, leave others aghast, and exhort everyone to come out of themselves. It would seem that all the works and all the authors of our literature are just so many possessions, and can be enjoyed only through the intervention of a critical self who bestows existence exclusively on the objects of his preference.

One of the surprising things about this book is that while it appears to be governed entirely by its author's whim, on the whole it finds itself in agreement with traditional views. Paradox has been more or less eliminated from it.[2] What is admired is what we are in the habit of admiring; what is violently singled out for scorn is what by general agreement deserves to be disdained. There is no point looking in this history for any exceptions that deserve to be promoted, or any fundamental revision of values. For Kléber Haedens, the seventeenth-century novel is not *The Other World* by Cyrano de Bergerac but *The Princess of Cleves*, and the most outrageous eighteenth-century author is Laclos, not the Marquis de Sade. Though he readily condemns Romanticism, in keeping with an already long-standing tradition, he redeems it piecemeal by displaying remarkable restraint and indulgence in the way he spares Lamartine and Musset, and even shows leniency toward Victor Hugo. When tolerance fails him, it is replaced by judgments that target authors or works of disputable quality. To be severe with Fénelon or Voltaire is to join a tradition that has always had robust defenders. And to say that Flaubert writes badly is to adopt a prevailing opinion that Proust is almost alone in challenging. His most original severity seems reserved for the *chansons de geste* and above all the *Song of Roland*, which he considers dull, written in impoverished language and lacking the charm of a good story.

Every era and almost every generation forms a judgment on French authors considered as a whole, providing them with either an accolade or an explanation. They bring unknown works back to life and consign to obscurity works that have acquired too much fame. People love or forget in accordance with the melancholy laws to which they sacrifice their liberty. Hence the importance of literary manuals, but hence too their frivolity. As Kléber Haedens so effectively puts it: "a history written in 1942 can bear no resemblance to a history written twenty years earlier, or to those that will be written twenty years later." We might therefore conclude that the one he offers us bears witness to the likes and dislikes of his time. That is possible after all. But the impression we gain is rather different. It would appear rather that this history accepts only reluctantly the enthusiasms under whose sway the generation it represents has fallen. That is particularly clear in the case of the great writers of the end of the nineteenth century. Rimbaud and Lautréamont are liked, but hardly praised to the skies. They are even considered suspect. Mallarmé, for his part, is not accepted in his entirety. He is seen as a worrying influence, and beneath the expressions of admiration that he attracts lies a whole network of reservations. And significantly, Verlaine's ingenuity receives exceptionally warm praise. Poor Lelian turns out to be superior to Vigny and the equal of Baudelaire. This twist may surprise the youngest among us, while the eldest will not find it uncongenial.

It goes without saying that Kléber Haedens is too free a spirit to indulge in feelings that are dictated by circumstance. Péguy is spoiled for him by the use that has been made of this solitary being over the past three years, and he continues to favor openly certain writers it has become habitual to despise. Similarly, he is suspicious of cliques. He wants to like what he likes on his own terms. This explains his reservations concerning Stendhal, whom he prefers to keep at arm's length rather than appreciate him in the company of unbridled zealots. The only line that he willingly adopts when coming to a judgment is that of the former neoclassical school. He heaps praise on its founders, adheres to its tendencies as closely as possible and seems to invite its views. No other exception to his wish to be free and his contentment with himself can be found. It is to this impetuous spirit of independence that his best pages are certainly due. There, without changing tradition, he renews it entirely from within. Hence, the writers of the sixteenth and seventeenth centuries are evoked with a poetic brilliance that grants them a second life. Neither learning nor critical intelligence or a sense of what makes a great work are sufficient to bring us closer to works that posterity has frozen in time. Neither is fashion enough to raise from the grave those fine shades that curiosity discovers there. It takes a kindred sensibility, the ability to recognize what remains young in what has aged, the capacity to open the way toward renewed duration for what is eternal, and last an animating spirit that only pure taste and vigorous literary sentiment prevent from collaborating in a grim comedy of rejuvenation. Classical works are the easiest works to conceal beneath the colors of the times. There is nothing more dismal than the artificial light beneath which they are placed so they may be seen more easily. They are made to resemble random realities that bear no relation to them. They are made to merge with the crowd. They are caught up in the sort of picturesque turmoil they have always shunned. That is the hell into which their glory, ensnared by a sun that shines on everyone, sometimes forces them to descend.

Kléber Haedens's method is entirely different. But it can probably work only for him. He moves from a writer to his works in a subtle way. He draws on biographical sources, narrates events taken from life, follows the river that once flowed, and gradually extracts from the outer adventures the deeper image that anticipates the creative adventure. Then he turns to the works, and by evoking them but not analyzing them makes them part of the very substance of the man. Poems, funeral orations, and novels change into figures, disintegrate into impressions, and create around the mind that produced them a radiant mist, the shadow of a light whose track we follow over the golden or snowy plains of literature. Sometimes anecdote vanishes: all that remains of the writer is the language of which he was master, he lives in the magnificent echo of a voice that is now silent, we encounter Bossuet; or else he is nothing but thought merged with silence, and, being without effect and without cunning, it can only be communicated if it is in itself identical to what we can find in our deepest selves, and here we encounter Descartes. When this meeting of inside and outside happens naturally, under the impetus of the critic's imagination, his art appears to be of the same nature as the creative power that it expresses, and he sketches portraits that are like the imprint of an invisible reality.

—September 22, 1943

The Influence of the American Novel

The remarkable book that Louis-René des Forêts has just published with the title *The Beggars* was written under the influence of American novels.[1] The author acknowledges this influence, and he has the modesty to consider that there are other grounds on which he may be criticized. At the same time, there are critics who seem afraid at the idea that the effect on the French novel of Faulkner, Hemingway, Dos Passos, and Caldwell could alter its true nature and make it betray its origins. It is quite obvious why the systematic imitation of a work or a genre should be a matter of concern. But imitation is not the same as influence, and the current state of our novel is such that it has nothing to lose by venturing down trails that have been so brilliantly blazed by the richest forms of contemporary novel writing.

It takes a certain amount of time to penetrate des Forêts's book. The world it creates is made up of superimposed stories or levels on which the action and the themes echo each other ever more profoundly. At the very top, the children playfully act out the story that in the middle is being turned into an awesome adventure by the adults; and at the very bottom, in a zone where the air is thin and events are a blur, isolated individuals yield directly to passions that others only experience under cover of violent action. The composition of the work is demanding, but the story itself is very simple. A group of boys with a young leader, Sani, at its head, organizes a large-scale series of games by the shores of the Ocean. They raid boats anchored in the port, they ride around the countryside on horseback, they conspire to seize power. This is the adventurous life they see grownups living, scaled down to suit their age. In the same port another gang has formed whose specialty is bootlegging. Led by an actor, backed by an old ship-owner and aided by a jailbird and an innkeeper, the association chalks up the raids until one evening the police arrest the band of accomplices.

A few seconds before the end, the actor Gregory Souvier is shot by a woman who is his leading lady in the theater. The passion of this woman called Hélène Armentière casts a dark light over the entire book. Abandoned by the man she loves, she hunts him down in a vain and desperate chase that he is not even aware of. Every step he takes finds her there, a smoldering shadow on whom he pours scorn. All he sees in such insistence is an indiscreet and short-lived passion, when in fact it is a fearsome sentiment whose fury is inflamed by solitude. Another solitary figure whom people call the Stranger passes through the world he inhabits without belonging to it. No one knows anything about him. Apparently he was once driven to crime by jealousy, but now, locked inside his obsession and his hatred, he yearns for folly to triumph, and is no more than a dangerous onlooker to whom no one listens any more. These two passions, pure and cut off from life, finding succor neither in reality nor in make-believe, reveal the desire that lies hidden beneath the seemingly more normal actions of the other characters. They too are drawn to the solitude of which they have an inkling, and the projects they embark on fail and collapse into the void.

Everything is a failure in this story, and everything leads to misfortune. The world of adolescence is no less under threat than the other one. One of the merits of the book is that it describes the adventures of the children without recourse to the false charm that generally makes them unbearable. The usual conventions are there of course: Sani, the leader of the gang, lives in a mysterious castle; he is a prince rather than a leader; his beauty and his force are exceptional. But this radiance does not save him from disgrace. The lust for power throws these young souls into turmoil, causing an association that was designed to endure to split apart in an undisciplined fashion. One episode shows the boys during an outing on horseback playfully hunting down their leader, who suffers an unfortunate accident as a result. The episode is significant. First, a leader exists only if he is being hunted; power requires of whomever assumes it a sort of expiation that he cannot avoid. Furthermore, play proves capable of a pathos and a seriousness that its tragic outcome places on a par with manly actions. The world inhabited by these adolescents lacks the brilliance of dream. Sentiments are not given color by a false light. In the case of both the youngsters and the grownups, a void that they are seeking to fill drives them to search outside of themselves for an unobtainable satisfaction.

The characters in *The Beggars* are in pursuit of something they can never attain. They hunger for what escapes them. And if they briefly seize hold of what they are seeking, they lose it or destroy it through a frantic impulse that they do not control. It is in this guise that fate plays a role in the tragedy. The presence of fate is expressed through a series of events that seem like echoes of one another. As we have seen, two main themes reflect each other throughout the book: The children use play to express what makes up the life and actions of the men; but a whole variety of coincidences, overlapping moments, and details makes us increasingly feel that a blind force is constructing order out of disorder, and introducing into human affairs a strange lawless harmony. Two other themes counterbalance each other: that of Hélène's unhappy love, which is doomed to destruction and eager for disaster, and the theme of the Stranger who, arriving from a distant land, brings with him the memory of a crime and a desire for solitude that is so extreme it is a madness. Last, just as playacting mingles with reality, theatrical sentiment combines with true passion. On stage, Hélène and Grégoire are Desdemona and Othello, and their jealousy is acted out simultaneously on several levels, where its effects are countered or inverted as they gradually draw the observer into an inextricable state of confusion, where what is true and what is false, reality and myth, are all no more than a single terrible nightmare.

These symmetries that can only have meaning if they remain partly hidden, these murky mirror effects, these musical combinations of theme have obliged des Forêts to resort to an exceptional mode of composition. He has abandoned narrative continuity and given each of his characters the task of evoking a small part of the story through his memories. Not only does that produce several accounts of the same adventure, but these stories also do not follow on from each other the way the events they recount did in reality. The result is a profusion of strangeness and shadow from which the book derives its character. For on the one side, the character who delves deep into his memories is not an objective historian; on the contrary, what he says results from his passion, he is locked inside himself and he sees only what he wants to see. But on the other hand, far from becoming clearer as they come together, the fragments of narrative form zigzags of image, an oscillation of incidents that shatter the picture and jumble together to the utmost degree the past, the present and the future.

It is easy to accuse des Forêts of borrowing from other authors, and indeed he makes no secret of the fact. The method he uses has been used successfully by English and American authors, and in particular by William Faulkner in two novels of his that are well-known in France: *The Sound and the Fury* and *As I Lay Dying.* We can see no reason whatsoever why a French writer should have denied himself the right to use this foreign technique for his own purposes. The first writer to tell a story opened the way for millions of others, and they have never been accused of illicit borrowing. The eighteenth-century novelists who followed the fashion for the epistolary novel had no scruples about using what was clearly an imitation, and twenty years after Rousseau's *The New Heloise, Dangerous Liaisons* provided a masterpiece in a genre that was already very hackneyed and almost discredited. Is the use of intercutting monologues more of a convention than a continuous narrative technique? Possibly, though every narrative displays a high degree of arbitrariness, and presupposes almost limitless goodwill and open-mindedness on its reader's part. All that can be said is that by employing an unusual technique a writer makes it visible, gives it an importance that holds the reader's attention and encourages him to call for it to be justified. If it turns out that the novelist could have written in a simpler manner, and that his choice of form is just a whim (or a wish to be original), he will seriously compromise the solidity and the interest of his work.

The reasons that led des Forêts to choose a new form are quite visible. The first is to be found in the common stock of gestures, actions, and sentiments that are repeated from one age to the next by men who are doomed to misfortune. Or more precisely, his aim was to translate a single aspiration and a single failure at several levels: his book is the novel of an obsession; his characters hear the same voice and reply to it with similar endeavors; they are caught up in the same vortex that isolates them from each other, even though it is the same vortex. They are separated by what they have in common. And this leads to the second reason why the novelist made his choice. Each of his characters is a prisoner of solitude; each one lives in a separate world. The monologue each one utters expresses a point of view that is incommunicable. Whether they join with others through their actions, like the children or the bootleggers, or remain locked away inside a solitary obsession, like the Stranger or the young woman, fate requires that they keep on going through life as though it were a narrow tunnel from which they are desperately trying to escape, and where they talk only to themselves. In this respect, the fundamental mode of their language is indeed monologue and not dialogue. They are unable to exchange anything but superficial impressions; they are powerless to go from saying "I" to saying "you" in any authentic manner.

If there were one reproach that could be leveled at the novelist, it is not that he has chosen an unusual form, but that he has not applied it in all of its rigor. In *The Beggars*, memories organize themselves too easily from one story to the other and form a group whose unity is patent. We sense the presence of the author as he coordinates the different details of the same episode. There is confusion only on the surface; the order that characterizes a coherent narrative wins out in the end so as to please the reader. More serious still is the fact that, though designed in each case to express the most intimate and least communicable of voices, all the monologues resemble each other in tone and language. From chapter to chapter, instead of varying, the form repeats itself. Whereas the separate narratives, in which an "I" who is both deaf and blind gives an account of things from the standpoint that is his, seek to give us the impression that they are closed rooms that do not open onto the outside, we ourselves move with familiar ease from one world to the other, without knowing the dreadful feeling of being out of our element that ought, each time we descend into the solitude of a new character, to wrench us away from our own language and make us obscure even to ourselves. By maintaining the unity of a particular form, that of his style, from one unrelated narrative to the next, did the author intend us to think that his heroes are both isolated and identical, yet identical without ever being able to become aware of the fact since all that they have in common is their isolation? It must be said that his art tends to encourage such an impression, but because it remains too embroiled in a clumsy lyricism, rather than lead us inside the solitude of the characters he has created, it leads us to the reveries of the author himself, who appears to have parted company with himself with the sole purpose of discovering himself again in the somewhat monotonous, hectic violence of his own language.

—September 29, 1943

The Mysticism of Angelus Silesius

The study that Henri Plard has just devoted to the great seventeenth-century German mystic Angelus Silesius is a work that raises the most important and difficult problems with a rare maturity of spirit.[1] It is clear and profound. While impeccably well informed, it always rises above its own erudition. As well as casting historical light on a subject that otherwise would not be fully comprehensible, it raises questions that go beyond history and in whose ambit the most acute spiritual torments come into focus. Such an effort not only presupposes remarkable awareness and intellectual strength on the part of the individual who has accomplished it, but it also implies an inner attentiveness whose effects cannot be gauged purely in terms of knowledge.

The life and work of Johann Scheffler, whom posterity chose to call Angelus Silesius, the Angel of Silesia, contain their own mysteries. They appear both strangely disengaged from the circumstances of their time and bound up with it even as they shun it, owing to a confusion that is merely its reflection.

Scheffler's life in itself is not a simple one. First of all, as a doctor who once studied in Holland and found his own religious disquiet awakening in that land of liberty and spiritual inquiry, he spent ten years in the grip of self-searching and doubt, the concrete significance of which we know little about. A first response to these hesitations is provided by his main work, the first five books of the *Cherubic Pilgrim*, which show us the progress and direction of his mystical enquiries. The second response is his conversion to Catholicism after a life of harsh combat, an intense and sometimes unsuccessful struggle in the cause of religious proselytism and endeavor. These two responses are of course not irreconcilable, but they remain distinctly different and, from a spiritual viewpoint, out of tune with each other. The fact that contemplation led him to confess a particular dogmatic faith can be explained, at least superficially, but then his adherence to Catholicism leads him toward action, and this action turns him away from the mystical rigor to which he was initially attached. As far as we can tell regarding experiences about which we know very little, and that lie outside of any clearly defined frame, it would appear to be a fact that for Angelus Silesius, mystical striving came before religious practice, and that through its demands, that practice gradually substituted another sort of light for the illumination he had sought for before entering the Church.

Our first instinct when we accompany Henri Plard inside this body of thought, as he seeks to comprehend solely on its own terms, is to see it as being very close to the mysticism of Meister Eckhart. The resemblance is not perfect, but it is very striking. It is all the more remarkable in so far as it cannot be explained by any direct influence. Scheffler knew almost nothing about Eckhart; it is thanks to Tauler and above all Ruysbroek that his heritage came down to him; the historical role of the Flemish mystic, who had vigorously criticized a number of the Master of Thuringia's claims, was to revive the main themes of his thought and ensure that they were passed on. He was himself the heir to what he fought against and sought to destroy.

However, the resemblance between Eckhart and Silesius is not just a matter of external influences, but it also derives from a less fortuitous affinity, an encounter that is justified, according to Plard, by "a similar mystical intellectual structure." What is important is not the active presence that one mind can bring to bear on another, by means of his work or works that are similar to it; beyond the level of such action it is a common principle and a parallel orientation that bring them together across the centuries, without them ever having come contact with each other.

The principle that is common to Silesius and Eckhart, and also other mystics such as St John of the Cross, is that man must necessarily seek God by means of nonknowledge [*le non-savoir*]. The principle that he shares with Eckhart in particular is that this search has theological consequences, and calls into question the very notion of God through a dialectic that has paradox as its principal. Supreme knowledge presupposes a progressive stripping away of knowledge. What we know creates an urge to appropriate it in us, it is transformed into an object whose limits are those of our own knowledge, and it conceals from us the limitless ignorance that we sense above and below us like a twofold yawning abyss. We must as it were progress from a finite ignorance that is commensurate with what we are, and that knowledge dispels as it develops, toward an infinite ignorance that transcends our condition, and is linked to our sense of a void that nothing can fill. What is the meaning of the expression: to know God? We know only that with which we can become identical. And to become identical with God requires of man not only that he shed everything that makes him man, but furthermore that he destroy everything that makes him think that he knows God. To lose oneself in every sense of the word, to experience death and put to death what one has and what one is, that is the sole path to knowledge. It is the path of negative theology, and Silesius invents nothing when he preserves it in all of its purity. All of his expressions, "All knowledge must be overcome," "God cannot be grasped," "The more you grasp him the more he escapes," express this loyalty to the mystical tradition that Plard sums up perfectly in these simple terms: Progress in knowledge is progress in ignorance. What should be added is that this absolute void of knowledge that alone allows us to unite with the void that God must be for us, this supreme vacuity, this icy impoverishment that embraces nothing in order to embrace everything, is ultimately indistinguishable from love, goes hand in hand with the total gift of love. Whence his admirable couplet:

> It is also possible to love without knowing.
> I love one thing only, and do not know what it is:
> And it is nonknowledge [*weil ich es nicht Weiss*] that made me choose it.

The man who can come to God only by reducing himself to nothing nonetheless links the notion of God profoundly to his human nature. First, God exists only in relation to man. That is a consequence of the dialectic of nonknowledge. But the name of God and all of the theological concepts that are linked to it have meaning and reality only for the man who receives, then conceives them. God is merely a moment of our ignorance, the manner in which, as creatures, we feel ourselves to be in a necessary relation to him. But if man as a creature is eliminated, what becomes of what he calls God? Naturally we cannot say, since we can only talk of God; the most that we can glimpse through ignorance is that the differentiated, Trinitarian, creator God must be transcended, that there is something beyond God, that this absolutely unitary God that exists before everything, this God who is empty of God and absent from all creatures, is the only deity who deserves both the names supernothing and superdivine. "I must climb," says Silesius, "higher than God in a desert." Up to this point, such apparently surprising statements are merely reference-points in a negative dialectic; in order to grasp God one must also forget what he is. But Silesius goes further, and like Eckhart, from whom he borrows the distinction between God and the deity, and even the image of the desert, he derives positive theological consequences from the challenge to the notion of God. If, before the creation, God is a pure deity and absolutely indeterminate, this leads us to the thought that the deity creates God for itself at the same time as it creates the world, that is to say the Word and all creatures. If the deity can only become an object of knowledge when it has become a personal God, and is seen as such by man whom it has created, this leads us to believe that God eternally creates the Word, the world and mankind in order to become aware of himself, to love himself and become conscious of himself, so that not only is it only possible to speak of God in so far as we speak of man, but the creation of man is linked to the eternal generation of God, the Word and the three Persons in divine consciousness itself.

These statements, whose equivalent can be found in Meister Eckhart, that reflect at the level of knowledge and at the level of God what an indefinite capacity for nonknowledge presupposes, and that are, in a word, the shadow cast by the absolute void of the human over the entire sphere of human reality, have the effect of enclosing the mind within a paradoxical tension, a harrowing confrontation between contradictory assertions that it must nonetheless maintain firmly together. And this search for truth by way of paradox again has its point of departure in the medieval theology of Meister Eckhart, and its later development in the philosophy of Nicholas of Cusa. Man is both infinitely separated from God and so to speak identical to him. He cannot reach him except through a leap of infinite transcendence, and nothing is more present in him than God. He is a mere nothing in the face of the supreme reality, and yet it is he who founds the essence of God. Eckhart has already said that the depth of the human soul is utterly impenetrable, and that in it there is a spark that makes it one with the primordial unity. Similarly, in Silesius, man can become one with the silent deity in this world, can grasp, at the heart of nothingness, a more unknowable nothingness and, deified in this supreme nothing, participate in the eternal creation that flows immeasurably from it. This extraordinary glorification of man is merely an expression of his supreme nakedness. There is nothing lower than man when he comes into contact with the immensity of this void; he is deader than dead; he is very precisely the dead God for which Christ provides the model; he is the one who has denied himself everything, including the ecstasy in which love unites with love in an identification that presupposes an initial duality. Plard brings out perfectly the necessity of contradiction, without which Silesius's thought would be unfaithful to itself by becoming immobilized. We should never be content to grasp only one side of it; on the contrary, it is the unstable axis around which, in a succession that seeks to suppress all movement, immanence and transcendence, glory and destruction, knowledge and love all rotate.

The manner of expression to be found in the exceptional poet that Angelus Silesius could often be corresponds to this persistence of paradox. *The Cherubic Pilgrim* is written in regular couplets, and it brings to perfection a form that he himself did not create. In the same period, the epigram is producing works that are similar in inspiration, and Czepko's *Monodisticha* show what benefit religious thought can derive from the concision of this didactic genre. Be it mystical or profane, there is no epigram without its "point," without the sharp shock of expressions that balance out as they clash with each other. It is in this disconcerting encounter that Silesius's thought acquires the enigmatic appearance that prevents it from being reducible to itself. An entire dialectic is played out between the two lines of the couplet, and through the juxtaposition of opposing words, through the correspondence between an idea and an image, through the rhythm that gives dramatic sense to a self-evident contrast, the assertion acquires both a form of the utmost rigor, and an oscillation that deprives it of any solid logical base:

> I do not believe in death.
> Even if I die each hour
> Each time I find a better life.

The images imbue these lines with the presence of an unattainable reality. No doubt they lack the radiant power, the pale ardor, veiled yet laden with fecundity, to be found in the poems of St John of the Cross. Silesius accepts the legacy of medieval mysticism, and the rose, the lily, crystal, gold, the lamb, and the dove pass gently through the same allegorical shadows as those that are found in the tender garden of Tauler. But without real invention, through a nuance of modesty that limits the singularity of his vision and adds mystery to its traditional configuration, he succeeds in plunging the simple words he receives into a new silence, so that the flame, the night and the sun are restored to their glory as flawless symbols:

> I must myself be a sun, with my rays I must
> Paint the colorless sea of all deity.

It would be vain, however, not to see that even in his language, Angelus Silesius comes under the influence of his time in a way that prefigures a no less significant influence on his thought. Sensual, violent images, wounds through which, before dying to the world, the body exhales its power and finds glory in its torment, bear witness to the effects of a divided thought that is drawn to baroque antitheses. The form chosen by Silesius reveals the secret of a dispersal that is preferable to unity. As Plard puts it so perfectly, these short epigrams that no external organization combines into more substantial developments, resemble the paragraphs of a mystical theology that has been invaded by a spirit of disquiet. They resemble scintillating stars that are incapable of proclaiming the pure constellation they nonetheless strive to form together. Furthermore, the mystical substance is itself altered by a literary spirit and by intellectual subtleties. Art deforms the energy it seeks to transmit, and analysis replaces vision with the methodical processes of knowledge. Just as the dispersal of formal inventions that remain separate from each other conflicts with the harmony of thought, so his thought finds it difficult to resist intrusions and inquisitiveness that are entirely mental. That is how Johann Scheffler, the last of the great German mystics in the medieval tradition, belongs also to those troubled times that saw the rise of the Counterreformation in opposition to Protestantism.

But the most serious and mysterious discord remains one we have already referred to: that between his mystical work with its fidelity to all the rigors of contemplation and love, and his later religious practice, which, while no doubt highly sincere and even admirable, remains almost entirely foreign to the ideal of the *Cherubic Pilgrim*. It could be thought that this sort of betrayal, that is all the more serious for being unconscious, may be explained by the violent religious activity and the wretched conflict to which his divided age condemns him. Naturally, this hypothesis is valid. However, the examples of Saint John of the Cross or Saint Theresa of Avila, who, though involved in the harshest sort of action, preserve the movement of their mystical lives in all its purity, make it difficult to accept it uncritically. It would be more convincing to examine Angelus Silesius's personal experience, the experience for which the *Cherubic Pilgrim* was meant to provide the speculative implementation. What was it when all is said and done? Was the pilgrimage as it is described ever undertaken? Was it pursued to its conclusion? Or does the work remain in certain respects a poetic one, and does it merely express a heartfelt yearning, a dream of thought that is content to imagine what might have been? There are only tentative answers to these questions, but we should remember the one that Henri Plard provides when he writes: "All that we can glimpse of his inner life shows him attempting to achieve union through asceticism, but it is unlikely that he ever succeeded, or that he accomplished his mystical pilgrimage other than in his thoughts." It is perhaps this lack that explains the literary and intellectual distortions in his work, and even more so, the lapses that mar Book VI of the *Pilgrim*, which was written during the polemical phase of his life. Angelus Silesius thus comes to appear like a mystic without profound mystical experience, obliged like William Blake to look to speculation and poetry for the upward soaring that his faith will subsequently fail to sustain.

—October 6, 1943

Autobiographical Narratives

In *Powers of the Novel*, Roger Caillois observes that the novel enjoys a true supremacy over other genres.[1] At the same time, between it and literature there is a sneaking opposition, and also an antagonism between the novel and society, whose dissolution it facilitates by separating the individual from it. These assertions are hard to prove. It is perfectly true that the novel appears to dominate literature through the attraction it exerts over the public, through the continuing preference that writers show for the genre and above all through the spirit of internal conquest that has allowed it to assimilate every other literary possibility to itself. It is also often true that once the novel has enriched itself with literature in its entirety, it seems destined to betray it: How many novels deserve to be considered as literary works? We have ourselves frequently had occasion to express doubts of that sort, and an examination of current output would tend to encourage such pessimistic theories. But do these failings stem from the nature of the novel, from the abuses that have corrupted it, from complacencies that allow it to imitate literary values without creating them, or from fatigue on the writer's part? Adopting a sociological perspective, Roger Caillois confines himself to general observations. He notes that the public's excessive appetite for adventure novels tends to make it find genuine works tiresome: he thus sees in the success of certain types of collection, for example novelistic biographies of great writers, a sign that there are more readers for the (wise and jolly) life of Montaigne than for the *Essays*, for the (painful) life of Baudelaire than for the *Flowers of Evil* and for the (prodigious) life of Balzac than for *The Lily in the Valley*. The interest shown in the novel encourages people to see all literature from a novelistic point of view, to prefer writers to their works and in writers to look only for adventures, stories, and an exceptional life.

Caillois also notes that the novel has no rules. It can do what it likes. Unlike the other genres it can be anything at all, and no obligations regarding content or form, no requirements concerning quality stand in the way of its exclusive obedience to the whim of whoever has decided to create a novel. This freedom is clearly remarkable. But is it unique to the novel? Has poetry not also striven to free itself from all convention and all external constraints? And if we imagine that it only sought freedom from formal rules so as to attain a deeper necessity, we can offer the novel the same excuse and see in the great works of modern novel writing an obedience to new rules, a furious search for conventions that are all the more imperious for being unique to each writer. In general, what Caillois says about the novel can be applied almost unmodified to literature as a whole; and when he denounces the sinister role played by contemporary novels, when he demonstrates the potential for dissolution that the instinct for anarchy and the urge to be oneself discover in them, he is repeating observations that were first directed against Romanticism, Symbolism, and all pure art in general. In reality, these accusations remain vague. Social formations are not stable, societies come and go; it is therefore likely that literature will play its part in these changes by reflecting them, encouraging them or else precipitating them. And this influence may be exerted in a whole variety of ways. Art for art's sake, a poetry that is as remote as possible from any demonstrative intent, is as capable of creating upheaval in social groups as a novel that adopts a revolutionary goal or lays claim to some moral authority. It may even be claimed that a work has all the more influence over society if it is conceived and shaped at a remove from society. Its perfect disdain poses a decisive challenge to collective existence.

In an interesting chapter, Caillois studies the categories into which the multitude of novels are usually divided. In his view, these classifications are either arbitrary or superficial. What is the point of distinguishing between the novel of analysis and the plot-based novel? Realist, poetic, fantastic, social, etc., these partitions are always overrun by the elusive significance of any work that is of some importance, and a novel by Balzac, Dostoyevsky, Kafka, or Virginia Woolf immediately bursts the bounds within which more ordinary works can be more or less confined. In place of these fixed categories, Caillois proposes a set of points of view that should allow the character of each work to be appreciated objectively. Hence he says, let us first identify the scale of the story, that is to say the number of characters who appear in it; then its density, that roughly corresponds to the minuteness of the narrative (while it is weak in an adventure novel, density can be very strong in a psychological novel); last, how far it extends in time and space. We should also note the level of attention to reality, the degree of inwardness in the narrative, and the relations between the writer and his heroes. To conclude, we should examine the wish to influence, that is to say, the way in which the novelist intends the public to react to his work. The advantage of these various indicators is that they leave aside all value judgments and make it possible to provide a classification that is more precise than is usual in critical descriptions. Their disadvantage is that they only appear rigorous. For example, how can attention to reality be defined exactly? Even if we agree to limit reality to the external world, what truth criterion should we choose? The art of the photographer is itself entirely subjective; our view of reality depends less on what we see than on what we read, so that a book can often seem unreal to us in so far as it contradicts the impression of reality that we owe to our[2] previous reading.

It should be noted that for readers as well as for critics, some prejudices concerning the novel are so stubborn that it is difficult to treat them as negligible. Why are we reluctant, for example, to consider autobiographical works as novels, not to mention intimate works, private diaries, or confessions? It would seem that truth in the novel is inseparable from an element of fiction: It can be brought to light only through the inventions of an imagination, and to borrow Caillois's criterion, there must always exist between the author and his hero a certain distance, a purely ideal interval that makes it impossible to identify the one with the other. The difference can be negligible. Memoirs not only dictate the form of a narrative, they contain an *I* that narrates itself, and there is no doubt that this *I* is that of the writer himself; however, if a degree of transposition remains possible, if more precisely the author leaves the reader free to imagine that after all, this autobiographical narrative is perhaps an invented story, the reader will accept the disguise and be content with a token alibi. Hence, in the final analysis, it is the writers will that prevails. Why do Rousseau's *Confessions* not constitute a novel? Neither its narrative precision nor the mode in which it is told would be enough to exclude it from the genre of the novel, were it not precisely that Rousseau himself intended to tell his own story, and summoned the public to be a witness to this direct revelation of his self. Would the text of the work have been exactly the one he published if he had inscribed beneath its title the word "novel"? Its significance would have been entirely changed, and literary history would probably not have encountered the long series of exceptional consequences that have placed this book in a class of its own.

The difference between Julien Blanc's book *Life Alone* and Pierre Molaine's *Samson Is Thirsty* is, first of all, the fact that while both of them appear to be autobiographies, only the first of them admits to what it is, while the second shelters behind the label "novel."[3] This difference gives rise to numerous others. It is undeniable that the reader does not read memories whose hero he believes to be imaginary in the same way as he would a narrative that deals with the life of the author. True memories interest him primarily to the extent that he knows about the person who is writing in advance. In this case, what he is looking for is a historical account. He is reassured by his familiarity with a great name; he takes pride in his knowledge of exemplary events. But if the hero of an autobiography has not yet played a significant role in history or in literary history, the reader is only interested in him if he sees in his story a series of facts that actually happened. It is that thought that accompanies his reading. He says to himself, these events are extraordinary, and they really happened; they had unambiguous meaning for someone who once existed, their value is that they are part of the world and so belong also to anyone who has lived. But at the same time, another thought cannot be ignored: What guarantee is there that the author is sincere? There is no such thing as an exact memory, and there are even fewer truthful accounts. Whatever the goodwill of an author, it has to come to an arrangement with the laws of literature, the temptations of imagination and even more so the mirages of a memory that, having retained a very intense impression of certain facts, rather than remembering the facts themselves, remembers similar facts that are capable of producing the same impression. Finally the quality of these real events, the prodigious nature of something that actually happened, is markedly weakened by the fact that the person who underwent them then overcame them by turning them into a book, has transcended them through becoming conscious of them as a writer. This is inevitable with this type of composition. The reader looks for the raw and as it were material character of events that are presented to him as being caught up in the density of things. He is in search of their contingent presence, their blind upsurge. He expects them to be revealed in the nakedness of an impossible fate. But what he finds when all is said and done is a literary life, since the person who lived it became a writer in order to tell it.

Julien Blanc may well succeed in overcoming all these difficulties. *Life Alone* is only the first volume of a work that will have several, and it is not yet possible to perceive its ultimate goal. The life it presents to us is one of the most pathetic that can ever be portrayed. This is due to the gravity of its ordeals and the unremitting nature of its woes; but it is due even more to the chaotic contradictions that run through it, and the constantly fruitless effort to find in society what it is unable to contain. Its hero endures the direst misfortunes. As an orphan, he knew his mother enough to adore her but not enough to turn his memory later into a rule of life; he is sent from pillar to post, from religious institutions to lay ones, from boarding schools to young offenders' institutions, and when the present volume ends, he is in prison. Childhood vices, the misfortunes of youth when it is exposed to the indifferent haste of grown-ups, the unhealthy impulses of adolescence are presented with a direct frankness that precludes all digression: there is no hidden level in his book, no play of shadow, no deeper resonance. A sort of wretched sadness or desolate impoverishment emanates from his style, and this impression would be even greater, were it not that the author's total disregard for any literary attempt at verisimilitude sometimes adds a comical edge to the most painful episodes.

Pierre Molaine's hero is very similar to the hero of *Life Alone*. Both keep their distance with regard to society, whose constraints they find unbearable and by which they are ruthlessly oppressed. Both have hung on to an ecstatic memory of family life, and of their mothers in particular, that makes all other social bonds seem worthless. They are the heirs of Jules Vallès's characters *The Child*, *The Graduate*, and *The Insurrectionist* and of those of Céline, with whom Molaine has certain things in common.[4] But what is unique about the "I" of *Samson Is Thirsty* is the fact that nothing happens to it, and the grudge it bears against society is entirely internal and appears to the external observer to be almost imaginary. Here, for example, are the facts that infuriate him: One day, three little girls began to laugh as he went by; a beggar woman to whom he gave some money forgot to say thank you; for no reason, his boss changed a word in a report he had asked him to write. These incidents are enough to unleash a torrent of invective, a whirlwind of resolve; he is determined to take vengeance on the crowd, to shoot his persecutors with a revolver. His hallucinatory sensibilities project images of his despair all around him, and he is convinced that people are after him, that they will allow him neither rest nor safety, that their sole purpose is to bring him down. Molaine's art lies in the way he makes these excesses seem highly plausible. His style is often remarkable. He captures perfectly the sarcastic verve of a man who, beneath his delirium, is describing a devastating truth that has meaning only for him.

—October 13, 1943

History and the Masterpiece

In his book entitled *History and Destiny*,[1] Gaston Roupnel both criticizes history and sings its praises. His criticism is severe. It rejects both erudition and the lack of it. Science is discredited for being obsessed with detail, and talent for only being capable of narrating and describing. When such infinite activity is devoted to incidentals, it spawns doctrinaire minds who have lost sight of their own ignorance, and statesmen who misread the future by repeating the past. It is a well-known fact that the love of history breeds turmoil among peoples and destroys individuals, that Napoleon perished for having sought to "put himself into history," and that nations that are too taken up with their former glories collapse because they neglect the present. Death comes from trying to go on being what one once was. Roupnel develops these remarks rather uncritically, and this leads him to extol the discipline of the historian. For history can be more than just the serious study of frivolous detail, or a brilliant account of great periods that are difficult to demarcate. It is essentially an experience of collective life, and the knowledge we may gain of it expresses human reality both in what it is capable of doing as well as in what it has already done.

History is not only made up of events and incidents. What we see initially is the surface agitation. The chaos of what is random and accidental, the stark drama of the adventures occupy the attention of historians as they vainly scrutinize them for possible ways of understanding and grounds for anticipation. For example, historians frequently describe the sudden invasions that imprint themselves on the memory of a people: The entry of the Germanic hordes into Gaul in the winter of 406 or the capture of Rome by Alaric in 410 are the sort of sensational episodes that history likes to focus on. But if, instead of being a sudden intrusion, the invasion takes the form of a slow infiltration, it is given scant attention and the history books ignore it. Thus it is that the insidious penetration of Germanic elements into the Roman West in the third and fourth centuries is glossed over, even though it altered the ethnic balance of the Western peoples. The same goes for the depopulation of the countryside in Burgundy, Franche-Comté and Lorraine during the Thirty Years War, which by severing communications between France and both Germany and Central Europe, opened it up to new influences.

The passing event is the surface manifestation of historical life. Structural history studies more enduring facts, along with the slower efforts through which the human world is constructed. These facts can be divided into several groups. Some concern demographic movements, changes in the volume and density of a population, in short the formation and material development of human communities. Others are linked to the way human groups function. Institutions, be they the monumental structures of the civil code or laws that are more short-lived, are an expression of the preeminent forms of social life; they correspond to general needs that have gradually stabilized, and having held firm against transient developments, evolved into routines and relics of the past. A third series of facts introduces us to even deeper and more obscure events. The anonymity of private life, social habits and customs, work in all its forms, are what make up its substance. "The object and the agent of this history is the individual without a name and without a history."

Roupnel attaches great importance to the activity that governs the secret life of a society; its essential events are those familiar innovations that renew the conditions of human economy. Work in the fields structured the forms of our social life, and by determining the structure of our countryside, the plow established its human status. In a series of excellent pages that recall his *History of the French Countryside*,[2] Roupnel shows that the use of different instruments profoundly modified the collective organization of life. The plough that created the countryside also immobilized it into its traditional forms. It required that it be broken up and parceled off into plots, and encouraged an enslavement to custom. Designed for light soil whose surface can be worked in a single furrow, it produced only inadequate harvests and established a regime of agricultural deficiency. In the end, it was this clumsy instrument rather than any human violence that was responsible for the long era of rural destitution. The hoe, on the contrary, is an instrument of liberation. It constantly transforms and improves the soil. It churns it up much better than the plow. It exposes it to the cool and the damp. Of course, it has a limited range; it is better suited to gardens than large estates. But in regions such as Flanders, where space is limited, it succeeded in making barren earth fertile, and it freed from the old system of land ownership a population that never took the easy option of sticking to routine tasks.

A historian can easily go on producing studies such as this, on the basis that the history of a people is determined not by political or military action but at ground level, in everyday life. Historical existence is a matter of wielding the hoe or driving the plow. Ancient France was merely an infinitely distended domanial expanse, an immense sweep of country managed as if it were a little plot of land. For as long as Roupnel confines himself to observations like these he says little that is new, but what he says has its uses inasmuch as it dissuades minds from adopting a superficial notion of history, and demonstrates the importance of the movement of ideas that has emerged from the work of the Bibliothèque de Synthèse Historique under the direction of Henri Berr. To explain a country by linking its development to a number of economic and social factors, to establish the framework in which the idea and function of the State take shape, to recognize the respective situations of the individual and society are all no doubt better ways of responding to the demands of history than by describing it in its dramatic moments, or searching for it in diplomatic archives. However, the historian's ambition according to Roupnel is to delve even deeper into the reality of collective acts. It is not enough to study structural history, it is also necessary to focus on historical continuity, to find the significance of the authoritarian force and the enlivening power that exist in time considered as duration. Where no effort at constructive coherence is in evidence there is no history. Traditional divisions are arbitrary. It was at the end of the seventeenth century that a German philologist from Halle, Professor Cellarius, had the idea of dividing human time into three periods: Antiquity, the Middle Ages, the modern era. That division continues to prevail everywhere, but it is merely a contrivance. Similarly, people readily believe that grave crises during which too much happens are separated from each other by empty periods when nothing happens. In reality, these empty stretches of time are just as important to the historian as the exceptional moments around which he weaves the fabric of his narrative; all eras have the same importance, all of them carry the same burden of responsibility and destiny. And no one can know the true beginning or the true end of human endeavor.

This continuity in history is an expression of the movement of forces through which the fate of a society is determined. But what are these forces, what is the meaning of this movement? On this subject, Roupnel's argument becomes somewhat confused. He thinks that by studying the successive powerful ventures of the group spirit we can discover the true movement of history. The totemic clan, the ancient city, the native land [*la patrie*], organized labor are the successive manifestations of a creative spirit that shapes societies and inspires collective destinies. They reveal what great themes govern social organization throughout the ages. From the way of life whose needs are met by the clan, to the family that gives the ancient city its close cohesion; from the land whose domanial use explains the origin of the modern *patrie*, to labor that is already creating a framework for the society of tomorrow, we can perceive the forms in which historical energy has been passed down, that incoercible movement that arises from the depths of the past to breathe life into the present and oversee the future. Roupnel firmly believes that history is a form of controlled evolution, that it has its own purpose and obeys it strictly. That is what he calls destiny. "Everything takes place," he writes "as if history talked sense to its events. . . . History only ever speaks the language of finalism." This notion raises numerous problems. It is a pity that Roupnel's literary eloquence has distracted him from writing a more precise study, and drawn him into an agreeable game of hide-and-seek between philosophy, the discipline of history, and the art of the pamphleteer.

In his book *Masterworks: Introduction to Humanism*,[3] it is also with reference to history that Léon Émery considers the question of culture. First of all, history teaches us by what means the most brilliant or most secure periods ensured for mankind the civilization of its minds and its customs. In the Greek cities of the classical era, a single book forms the basis of all teaching: the Homeric epic provides children not only with grammatical examples but also the purest gems of poetry and countless ideas on geography, cosmography, and religious morality. Homer, as Victor Bérard has written, is the Greek Bible.[4] The Middle Ages provides the same example of a pedagogical culture founded on unity: a few fundamental texts taken from the Bible and the Gospels, and skillfully combined with elements of Aristotelian knowledge, make up what amounts to a single book from which a coherent representation of the world can be derived. It is that worldview that can be found in the learning of the universities as well as in the *Divine Comedy* or the images inside cathedrals. Émery believes that no valid educational system can exist without the guarantee of simple principles expressed in great works. The absence of basic texts appears to him as the main weakness of our educational culture: there is no fundamental work capable of bringing the mind into relation with itself; no moral system to organize consciences; no scientific culture to provide thought with shape and assurance. If the modern mind suffers from a lack of discipline, it is because teaching suffers from a lack of order.

Émery is thus in search of a Bible. And he finds it in the greatest works of humanity, those in which the different moments of Western civilization have been expressed along with all of their values, works that are epic in character. The reading list he proposes goes from the *Iliad* and the *Odyssey* to Hugo's *Legend of the Centuries*, and contains those masterworks that best reflect the moral and religious ideal of each epoch: *The Oresteia*, the *Gospels*, *The Divine Comedy*, *Don Quixote*, *The Tempest*, *Athalie*, and *Faust*. To these works he adds others that are not literary but that, like Chartres cathedral, Rembrandt's paintings, or the Ninth Symphony possess great powers of collective or universal representation. Émery analyzes the works he recommends we should know. He clarifies their more obscure aspects. He opens them in search of the human sentiments whose exploration is the goal of all humanism. This effort at initiation is conducted with great discrimination and without a shadow of complacency, and on the whole it deserves a sympathetic reception. The commentaries do not detract from the works they make use of, and some of them, such as those devoted to Homer, are excellent. What remains open to doubt is the effectiveness of this effort for the dream of unity that the author holds dear. Émery believes in the unity of history. He believes that the great works in which humanity has expressed itself impose an idea of order and can assist the mind in its search for balance and harmony. He sees in exemplary myths and fables the expression of an ideal that has acquired precision and perhaps reached fruition there. It is risky to base hope for a renewal of educational culture on assumptions such as these. It will always be legitimate to ask if children who read the *Gospels*, *Don Quixote*, or *Faust* and understand their meaning derive a harmonious view of the world from them, or whether on the contrary they do not find in them forms that are an expression of profound disorder, fragments of a universe in which no amount of pedagogical effort can realistically reveal any unity.

—October 29, 1943

A Study of the Apocalypse

In troubled times, minds that cannot bear the uncertainties of the future discover a need for prophets. But they go looking for these prophets in the past, and the more ancient—and formidable—the oracle, the more they see parallels between it and history. It is in part to its sublime language, to the authority of its writer and to the scale of its revelation that the Apocalypse of Saint John owes a curiosity about it that centuries of study have failed to exhaust. But for minds that are not always godly, it also owes its prestige to the age-old nature of its response, and to what is terrifying about it. Who does not sometimes believe that the end of time is near, and that the worst ordeal is about to happen? Everyone has the secret wish to link his own end, of which he has an inkling, to the end of the world, about which he is less certain.

The study that Father Henri-Marie Féret has just published, *The Apocalypse of Saint John: A Christian Vision of History*, leaves no room for such idle frivolity.[1] It is severe and rigorous. It reduces the role of prophetic revelation to a minimum, and gives an increased role to doctrinal and religious teaching. Though it adopts a strictly orthodox point of view, it is of interest to any mind that has fallen under the spell of the great Johannine symbol, and that looks to it less for knowledge of the future than for a profound insight into the unchanging realities of history. What is more, Father Féret's reading, illuminated as it is by the best critical commentaries, in particular those of Father Allo, allows a better understanding of the structure of this impenetrable book, and before interpreting its obscure allegories, it identifies the reasons for this obscurity in the original method of its composition.

The starting point of this study is the fact that in writing the Apocalypse, John wanted above all to enlighten the faithful who, owing to circumstances, were confronted with great ordeals and serious difficulties. It is therefore in relation to contemporary events that its message should first be interpreted. For Christian communities at the end of the first century, it was a book whose general message was very clear, and contained allusions that were perfectly intelligible. Though perhaps enigmatic in the eyes of the persecutors, whose unfamiliarity with biblical tradition meant they were unaware of the subtleties of traditional language, it could not fail to be accessible to Christians, who were still imbued with the spirit of Jewish scripture and could readily recognize the meaning of allegories for which the events they were living through provided the key. Father Féret clearly sets out the circumstances with which the Apocalypse is associated. With Domitian there began the first persecutions that were capable of putting Christian faith to the test. First of all, they were systematic. They were no longer just a matter of local opposition or unmotivated cruelty. Domitian persecutes believers because he himself is god, and he demands to be honored as such. Strange to say, this deification of Caesar presents Jesus's disciples with a serious question of principle. What is Christ's teaching in fact? Having replaced the messianic doctrine of Israel with faith in a purely internal kingdom of God, Christ refused all truck with the world and formally distinguished between the religious order of things and the temporal one. There is thus no opposition between Christ and Caesar; as a Roman citizen, Paul has no difficulty reconciling his political loyalties and his religious faith. But with the ambitions of the new emperors all that will change. On the one hand, events will see Rome rise up in all its might against the Church; the empire that stretches to the ends of the earth is now the adversary of a religion that it threatens with extermination. On the other, the political order and the religious order now become indistinguishable; the temporal realities that Christians claimed to ignore while at the same time respecting them are not satisfied with their allotted portion. What sense can loyalty to Caesar have if Caesar lays claim to the title of Lord (Kurios) that faith reserves for God? And what practical expression can the purely spiritual kingdom of God be given, if the facts make clear that the political and the spiritual are always intimately joined? Ought there not to be a return to the theocracy of Israel, to a dominion that is both religious and political under which all human societies must be brought, willingly or not? Clearly, it is the whole problem of the meaning of Christ's kingship that Domitian's persecutions raise in the minds of fearful Christians.

The Apocalypse provides an answer to these doubts. It responds to them first by affirming the glory and triumph of Christ. In no other religious text does the figure of Christ appear more closely linked to the splendor of victory. King of kings, lord of lords, it is through terrifying visions that he offers a glimpse of his power over time. If he has the characteristics of a priest, he also possesses the majesty of royal power. He is at a pinnacle of glorious transcendence. Above and at the dawn of history he reigns in an apotheosis that recalls the vengeful theophanies of the Old Testament. But this reign that is exercised through truth and the word, in accordance with the teaching of the Gospels, and not by means of temporal arms, concerns not only individuals but also the great collective powers. Christ is king within men's souls, but he is nonetheless also the master of nations and peoples. And he is so because he holds the key to history. Everything that happens historically bears the mark of his designs. It is from this angle that the great visions of the Apocalypse, in the course of which history is revealed in its abstract generality, can be explained. The first pages of the revelation (after the prefatory address to the Churches), the opening of the seven seals, bring to light the permanent factors of history as the Christian mind should interpret them. These real components, expressed primarily by symbolic horsemen, are the propagation of faith and war, the prayers of the saints, and famine, cosmic cataclysms and human cataclysms (plague). To the question, "How is history made?" John replies: through war, through economic struggle, through the destruction of the body, but also through the victory of the Gospels and the constant intervention of spiritual values.

All of these elements depend on Christ, and the plagues themselves are the manifestation of justice, for which history provides the opportunity to punish the wicked, "those who inhabit the earth" as the book calls them, and above all to increase the number of the chosen. The fact that evil exists is the great drama whose effects human history endures, and by which its development can be explained. The entire central section of the Apocalypse describes the struggle between good and evil, Satan and the Church, and shows the action of demonic power within the vicissitudes of passing time. The struggle begins in heaven, and then carries on in this world where, uncertain till the outcome, it only concludes to the advantage of the Just because God puts a hasty end to history. The symbolism of this lesson seems fairly simple. The great dragon is the tempter from the Bible. The two Beasts he summons up to torment mankind are, on the one hand, the Roman emperors and their persecutions, and more generally any political power that lays claim to spiritual dominion; and on the other, the false prophets, the magi and the *mystes* whose secret religions proliferate in the East at that time. Of course this description of evil is nothing new for the Christian communities, who learned about it from the stories of Genesis and the synoptic Gospels. But what is peculiar to the inspired message is the role it grants the demon in collective life and the movement of history. Saint John does not reveal the action of evil in men's souls; he confines himself to showing what dominion the demonic powers can exert over collective realities, through what channels they operate (false religious or philosophical doctrines, and blasphemous claims on the part of political powers), and what defeat will bring their supremacy to an end. For if, from an individual point of view, the triumph of evil remains possible until the end (each person being capable of yielding to it), from the viewpoint of history, the triumph of truth is certain and salvation here and now is assured.

The final part of the Apocalypse turns to events, and eschewing general descriptions, it renews contact with passing time in order either to follow it or to be ahead of it. This is the prophetic part of the book. Father Féret seems rather inclined to minimize its importance. Nevertheless, here are the directions he discerns. John identifies three stages in the unfolding of the future. During the first stage, the Church comes up against the power of the Roman Empire, but one day Rome succumbs, the great whore disappears along with its useless wealth and its corrupt glory; the allusions to the Roman emperors are perfectly clear; the mysterious Beast that many an interpreter has sought to identify is Nero, whose name in Hebrew characters corresponds to 666. The second period is that of the ten kings who, having contributed to the defeat of Rome, prolong its diabolical heritage and struggle against the Gospel on behalf of the same errors. Who are these ten kings? Clearly, they are all those political powers that have introduced the principles of idolatry into the organization of society; the number is symbolic, and it is difficult to know how long this final struggle between the lord of lords and the heirs of the Beast will last. What is clearer is the fact that during a third period, human history, delivered from the action of the devil, sees Christ's reign established along with a society that conforms to its laws. For a thousand years, truth is triumphant, and Christian civilization is unanimously recognized. Not only in heaven but also on earth, the kingdom of God is established. This is the response to Domitian's persecutions and the apprehensions they arouse. No, divine royalty is not an internal illusion. It will impose itself on this world and it will be manifest to all. It is only after "this fullness of time" that another outbreak of evil will occur, to be followed by the Last Judgment.

With its tendency to see the Apocalypse as a discourse on history, Father Féret's interpretation focuses, not always knowingly, on the difficulties experienced by the Christian mind in the early days of the Church, when it came to representing historical duration. To a certain extent, John's book is built on the idea that history is finished, and that, once the Messiah has come, no future is any longer possible, and no real events. Henceforth, nothing happens. If all of the visions of the Apocalypse lead to the end of the world, this is not only because that perspective is inseparable from the prophetic genre, it is also because, for the Seer of Patmos, the last days have already come and we have entered the cycle of eschatological events. The judgments we are subject to only just anticipate the Last Judgment. And it is divine pity alone that extends our days in order to increase the numbers of the elect. We can see how the Apocalypse, accepting the Jewish notion according to which the sole motor of history is messianic hope, suddenly relegates history to the past from the beginning of the Christian era, or more precisely, collapses past present and future into a single vision. But at the same time, the apostle is fully obliged to observe that history goes on happening, that it happens through torments and persecutions, that the Kingdom of God is still far from being about to come. He therefore seeks an explanation for this survival of history in the struggle between Good and Evil, the Church and Satan, a struggle that is simultaneously always victorious, since the triumph of the saints cannot be called into doubt, yet begins again ceaselessly, and is only brought to an end through the unilateral intervention [*coup de force*] of God. Furthermore, through the vision of a thousand years of Christian happiness on earth it restores a future perspective and the possibility of further waiting. There is no need to wait for Christ any longer, but the coming of his reign must still be awaited. That is why history is not over.

Father Féret insists on the optimistic message of the prophecy. He even sometimes insists, possibly dangerously, on searching through the twenty centuries of our era for signs of a progress that is far from evident. In what period foretold by the revelation of John do we find ourselves today? Have we gone beyond the stage of the ten kings? Are we still in the millennium during which the principles of the Church hold sway? In our view, critics tend in general to prefer not to offer too literal an interpretation of these thousand years of Christianity, and to see in them the ordinary progress of the Church militant. Father Féret differs from these commentators, and if he does not foretell a second coming of Christ, he readily asserts that the theology of Johannine history presupposes this pure triumph of Christianity among societies, institutions and the general rules of life. "If this sentiment is correct," he writes, "it must be concluded that we still find ourselves in the period of the ten kings as foretold by the Apocalypse." He adds, albeit cautiously, that the era when Christianity will fully flourish is now perhaps not far off. It is impossible to choose between these estimations, requiring as they do an entirely personal act of acquiescence. But what these judgments make clear is the fact that the book of John, so full of ambiguity when it describes the progress of history, is no less uncertain when it comes to revealing its meaning. Optimistic this theology may be, since it affirms the ultimate triumph of the Church above and beyond the world; optimistic too, insofar as it foretells the downfall of idolatrous peoples and the period of Christian purity that the faithful may once again start to hope for in a sort of messianic waiting. But at the same time, and contrary to what Father Féret believes, such a view of history remains alien to any conception of progress. There is no continuous progress or chronological improvement in societies. On the contrary, history is merely a long series of acts of divine punishment, moral disasters, universal cataclysms. It is a drama in which everything is constantly crumbling, where no value is ever established once and for all, where the devil in chains is replaced by a freer and more powerful Satan. And even after the first resurrection, which sees the return to earth of the Just who are called to true victory, evil is not conquered. It is once again the master of the world, and the forces it unleashes, the powers with which it tempts mankind are in no way diminished by the recent reign of Christ, which seems to have left no trace in either institutions or societies. On one side, there is the certainty of victory even over political powers, Rome and its successors; on the other, an unending combat whose outcome is always in doubt, and that gives Christian civilization only a brief moment of respite. It is between these two visions that the Apocalypse swings, in a paradoxical evocation of history that describes what history can be when the end of time has come.

—November 3, 1943

La Fontaine without the *Fables*

In the delightful lectures on La Fontaine that he gave in 1938,[1] Jean Giraudoux showed that among all the temptations with which the muses had strewn the poet's path in order to prevent him from being himself, that is to say from writing the fables, the temptation of literature was the most dangerous because it was toward tragedy, comedy, epic poetry, opera, the elegy, poems of all types, in fact to all of these major genres that La Fontaine felt naturally drawn, inopportunely aware of a heroic vocation that he did not have. We may thus quite reasonably dream of the disaster represented by a La Fontaine without fables. What figure would he have cut on Parnassus? Would he have been irremediably lost among the minor poets, or worse, among those false great poets who are false only because they wished to be great? Such speculation is of course unreasonable, but it is sometimes enjoyable to indulge in it, because it secretly reassures us that in any case La Fontaine would have been an unparalleled poet, sure of himself even when distracted and remaining natural even in the most contrived artistic forms—in any case: La Fontaine.

The edition of his works that Pierre Clarac has completed for the Pléiade collection helps us to play this game.[2] In the second volume that has just appeared, and in which, to quote the bookseller-publishers of 1729, all of his works that could be collected together can be found, both the verse and the prose, but excluding the fables and the tales, we have a La Fontaine without fables. We encounter the poet as he struggles with his temptations. Clarac's labors, lovingly and studiously pursued, have a perfection that facilitates our reading without ever weighing it down. The notes are full, but the reader who prefers to remain ignorant can ignore them. The critical judgments are based on impeccable erudition, yet they never come across as peremptory. We follow them without even realizing we are being guided, and with the feeling that we are being faithful to ourselves. In short, it is the book of friendship that this wisest and simplest of poet's deserved, he who could least do without commentary while also being least able to endure it.

Clarac is well aware that several precious texts are still unknown to us. What bibliophile has not dreamed of the letter from La Fontaine's grandson Charles, who wrote to Fréron one day: "Can you believe that one day I found some letters of my grandfather's at the foot of the Pyrenees? I have some of them on my table, some are in verse and some in prose. In addition, I have about five hundred letters of Racine's, forty by Mme de La Sablière that can be compared to those of Mme de Sévigné and have more to say to the heart; last, letters by all of the famous people from Louis XIV's reign, from 1676 until 1716." None of these wonderful texts that must have been located in the Château d'Usson, in the papers of M. de Bonrepaux the king's envoy to England, has been either published or preserved. More fickle than his grandfather, the frivolous grandson's promises regarding their publication led to nothing. Their loss comes after that of the *Hymns*, some autobiographical remarks about Maucroix's *Asterius*, the manuscript of the *Merry*

Men of Beau-Richard (*Les Rieurs du Beau-Richard*) and that of a few other works that are not even definitely by the poet. Among the writings whose burden this edition happily relieves him of once and for all, mention should be made of all those comedies that tradition attributed to him under the name of Champmeslé. Some of these plays, such as *Ragotin* and *I Take You By Surprise* (*Je vous prends sans vert*) are dull, and the only thing they had in common with genuine dramatic works by La Fontaine was their lack of success. Today we can see the uncertainty of their attribution, based entirely as it was on the entrepreneurial talent of a bookseller and the laziness of historians. Another legend that Clarac tackles in order to destroy it has rather more about it. It is the legend that makes the four great classical writers, Racine, Molière, Boileau, and our poet, the four friends in the novel *Psyche*. Unfortunately, these fantasies that have charmed literature for centuries do not stand up to scholarly examination. The only friendship of which we are certain is that between La Fontaine and Racine. In Boileau's case there is no certainty, and if the fabulist always admired Molière and often said so, it is difficult to believe that he ever had anything to do with him. "No serious document," claims Clarac, "allows us to believe that La Fontaine, Molière, Boileau, and Racine ever formed a 'society of friends,' and even less a literary school."

As he went in search of the fables, to what genres that exceeded his vocation might La Fontaine have been tempted to devote himself, and so fail? There would appear to be few. It is true that he was drawn to the genre of poetry termed heroic, "the finest of all," he said, "the most florid, the best adapted to ornament and to those bold and noble figures that make for an exceptional language, a language that is charming enough to be called the language of the gods." But as commentators have remarked, just as there are two lyrical styles in the seventeenth century, that of Malherbe, that of Voiture, there are also two heroic styles, that of Homer and that of Ovid. And for La Fontaine there were no two ways about it. He is infinitely fond of

Homer whose naivety and nobility, naturalness, and power represent for him a true image of poetry, but it is Ovid whom he follows, it is from Ovid that he borrows his rustic scenes and tales of love whose heroes are gods. Was it a mistake to imitate him? If so, the fruits of that mistake are entitled *Adonis* and *Philemon and Baucis*, works that give seventeenth-century poetry an inimitable voice, the purest and most tender that can be heard in the vicinity of Racine. After Paul Valéry there is no need to seek to justify these expansive beauties, whose effect on our sensibilities is as intense today as it was at the very beginning. It is true that alongside these two poems whose loss the *Fables* could not compensate for, there are others that it is less easy to prefer. *The Epic of Quinquina* was of little service to him in his search for fame, and the *Poem of the Captivity of St Malo* seems like the peccadillo of an old man, a sin of old age that seeks forgiveness for more serious ones. These compositions certainly do not deserve to be rehabilitated. But if they have faults, at last these do not stem from too lofty a tone or too ambitious a search for symbols. *Quinquina*, a 1,200-verse treatise on fever written with the aid of medical manuals that were in vogue at the time, is a wager that the poet carries off with good humor. Scientific poetry, or at least the type that juggles unfamiliar words, always appealed to him. His verse accommodates it without difficulty within a variety of rhythms, and it is still possible to enjoy admiring how precise this poetic language can become in order to describe phenomena that are as difficult to grasp as the circulation of the blood, the progress of bile, contractions of the muscles or the act of shivering. Nothing in this verse is worse than certain of the bad fables, and everything is better than the awkward flowers of Delille's poetry. As for the Jansenist poem, there is no rigor of inspiration to lead La Fontaine down paths where his lightness of touch and his natural approach run the risk of disappearing; on the contrary, it is La Fontaine's poetic freedom that makes him connive with such humdrum originality, and allows him naively to invent the episode of the saint meditating at the funeral of an ant, or that of the charming shepherdess who, so as to appear ugly and flee the perils of too great a beauty, lets herself become bronzed by the sun, "to the affront of a tanning exposes her charms."

La Fontaine wanted to write a tragedy. Its title is *Achilles*, and it is most likely that it would have remained a rather languid one. But the poet was wise enough not to pursue it beyond the second act, so proving that even when he is tempted to stray, his fickleness ensures that he will soon come to his senses again. Clearly, the tragic does not appear to be his natural tendency. The discreet nature of his sentiments, the fact that his complaints are always of the gentlest and most restrained kind, the regrets that out of delicacy he keeps from turning into revolt, all destine him to write poetry that has more affinity with sensuality, idylls, and elegies. Nonetheless, it is impossible not to dream of the perfection of those alexandrines whose purity is never lifeless, and contains, along with the most transparent and harmonious of music, an as yet still hesitant truth that is always on the point of revealing itself? When we listen to the lament of Venus before the lifeless body of Adonis, what we hear is tragic song in its familiarity with silence, and ten years in advance, these lines anticipate the voice that will not fall silent until after *Phaedra*:

> So my love was unable to make you love life!
> You leave me, o cruel one! At least open your eyes,
> Be more sensitive to my sad farewells;
> See with what suffering your lover is afflicted!
> Alas! I cry out in vain: he will not hear my complaint.
> By eternal night he is forced to leave me;
> Neither my tears nor my sighs can stop him.[3]

La Fontaine liked the theater and would have liked to find success there. But if his instinct takes him toward Terence, whose *Eunuch* he translates, it also takes him to the delightful pastoral poems and eclogues for more than one voice with titles such as *Daphnis*, *Galatea*, and *Astrea*. If he and Opera do not go well together, it is because his poetry contains its own melody and is smothered by "the score of clavecins, the hundred violins" that are brought on "for the audience's pleasure." However, it strikes him that his art has affinities with dance, which he calls "the flute, the oboe, the charming theorb," and his appreciation of Lully, whom otherwise he detests, is less a sign that he is drawn to a fashionable genre than a sense of the gracious forms of which he feels capable, that beguile the imagination like a difficult combination of gesture, song, and word.

La Fontaine is often criticized for his odes and his paraphrases of the Psalms. It is true to say that there are some that are only likable up to a point. But in this genre, where he is only as prolific because he is obliged to satisfy powerful people, it is admirable to rediscover him in his simplicity, his agreeable inventiveness, his easy familiarity and his inimitable guile. Giraudoux is unhappy for example about the excessive nobility of works in which Turenne becomes Mars and Condé becomes Alexander. But on the contrary, what could be more spontaneous and less stilted than the epistle to Turenne that begins with these comical lines:

> You have written, my Lord, an opera.
> What, the old duke, followed by Caprara?
> What, bravura and cunning?
> Great is the glory, and so is the killing.

Or else this other one, which contains a mysterious inkling of the Salzbach drama:

> What so my Lord, always fresh combat!
> Always danger! Do you therefore think
> You cannot die? Everything dies, all heroes pass.

As for the regular odes, they never escape the boredom that improvised mythology inspires, but with them, as with the translations of the psalms, a note of truth and mildness, of candor and purity always prevails over artifice in the end, and exonerates the poet's efforts. Who could not recognize La Fontaine in a *Dies irae* whose music has become so calm and almost inward:

> Have me placed on the right, among the sheep;
> Separate me from the reprobate and accursed goats.
> You see my contrite heart and my humble prayer;
> Help me to persevere with this just remorse:
> To you I entrust my final hour;
> Abandon me not when I go to join the dead.

La Fontaine's primary literary temptation was probably not his liking for sublime genres. If in order to keep the appointment he had with the fable he more than once took a road that seemed to lead him away from it forever, it is because above all he liked diversity and change. A single genre, even the noblest, could never be to his liking, and he would have always preferred the more obscure deployment of several talents to any glory acquired in just one genre. "Diversity is my watchword." The collection of his "diverse" works is an expression of this variety, for which Mme de La Sablière reproached him though to no avail, and that acted rather as a goad for his uneasy soul. From the novel *Psyche* to the *bouts-rimés*, from the elegies to the epitaphs, from the satires to the historic disquisitions, from the travel accounts to the epithalamia in the style of Nostradamus, he tried out every form and conformed to every rule without ever betraying his art. The labor that such a wide and varied output presupposes is infinite. The few working manuscripts that have come down to us show that the choice of each word required interminable study on the part of this relaxed and uncomplicated poet. The two acts of the tragedy *Achilles* that were eventually abandoned are covered in corrections, overflowing with changes of heart, embellished with erasures that all point in the direction of greater precision, a more appropriate use of a terms and a purer level of verification, each of which is taken to perfection. Such is the effort of a poet who is generally considered idle and distracted. We can be sure that fewer have worked harder than he did, and we may find the secret of such studiousness in his mysterious confession to Maucroix: “I would die of boredom if I stopped composing.”

—November 13–14, 1943

Baron d'Holbach

The important book that Pierre Naville has just devoted to Baron d'Holbach is not only an objective study whose analyses clarify the main concepts of the eighteenth century almost exhaustively, but it is also a book with a mind of its own, one that takes the side of what it studies and combats rather violently the adversaries it considers to be dangerous.[1] In numerous pages, the author reveals the ingenuity of his preferences. If he admires Baron d'Holbach, it is because he accepts his ideas. Like him, he is a materialist. Like him, he considers religious beliefs to be false and harmful. Like d'Holbach, he is not neutral about what he believes, and he is tenacious in the way he asserts it and seeks to convince others of it. There are advantages and disadvantages to this approach. Sometimes, persistent apologetics can weaken a book that only appears to be partial, and that in its essentials is a very serious and well-documented study; but it is doubtful whether the Baron "always took the right path," met every objection and displayed faultless clear-sightedness and penetration of mind. To be so unassailably right can be tiresome. In many respects, Naville's viewpoint appears narrow. He easily forgets that the strongest anti-Christian arguments in the twentieth century are also the most strenuously antimaterialist, that it is not just nineteenth-century metaphysics that "consigns d'Holbach's system to oblivion," and that the conclusions that sometimes make our era echo the critique of religion found in the *Encyclopaedia* presuppose ways of thinking and types of hypothesis that are quite different. Naville pays little heed to all that. Modern science, with which he is very familiar, provides solid proof of his convictions in his view. He adheres to it decisively and uncompromisingly.

In the case of his book on d'Holbach, more than for his study of behavioral psychology that we have had occasion to mention,[2] such firmness of opinion has the advantage of sparing us one of those lifeless studies written by historians of the sort who will turn their hand to anything. His book is not the result of erudition that shows no interest in its object. Its goal is to bring to light a philosophy and a man who are worthy of attention, and who have until now been unjustifiably kept in the shadow. Has d'Holbach really been the victim of a conspiracy of silence? Possibly so: He has never been studied or published seriously. In the manuals, his name sits alongside that of Helvétius, and both are insufficiently known about. In his lifetime, this verbose yet secret author wrote or translated more than fifty works, yet his name is never uttered in relation to a single one of them. As a friend of the Encyclopedists, he boasts an important position. He is rich; he has a salon. He is in contact with numerous brilliant people. He is "the major-domo of philosophy." But his true role as a publisher and an author, having remained a secret during his lifetime because of the dangers it could have caused him, brings him little glory after his death, and indeed leaves him with a dull and unfortunate reputation. His involvement in scandal brings him no luster. His books may well be banned (as they were until 1838), but this does not make them readable. In the nineteenth century, few philosophers discussed him. Goethe called his *System of Nature* a dull and insipid book. Hegel is almost alone in devoting serious study to his contribution to the history of thought. Naville is no doubt right to believe that the strength of his atheism was partly responsible for this unmerited discredit. But other motives inevitably come to mind. Diderot, who was scarcely less anti-Christian and just as much of a materialist, has gloriously risen above what was odious about his opinions. True, he has his style to thank for this, and it is sometimes brilliant (if not "the finest in the French language" as Naville claims). It is also true that the Baron's style is ponderous, labored, and far inferior even to that of La Mettrie or Helvétius. It is pointless to try to rehabilitate it. It is not without its worthwhile turns of phrase. But as a whole, it is confused and shapeless. Repetition drags out every development. The structure becomes turgid. It is a miserable crawl across an interminable plain, a permanently vanishing horizon.

D'Holbach's merit does not lie in having invented a new system, unique to him and the fruit of some original insight. Most of his ideas are also to be found in all eighteenth-century philosophy. There is hardly a single one that he did not inherit from predecessors or contemporaries. He shares them and discusses them with Diderot, and many pages of his works were even written by the author of *Jacques the Fatalist*. Naville describes his main book, *The System of Nature*, as a popular digest of the materialist and atheist doctrines of the majority of the Encyclopedists. This critic has brought out very well all of the influences that converge in a work that makes them both clearer and more systematic. The first half of the eighteenth century is well known for having seen the appearance of numerous occult manuscripts that criticized religion and proposed a nonconformist philosophy. "Coteries" are formed in which scholars whose official opinions are utterly reliable secretly carry out more freethinking studies. Around Boulainvilliers gather academicians like Fréret, Du Marsais, and Mirabaud, who develop certain tendencies in Spinoza and subject religious revelations to rationalist scrutiny. Lone scholars such as the famous vicar of Étrépigny, Jean Meslier, abandon Christianity out of a sense of social injustice, and his posthumous manuscript, *Testament*, a toned-down version of which is published by Voltaire, is widely read and circulated. But the decisive influences are those of the philosophers, in France with La Mettrie and Helvétius, but above all in England, where Hobbes, Locke, Hume, Toland, and Anthony Collins assembled and perfected in near-definitive form all of the arguments that materialist empiricism will go on to defend, namely that man is governed by the same laws as nature, that action and movement are essential components of matter, and that thought is a mode of physical reality.

D'Holbach gave all of that systematic form, abandoned claims that were too vague, took materialism to its conclusion and sought to found his philosophical synthesis on thorough scientific enquiry. He pays particular attention to the German chemists and mineralogists and translates numerous works of theirs; and he adopts the principles of Stahl's universal chemistry, which is currently in vogue but will soon be made redundant by Lavoisier's experiments. What is the significance of all this effort? In *The Bourgeois*,[3] Bernard Groethuysen has shown that the primary goal of the *Encyclopaedia* was to seize hold of the world by reducing it to a collection of scientifically identified objects. This involved drawing up an inventory of knowledge in order to declare the annexation of the world by man. Two sorts of thinking come together in the Encyclopedist: He gathers facts and calls on those who know how to organize these facts in an encyclopedic order, on the understanding that once this task is done, he will have replaced a universe whose deepest reality was assumed to be beyond him, with a new universe that will be fully known to him. He thinks therefore that the unknown that is in the world and that surrounds the world, embracing it and haunting it, will disappear when he has transformed the world into a set of objects that can all be understood by him, in themselves and through their relations. And this is the second sort of thinking: This unknown world, reduced to a world of the known, will henceforth be at the disposal of mankind. Man will be in possession of it. He will be its master. He will enjoy full property rights over it. The Encyclopedist wishes to know the world in order to appropriate it. That is a key expression of the bourgeois spirit.

The materialism of Diderot and d'Holbach follows logically from this state of mind. Mankind can only exert control over the world if the world is a collection of objects. Only things can be possessed. It is therefore over a world of things that mankind will reign. But what of man himself? What is he? What is his truth? Well, replies d'Holbach solemnly, a man, too, is a thing; he is of the same nature as what he possesses; he is governed by the same laws, part of the same realm, the realm of science that grants rights of ownership over all things. That is the significance of monism. D'Holbach offers a rigorous formulation of it that is remarkably precise: "Man," he writes, "is a purely physical being; moral man is simply that being considered from a certain point of view, that is to say in relation to some of his modes of action that are the result of his own constitution. . . . Moral man is man acting under the influence of physical causes that our prejudices prevent us from recognizing." All of his work is a development from this statement. It is a philosophical effort to overcome the mind-body dualism, and a scientific effort to apply to mankind the knowledge that is revealed by the study of things. If he rejects Cartesian mechanism as a system of scientific explanation it is because he requires a suppler system, one capable of more spontaneity and more variety, within which can understand animate and inanimate nature, as well as that of man. The world appears to him fundamentally as an organic, dynamic reality. And his atomism, differing radically from the classical atomism of Epicurus and Gassendi, is defined in terms of the biological and chemical combinations of living matter rather than of the properties of geometrical and mathematical matter, which is to say: extension.

Of particular interest in d'Holbach are the antinomies that the rigor of his system makes very stark, and unlike other authors, he makes no effort to scale them down. In accordance with the tradition of the Encyclopedists, the Baron wishes to seize hold immediately of this new acquisition called man and subject it to his utilitarian designs. His system, says Naville, is just as much an ethic as it is a world system. It is a response to practical concerns, and seeks to make large-scale action possible. It is clear that if man is nothing but a thing, he can be modified scientifically—through education and the cultivation of habits—the way objects are modified by being adapted to the needs and wishes of mankind. However, to take possession of man in this way, by appropriating a being that has become a thing, has a consequence that the Encyclopedists find deeply repugnant: Once a man is no longer an existence but a thing, no longer a subject but an object, it becomes possible and legitimate to make use of him as if he were a thing, to turn his labor into a value that can be entirely expressed as a price, a merchandise that is identical to all others. The materialist *Encyclopaedia* made man into the absolute owner of the world, its proprietor, but it also subjected the proprietor to the common laws of property.

This was something about which Hobbes had a deep understanding, when in *Leviathan* he suppressed every freedom enjoyed by the citizen and gave the state tyrannical discretion in affairs of human morality. But it is also something that the eighteenth-century *philosophes* cannot accept, for while they are asserting universal determinism they are also pursuing a struggle for freedom that provides them with their primary justification. It is therefore clear to what sort of antinomy Baron d'Holbach's faith in materialism leads. On the one hand, he makes mankind into a natural object, and thus an object of use—and this is why his philosophy sometimes looks like a type of fatalism. On the other hand, he does not want mankind to be treated like a thing, and he grants it separate status while requiring that men respect freedom in all its forms: freedom of conscience, constitutional freedom and, to a certain degree, economic freedom. Another version of the same antimony can be expressed as follows: If human beings are restored to the world of things, they are again what they have always been, they live in the present they way they did in the past, they are totally deprived of a free future that would allow them to escape what determines them. An object is always what it is. It is eternally its own repetition. If it is modified, if it becomes something other, it becomes another object and begins again, in the past, what is an eternal present. Between its homogeneous moments, linked as they are by a simple external relation, there is no true continuity, no movement toward the future. Consequently, for mankind that is subject to the timescale of things, there is no possibility for progress either. Materialism of the d'Holbach variety, with its tendency toward fatalism and what is despotic and arbitrary, also has a pessimistic tendency. This tendency is visible in his work in numerous interesting observations, but it conflicts with the faith in progress and the assertion of victorious reason that inform the great eighteenth-century theme of hope. In contrast to the knowledge of a being that must necessarily preserve itself in the form of a quantity of movement, force, or energy or else inevitably descend into perdition and death, there exists the belief in a future that can be forged, in a process of progressive innovation and indefinite liberation.

It cannot be said that d'Holbach overcomes these antinomies, or even that he has any deep awareness of them. By presenting the problem of liberty and progress to him in purely practical terms, the fundamental project that his era prescribes for him makes him blind to its own contradictions. To be free is above all to be free of all religious subjection. Freedom is political freedom, and it will shake of the bonds of Christian religion and reveal the truth of materialism. Furthermore, like the other eighteenth-century *philosophes*, d'Holbach introduced into nature considered no longer as a constructed mathematical mechanism but as a concentration of organic forces, a sort of spontaneity that made the idea of indeterminate movement into the future appear not inconceivable to him. The intellectualism of the *Encyclopaedia* is associated with energy and power. At the heart of reason, it preserves a preponderance of irrationality. It is all passion and enthusiasm. (Hence, the glorification of energy to be found in Stendhal, who was the heir to the ideologues.) Nonetheless, it is clear that a fundamental difficulty remains at the heart of the system, and this is a serious impediment to its liberal claims. To make mankind into a thing that can be studied like a thing is to ensure that it can be used as a thing and exploited as a thing. All of the social contradictions in liberalism can be found in this statement. And their starting point is the *Encyclopaedia*.

—November 27–28, 1943

The Pure Novel

The journal *Confluences* has published a special issue devoted to "the problems of the novel," and it contains everything that the curious reader and the attentive critic could wish for on the subject.[1] It cannot truly be said that this collective volume encourages clarity of thought, or that it expresses a precise view of the novel in any coherent way. It is quite clear that the writers of every sort who have contributed to this study rarely agree about the subjects it raises. Some are committed to traditional views; a few others take a bolder line. Most of them resort to rather vague definitions to promote the very distinct preferences they find within themselves, and that stem from their tastes as either readers or novelists. Such confusion is not without its charm. It is perhaps even of some interest. For beneath the disorderly judgments and vague vocabulary, the attentive reader will just be able to discern one or two of the fixed points where what is at stake is the fate of the novel as a genre.

Edmond Jaloux considers that between the nineteenth and twentieth centuries a fundamental difference emerges. The novels of last century do not call into question what is generally taken to be reality. The world represented there resembles the one in which everyone is accustomed to living. In it, men are more or less what current forms of imagination and observation consider them to be. In this sense, there is a continuity between the works of Balzac and Stendhal and books by Roger Martin du Gard, Jules Romains, and Georges Duhamel. All belong to the same tradition, to the extent that their aim is to respect the traditional structure of the world. With a few novels of our time, this situation changes. The novelist's vision becomes separated from ordinary vision. The author starts with the suggestions of his sensibility and no longer tries to coincide with the appearances of everyday reality. On the contrary, he distances himself from the universe in which everyone recognizes himself. The inventions of the novel should not be tied to the world of familiar things according to him: They are connected to what is not known, to what it is impossible to know.

Edmond Jaloux is right to consider this an important point. It provides a simple definition of the two main directions open to the novel. We may leave aside the fact that these tendencies cannot totally differentiate between nineteenth-century novelists and those of our era, since most famous novels today belong to the tradition of yesteryear, while the work that challenged that tradition most powerfully, *Maldoror*, was written in 1867. On the other hand, we must be wary of being taken in by the excessively simple nature of this definition. The difference between Balzac-Stendhal and Lautréamont does not come from any greater or lesser intensity of personal sentiment, from a more or less straightforward subjection to an irreducibly inner vision. It is likely that the great novelists of nineteenth-century tradition based their writing on personal reactions that were just as extraordinary, on dictates of the imagination that were just as peculiar as those of the most outlandish writers of the Surrealist era. Indulging in a little paradox, one could even identify in both Stendhal and Lautréamont a number of common points of departure: the same explosive sense of time, the same addiction to willed metamorphosis, and an identical devotion to an extreme power of effortless overcoming. Except that Stendhal expresses this fundamental sentiment through a world of appearances that perfectly reflects the society of his times, while Lautréamont derives from it a world that clashes with the world of common experience, rejects illusion, and entails a violent disruption of image and impression.

Whatever the role that imagination plays in it, the Balzacian novel (to give it arbitrarily a name) introduces into the system of fiction enough recognizable elements for it to be possible in principle for the real existence of the reader to have a place there. To an inside conceived by an imagination and a sensibility that are singularly remote from the everyday model, corresponds an outside that conforms to that model. In the Lautréamont novel (to give it a name also), the inside no longer seeks a connection with resemblance; it is oblivious of the elements of verisimilitude that everyday existence presupposes; it wants to shape and mold the form that will make it manifest without regard for habits and customs. The outside must reflect the inside, and not practices that are in any case artificial or the general but arbitrary beliefs that form the basis of life in society: this is the new ambition that sets the twentieth-century tradition against the nineteenth-century one. As a result, since the rule of verisimilitude has lost its value, the novel can now transform reality, not just paint it in different colors but change its structure, overturn its laws, empty it of all intelligible light. It now secretes its own world as it sees fit. It is in control of what appears. A unity of its own choosing and references it has no need to justify provide the focus that allows it to compose a new nexus of figures and events. Its freedom may appear absolute. But it is limited by this basic requirement: to bring together, without fakery, the inside and the outside of novel creation.

This rigorous correspondence makes it possible to understand what was meant by the pure novel. The expression "pure novel" is generally attributed to André Gide who, in the *Diary of the Counterfeiters*, went in search of the meaning of this expression. If we pause at one or two of the definitions that his hero, Édouard, puts to the test, it is clear that they all relate to similar ideas. The most significant of them is no doubt this one: "I am beginning," the novelist has Édouard say, "to form an idea of what I would call the 'deep subject' of my novel. It is, it will no doubt be the rivalry between the real world and the representation we give ourselves of it. The manner in which the world of appearances impresses itself on us, and the manner in which we seek to impress on the outside world our own individual interpretation together make up the drama of our lives."[2] And elsewhere he proposes another, rather different formulation: "In fact this will be the subject: the struggle between facts as reality presents them and ideal reality."[3] These definitions are far from satisfactory, and what is more they are highly ambiguous: "ideal reality," "individual interpretation," these are expressions that fit perfectly with the habits of everyday realism; in fact, however, we are already some way down a path of inquiry that will lead to the pure novel. What constitutes the drama of our lives, according to André Gide, is also the particular drama of the novel genre: The art of the novel will not always tolerate having to conform "to the world of appearances"; it is in competition with the reality that belongs to "everyone"; it requires its own particular appearances, those that can be deduced from the rhythm and inner vision of the novelist, and not those that the vision and the practical habits of the reader impose on it. What is a pure art? An art that seeks to obey an exclusively aesthetic criterion, and which, instead of combining the representation of things with certain laws of sensibility, dispenses with imitation and even with sense-making conventions altogether. The novel thus does make a serious claim to purity to the extent that its ambition is to create, if necessary, a system that is absolute, complete, indifferent to the usual circumstances in which things exist, constituted by intrinsic relations and capable of sustaining itself without drawing on anything external to it.

Naturally, expressions such as pure art or pure novel are themselves rich in ambiguity. Paul Valéry always acknowledged that the arts of language were not capable, as music is for example, of founding a separate universe or a strange realm that would be self-sufficient, exist in and through itself and signify nothing but itself. The purity of poetry does not entail the destruction of language considered as a sign-system, but the creation of an order out of the complex group constituted by signs and sounds that, as well as signifying something, finds its justification in being an organized unit of rhythms and sounds. Similarly, the pure novel is quite willing to bring together sensibility and resemblance or sensibility and comprehension in a single work, but its aim is to organize resemblances and general notions in relation to the inner suggestion that they are meant to translate, with no other goal than to make the translation accurate. The purity of the novel does not entail stripping itself, as Gide's Édouard puts it, of all the elements that do not belong specifically to the novel, of excluding external events, accidents and mishaps, or else of suppressing character description and even characters themselves; but rather of making all these elements dependent on the personal order it is their task to make manifest, subjecting them in the strictest manner to the intention whose projection in time, whose shadow projected onto the outside world it is their task to be. It is easy to point out that those novels that are least concerned with external verisimilitude nonetheless give a substantial role to numerous details provided by everyday observation; that *Maldoror*, to turn to it as an example once again, is entirely taken up with familiar images, recognizable figures, and trivial detail. This goes without saying. The aim of the pure novel is not to create a world whose material is alien to the one in which we live out of habit, or even systematically different from it; what matters is the order, the way appearances are combined and the reference points that give direction to all of the familiar images according to certain specific perspectives.

It is noteworthy that one rarely hears speak of the novel without also hearing the word "world." The defenders of objective storytelling, as well as those who seek the reality of their fictions in the realm of the imaginary, all agree on this term. "Novelists," they say, "seek not to write a novel but to create a world." If the use of this term is so widespread, this partly reflects the preoccupations of contemporary philosophy. A serious study of the novel, even of the pure novel, would set about establishing what demands lie hidden beneath a notion that is simultaneously clear and muddled. It would no doubt become clear that if there is no novel without a horizon of being that expresses it, that does not mean that the novel must always take place within the world we know—or in a similar world to this one—or that it has any need of the circumstances of "life," or that it necessarily contains characters whose make-believe existence can be identified with that of the reader. In fact, if the novel always has an outside, this is because what we call its inside, the inner pole provided by the vision of the novelist, the explicit or implicit sentiment whose dictates he follows, is itself inseparable from the concrete structure within which it develops. It truly is a pole, an oriented direction out from which lines of force radiate and are then scattered and unfurled in order to give the impression of an ensemble, a figure, of that situation peculiar to a mankind around which there is always a horizon. In other words, the world of the novel seems to be linked to two fundamental elements: It is an order, a system of relations, organized in the image of the human situation in order to express its meaning; and as an order it is not static, because it is revealed through time, it has duration, it gives duration reality.

One might ask what reasons lie behind this search for the pure novel, which, as Édmond Jaloux observes, has perhaps not always given rise to exemplary works but is the most significant contribution that contemporary novel writing has to offer. Such a question would require infinite discussion, as indeed would the entire problem of the pure novel. But two rapid observations may be made. First, such a notion is linked to a certain type of creative mind. If, following Gundolf[4] when he distinguished between the attractive creator and the expansive creator, we see in the first the mind that fashions the universe according to its self, that draws the universe toward it in order to reconcile it with its self, that becomes its center the way Dante did; and in the second, the mind that pours itself out into the world, relieves itself of its own excess in order to enliven and possess the world the way Shakespeare did, we may deduce that the author of the pure novel belongs rather to the attractive type. He, too, seeks to make his self into the symbol of the world. He draws it to him in order to refashion it according to his outlook. He accepts what it gives him merely as raw material that he must reconstitute and organize. Balzac, on the contrary, is an expansive genius; he breathes life and strength into a reality with which he is satisfied, he extends himself and overflows into the frames that the universe has already traced out. Having made this distinction, the question remains: Why in the pure novel does the attractive mind draw the world to itself not so as to give it the harmony of a center, but to do violence to it, annihilate it, and replace it with pale illusions. It is because, first of all, the creative mind lacks power. "In the attractive mind who is not a Dante," writes Gundolf, "it would seem that the world is lacking." But it is also because the world that must provide the material for the creative self today appears exhausted, it has lost its originality and its objective truth, its sole presence is that of an insubstantial, impure system whose appearances the mind is tempted, not to say forced to reject in order to restore meaning to it and express the original experience that belongs to it. That is why the pure novel, whatever its failures, deserves more attention perhaps than well-rounded works of objective narrative. It is in search of the unknown. It demands what it is inaccessible. We may therefore apply to it this observation by Édouard in *The Counterfeiters*: "I have often thought that in art, and in literature especially, only those who launch themselves into the unknown really count.

New territory cannot be discovered unless from the start, and for a long period, we are willing to lose sight of land entirely. But our novelists are afraid of the open sea; they merely hug the shore."[5]

—December 4–5, 1943

The Lament of the Shadow

One day, Zarathustra met his shadow and heard it lament: "*Where* is—*my* home? For it do I ask and seek, and have sought, but have not found it. O eternal everywhere, O eternal nowhere, O eternal—in—vain!"[1] This lament is one that the shadows of our own time repeat in their turn. The fact that there are so many books devoted to knowledge of the mystics (very good translations of Dionysius the Areopagite and the blessed Henry Suso have just appeared),[2] and that so many novels have taken as their theme the quest for a spiritual life, is a sign that must be given its due, though its significance should not be exaggerated. There is often a good deal of naivety and even some complacency behind a quest such as this. The unhappy mind feels a need for consolation, and it will yield to hope of any sort in order to flee its anxiety.

It is important, therefore, to single out those works that show greater seriousness and are more demanding. Marius Grout's work is remarkable for the consistency of its preoccupations, and it has the merit of tending constantly toward a horizon where literature turns into meditation, personal experience, and self-examination. Marius Grout does not write to provide literary pleasure; even less so do his chosen subjects reflect a simple desire to publish books; there is nothing reprehensible about such motives in themselves, but the writer who decides to explore themes in which human destiny is at stake cannot be satisfied with them. Between him and his work there must be closer bonds; the risk he runs must be greater than that of merely writing an imperfect book: He himself is at stake, his own self provides the stakes; if he loses, he loses himself. *When the Man Passed By* is at once the story of a man, that of a village, and the story of a myth.[3] The man resembles those strange individuals who are the apostles of a new faith whom Selma Lagerlöf portrays in *Jerusalem* or *The Holy City: Jerusalem II*.[4] He comes from a land of mists that we never see and can only picture with difficulty: it is "beyond the rivers," and he goes off to an even more mysterious land that he calls "the Islands."

Before leaving for good he lingers a while in a village and tells of the islands to which he plans to go. There live better men than us, entrusted with secrets that we do not know. If the Bible alludes to them, no one has yet been able to reach them, yet they do exist; they stand for a truth that we can reach out to; they offer the promise of a happiness we can attain. The traveler lives a simple life like everyone else; his presence alone is enough to teach both the children and the farmers to see the beauty of the world; he sculpts objects that he calls "things from the Islands": they resemble nothing; they are pure, free forms that give pleasure through the dream they realize, and people credit them with miraculous powers. Gradually, the village awakens in response to this presence; some people are friendly and they, too, begin to place their hopes in this voyage that will give them the Islands; but others judge it to be harmful, and blame it for a number of calamities that afflict the village: the traditional powers represented by the priest and the schoolteacher condemn the man; people throw stones at him and threaten to set fire to his house. He is obliged to leave, driven out by resentment, and he goes off in search of the vague regions in which he has placed his hopes.

At this point in its development, Grout's novel hesitates. We lose sight of the traveler. The village falls prey to a mysterious folly. It is stricken by plague, hatred divides it, and nocturnal obsessions convince people that the dead are rising again. Like a consoling thought, the memory of the man who must restore peace to those who have lost it lives on in the midst of this disaster. But alas, where is he? Will he return? Initially, news reaches the village: He has reached unknown regions where people practice extraordinary arts and follow surprising beliefs; but these are not the Islands. Then the news arrives less frequently. People believe that the traveler is plunging deeper into territory that is ever more mysterious, ever more remote; he is constantly having to learn new languages, cross new oceans, and plan new routes. One day, he loses the young woman who is his companion and the child she had given him. A doubt enters his mind: Will he ever return? Will he even have the strength to reach his goal? Soon silence falls. But one evening, the traveler returns. He reveals to the old woman who takes him in that he has failed: He found nothing. There is nothing. There is no "dwelling place" for mankind, and since he gave the people of the village false hopes, he wants to tell them now of his disappointment. So he calls them together, but in a last twist, just as he is about to speak he dies, and the old woman, falsifying his message, declares on the contrary that he has found the Islands, and what he was about to reveal to us was the path that leads to them. This false message is enough to restore the farmers' faith. The village comes back to life, a new religion is founded, and each year, young people go off in search of the Islands. The sense of the marvelous, in whatever guise, expresses the reality of life.

The meaning of Grout's book is not as simple as its form might lead us to believe. Like his previous novels, this one is the story of a failure, and the failure is ultimately a success. In *Advent Music*,[5] we encountered a schoolteacher who sought to awaken an interest in miracles in those around him with the aid of rather crude stratagems. This marvelous undertaking ended rather badly, but seeing the significance of his failure, the poor man ultimately achieved a sort of sainthood, and having gone blind, surrounded by a veneration he was unaware of, in the end he unwittingly fulfilled the mission he believed he had been given. In *When the Man Passed By*, the two themes are intertwined and appear to intersect each other only at random. That is one of the ambiguities and probably one of the weaknesses of the book. The man's quest is a failure. On his return, like Zarathustra, he has only one piece of news for us: God is dead, and it is not in a state of elation and through the liberating power of laughter that he brings it to us the way Nietzsche's prophet does, but in a state of fatigue and discouragement, and already in the shadow of death. What does this failure mean? Was the traveler's mistake to want to find, rather than be content to seek? Or should he have lived alone? That is what a mysterious visitor tells him: "You can tell him that if he finds something, he can go on looking. And if he has found nothing at all, you can tell him to look even further. But alone." The meaning of this fruitless journey thus remains vague, and that is why the triumph of the marvelous that restores the will to live to an entire small community by means of a hoax is itself ambiguous.

What Marius Grout is trying to show can easily be grasped: men cannot live without a dream of transcendence, miracles do not need to be true to be real, the marvelous exerts a radiant power that overcomes the lie on which it is based. These are pathetic hopes, since beneath the thin veil of illusion they border on despair. But what is this marvelous? What interest is there in a fable that only succeeds by chance? And if men need an ideal that takes the form of a fable in order to live, the question arises: In the end, do men really need to live? In his latest novel, *The Return of the Divine*,[6] whose poetic density is often extraordinary, Audiberti also compares hope in the sacred to a conjuring trick. But in his case, the conjuring trick is art itself, the power to transform everything, to change appearances into values and values into unutterable powers. Magic and poetry: They are the truth of mankind. His last word is thus a sort of reply to Marius Grout: "Humanity," he says, "is waiting for the divine. It returns. It does not return. And that is its drama. And that is its game."[7]

—December 10, 1943

The Novel of the Gaze

No reader capable of being touched by what he reads will open Simone de Beauvoir's novel *She Came to Stay* without recognizing what makes it both pathetic and natural as a work.[1] But perhaps there are those who will fail to see that it is a novel that differs markedly from others, one whose project is not to deploy types or bring characters to life but to illustrate, by means of a seemingly quite ordinary story, a situation that is typical of mankind as a whole. Although all such epithets are rather empty (and what is more, partly false), it is possible to give an idea of the importance of *She Came to Stay* by saying that it is, after Jean-Paul Sartre's *Nausea*, the second novel to be inspired by phenomenology.

A feature of this book is that its meaning can change completely, depending on the level of analysis that we bring to it. Its perspectives are very simple, and the author's intentions are not hidden. But despite its precise outlines, it is entirely at the mercy of the whim of its reader who, depending on his ability, will see it as a social novel, a character-based novel, or as what it is in fact: the novel of humanity when it undergoes the tragic experience of the other's gaze. It may be that, considered as a social and character-based novel, *She Came to Stay* will appear unpleasant and vacuous. The fault in that case lies with the reader who looks for nothing else in it. The three characters whose encounters are tirelessly described to us, the setting in which the same cafés, the same nightclubs, the same hotel rooms pass repeatedly before our eyes, the descriptions of a world where we observe the success of a young theater manager during the year that precedes the war are all so close to life that they seem to have been borrowed directly from it; but in themselves they are of minor interest. Why bother, some might say, to give us a new version of the traditional ménage à trois, one of those plots woven out of complacency and ambiguous sentiment? Why show us these backstage quarrels, these petty amorous tiffs? What is the point of this dull affair in which two women who are jealous of each other vie for the same man, while he is willing to have both of them? In fact, these objections make no sense. Simone de Beauvoir has chosen events that can adapt to any scheme. She has shown them and organized them in order to bring out the authentic drama they contain. The realism that she observes allows her to make do with a banal situation, and this she describes with considerable concern for verisimilitude and precision of tone.

It is quite conceivable that some readers will admire the authenticity and mysterious depths of character to be found in the novel. The three basic characters are protected from analytical curiosity by the way they move and by a capacity for sidestepping, each of which makes them elusive. They are not originals. Neither, however, are they bland characters onto whom the reality of a consciousness has grafted something individual and exceptional. There is no attempt to make them either banal or strange. The love that binds Françoise and Pierre expresses what is clear and strong about their two natures. People spontaneously describe Françoise as upright and loyal. But she is also protective of her happiness, and concerned to keep things in balance. She is involved professionally with Pierre who is an actor-manager, and leaves him free to indulge his fancies, since she herself is reluctant to let commitment undermine the happy life she has made for herself. This arrangement very soon comes under strain with the arrival of Xavière, a young friend from the provinces. It is she who has come to stay. Who is this little girl, so self-effacing, affectionate, and timid at first, but who soon takes things by storm, sowing disorder and provoking drama? The variability of her character conceals what she really is. Sometimes she is charming and entirely responsive to the feelings she arouses; at others she is reserved, arrogant, and perverse. It is difficult to know in what light to view her. In some respects she is a simple being; she lives for the moment; she welcomes everything she encounters; she rejects long-term projects and the convenience of habit. But at the same time she is far removed from any genuine spontaneity. She is elusive toward what she embraces. She is tyrannically possessive and impossible to possess. The individual she is exerts an attraction over Françoise and Pierre that is mixed with unease. The timid guest becomes a jealous friend, a supreme power that demands submission and punishes independence. They vainly try to build a happy three-way relationship. Everything would collapse into chaos were it not for Pierre's calm strength and Françoise's loyal friendship, which together preserve the happy peace they have chosen against this predatory outsider.

It is clear that the true drama does not take place between these three characters as they clash in their pursuit of each other, but in Françoise's consciousness alone. The entire book develops exclusively from the young woman's point of view, and although the story is told objectively in the third person, it is in relation to a hidden *I* that its perspectives evolve and its angles vary. For Françoise, this young guest is not just an alarming friend who encroaches on her intimacy and threatens her happiness. Nor is she simply a disagreeable partner who judges her behavior, questions her way of life and in the name of a harsh version of liberty, ruins the confidence she has placed in a stable form of happiness. Or rather, it is through these images that she discovers the alarming truth that her little provincial friend represents for her. It is in the display of her jealousy and the experience of her self-centeredness that she experiences something much more serious and decisive. The intransigence of this willful creature, her possessive rages, her stubborn, tiresome feelings would all mean very little, were it not that these character traits reveal to Françoise's anguished consciousness the unjustifiable and therefore unbearable fact that, face to face with her, someone exists, someone who is an inalienable consciousness like her, a pure presence, an indestructible reality, someone who sees her from without and against whom she is powerless and helpless. Françoise experiences this very simple fact: She does not live alone in the world, but she also lives for others. This is indeed a very simple experience, and to the average person, the upset it causes and the dramatic truth that embodies it will appear ridiculous. But the average person does not experience this revelation of the other's existence. He knows that the other exists, and he is at grips with him daily through his actions; but rarely does he go so far as to experience the singular nature of these relations, or else he only glimpses it in fleeting circumstances whose meaning briefly surfaces during instances of momentary sentiment. For someone like Françoise, by contrast, for one who is openly exposed to the presence of the other, this situation appears scandalous and impossible. It is a sort of drama with two endings. This Xavière gives whoever crosses her path the impression that she is an immovable presence, a reality that can not be erased, modified, or utilized. She is a soul upon whom "no one has any purchase." She is a closed, inaccessible presence, as her intransigent character makes evident; she is nothing but unknowable existence, "the explosion of purity and liberty" that is found in all men who are not me. The fact that outside of us there exists a consciousness that escapes us, that constitutes an insurmountable obstacle for our desire to appropriate it, like a sort of meteorite plunged into the earth and whose strangeness is all the greater for providing an exterior picture of what we are inside: such is the truth that we can only encounter in anguish, and before which we quickly close our eyes, blind to what there is of ourselves that exists in others. That is Françoise's discovery. "I discovered," she says, "that she had a consciousness like mine; have you ever had the experience of feeling another person's consciousness as if it was inside you?"

The other side of the drama is no less daunting. If in Françoise's presence there is someone who says *I*, at the same time she is obliged to acknowledge that for this inaccessible *I* who places a restriction on her liberty, she herself is no more than an indistinct *someone* [*on*], something that does not exist or that exists, precisely, as a thing and not a person. That is no doubt an experience that we all encounter frequently. When we say of one of our friends: "He doesn't care about me, in his eyes I don't exist," we are expressing the suffering and astonishment we feel when we are treated not according to what is irreducibly true about us, that priceless treasure we keep hidden away in the dark, but as one being among others, in other words as an object that people get to know by appropriating it. Xavière's voraciousness, the unrestrained imperialism that Françoise sees in her, is the innocent name that Françoise gives to the condition of being changed into an object, of being a consciousness that has been solidified into a thing. This misfortune takes different forms. Sometimes the young woman loses touch with her inner strength when she encounters this vital, self-assertive being. She becomes no more that "a white mask"; she drifts, naked and empty, across the surface of the world; fascinated by the sight of the other, she allows herself to forget the rich resources of her own existence considered as a force for self-assertion and renewal. At others, Xavière's gaze turns her into a stranger in her own eyes. Someone is judging her from without. If she keeps her distance, another attempts to confine her within the bounds of unchanging truth, to define her with images that are permanently attached to her henceforth unchanging person, and that she will never be able to put behind her. And it is against this enslavement that she rebels. To the woman that another wants her to be, immobilized by her character and a prisoner of her actions, she says no. Is it possible to escape the other? Perhaps, if by means of an act that we assume entirely we succeed in becoming conscious of our liberty. The final pages of the novel describe Xavière's end as Françoise resolutely rids herself of her presence by killing her.

Simone de Beauvoir's novel is an illustration of Jean-Paul Sartre's analyses of our "existence for others," which provide an admirably clear explanation of the most intractable and obscure dramas of human existence. The situation portrayed in *She Came to Stay* is even quite similar to the one to be found in *The Flies*,[2] and it would probably be a misreading of the end of the book not to see in it a call for the liberation of consciousness. In a way, Françoise's tragedy like that of Orestes is the tragedy of a being in search of its liberty. Before meeting Xavière, as is the case for Orestes before he comes to Argos, Françoise scarcely exists. She lives parasitically on happiness and tranquility, transferring onto another the responsibility for what she should be alone in being. Xavière's appearance is the ordeal that makes her conscious of this inalienable possession, through the loss of it with which she feels threatened. It is through the other that she rediscovers herself, and it is in a state of bondage that she finds what is authentically hers. The unease she feels beneath the gaze of her young friend is the anguish of a consciousness that discovers it is absolute at the very moment when someone tries to reduce it simply to one point of view among others. This makes clear how we should interpret the rather brutal denouement of the book. If she kills Xavière, it is not because Xavière is someone other, so that by killing her she will be able to be free of the other altogether. Such an approach would be both absurd and crude. In reality, she only rids herself of the other, only overcomes the other, because she seizes her liberty at its source, and she becomes free only through an act that is both scandalous and decisive in which she risks herself totally, an act that she carries out alone, face to face with herself, and with total liberty: the murder of Xavière, an act that is identical in certain respects to Orestes's matricide. In other words, the slave does not become the master because he kills the master, but because by killing him he risks what up until then had enslaved him: his life, his peace of mind, his uncomplicated relation to the world. (It should nonetheless be noted that the way Françoise crushes "the hostile presence," in a furtive, untraceable, risk-free act, does not constitute a true ordeal, seen from without—"In any case," she says to herself, "there won't be any proof"—but rather brings out the desire for security that is one of the character traits of the young woman.)

The art form chosen by Simone de Beauvoir is one of detailed realism. She has a natural talent for it, and she expresses herself with considerable ease. One might wish to explore whether this form has not obliged her to distort her subject. For example, if her book can be seen as a character-based novel, this is because there are grounds for this. It is in the guise of a character type, an independent, susceptible character, that the author presents the figure of the invited guest; but it is clear that what provides the substance of the book is definitely not the mood or jealousy of an individual; beneath such particularities, it is rather her bare existence, her existence as a free consciousness and an elusive force. This ambiguity is all the more dangerous in that Françoise's discovery should, precisely, prevent her from seeing her friend from without, that is to say in terms of her character. Suddenly the inside of a being is revealed to her, and she lives under the spell of that presence, of the invisible gaze of an eye that is constantly concealed by its vision. Simone de Beauvoir has remained faithful to the conventions of her subject in so far as she has organized the novel according to the approach that is Françoise's own. The only direct analysis concerns Françoise's feelings, and most of the events are shown to us as the young woman could have seen and experienced them. This unity gives the novel considerable consistency. We know the other characters only through what they say, through the enigma of their voices and the density of their conversations. This produces interminable dialogues that the author develops skillfully, and that could eventually overwhelm the fabric of the book, were it not that, as she determines, they sometimes convey an impression of ease, and sometimes one of anguished emptiness.

—December 18–19, 1943

Tradition and Surrealism

Louis Hourtiq is a renowned art historian, known for his sometimes courageous hostility toward almost all modern art, from the Impressionists to the work of young painters today.[1] He has recently defended his ideas in a new book that shows them in a rather curious light. In *Art and Science*,[2] he seeks to demonstrate that there is a natural link between artistic disciplines and the goals of science. Initially, at the origin, the artist and the scientist are no different from each other; a flint ax is a magnificent work requiring considerable talent (as is the spoon, deemed beautiful by Socrates because it allows us to scoop up a mouthful of soup). Greek art presupposes an intellectual curiosity that makes the artist an unwitting expert in mathematics, mechanics, and anatomy, all of which are natural sciences. The Greek temple displays an obvious kinship with geometry: simplicity of structure, regularity of outline, and precision of detail. It reflects the purity of abstract forms, and to describe it exactly is to employ definitions taken from the science of plane surfaces and solids. Does that mean that architects draw their inspiration from geometers? Not at all: The Greeks were building their temples three centuries before Euclid, and putting all the elementary notions of the spatial sciences to use on their building sites.

Greek sculpture displays an extraordinary knowledge of the human body. The solidity of Polykleitos, the serenity of Phidias, the languor of Praxiteles, and the vivacity of Lysippos all come less from a fertile imagination than from impeccable knowledge. Sculptors are in possession of anatomical truths that will be inaccessible to scientists for more than a thousand years. Though their art owes nothing to dissection, it predates most of the surgical discoveries that will come later. After a period of dormancy during the Byzantine period, we see art triumph strangely again in the form of realism, which is a science before science was invented. Gothic architecture is based on a mechanical empiricism and an implicit knowledge of laws, each of which is a sign of unprecedented progress in comparison with common belief. The sculpture and painting of the Renaissance are more rigorous than the science that is nonetheless beginning to make major advances at the time. In the fifteenth century, while painters are imposing a rationalist vision on the world in which everything visible obeys mathematical laws, the imagination of the physicists is still hampered by supernatural principles that explain the specifics of motion in terms of occult qualities or various "demons": in short, there is more theology and more animism in Kepler's physics than in the universe conjured up by Paolo Uccello and Mantegna. The hero of this art of supreme knowledge that provides an explanation of the world and foresees future developments is Leonardo da Vinci, who, having understood that painting is a universal power, combined art and science as no one has ever done since.

It is clear what familiar views can be justified by these remarks in Hourticq's mind. If what we term artistic beauty can also be called truth in the field of knowledge—if, for example, history shows painters and sculptors that they owe nature the same scrupulous reverence as the sciences whose discoveries they anticipate—then it follows that art is fundamentally realist in nature, that the use of imagination and fancy constitutes a risky adventure, in short, that the plastic arts are essentially arts of imitation. These are the familiar tenets of the so-called school of sincerity in art. But Hourticq's attempt to enlist the entire history of art in his cause is perhaps not without its difficulties: He is required to leave aside Eastern art that enchants the eye and encourages us to dream but, according to him, does not awaken our intelligence; he is obliged to be especially severe toward Byzantine art, "the only case where a rich and durable school of art does not find its beauties in the domain of truth." But even among the Greeks themselves or the great classical artists, the works do not always conform to the obligations that a strict adherence to realism would impose. The chapter in which Hourticq examines the mythological bestiary is rather curious in this respect. Faced with the Erichthonius of the ancient Parthenon, a man with the body of a snake, or with the minotaurs, centaurs, and other monsters with which the Greek imagination was fertile, the learned historian feels certain scruples. Did the sculptors respect anatomical truth? Did they not do violence to nature? Of all these inventions, only that of the centaur appears valid to him, even though, as he remarks somewhat ruefully, many of the organs of this magnificent hybrid are present twice. Later, Hourticq sees artistic inventions based on Christian symbolism as equally dangerous, and he anxiously scrutinizes masterpieces by Dürer as well as the wonderful Angers tapestries, in which Jean Bandol and Nicolas Bataille transposed the impossible visions of the Apocalypse as accurately as possible. (Hourticq gives us the opportunity to welcome the very fine book that André Lejard has just devoted to this masterwork of French mural tapestry, which is still almost unknown.)[3]

What is very odd about Hourticq's argument is the fact that he appears to be in agreement with the people about whom he is most wary: those "doctrinaires" whom he calls "deformers and surrealists." What is his book saying, basically? That when art is authentic, it is inseparable from knowledge, that there is in the artist a magical power that allow him to discover things that are hidden and gain knowledge of the secrets of the world; art does not depend on science strictly speaking ("It is always a dangerous moment for art," he writes, "when the precise knowledge whose development it has encouraged shines its all-seeing light on the uncertain domain of instinct"); rather, it is science that is derived from art, that in any case often feels it is an anachronism in relation to art, weighed down by prejudice and a prisoner of error. But while Hourticq perhaps does not realize it, his thinking on this subject coincides exactly with that of the Surrealists. It is André Breton who wrote with characteristic peremptoriness: "I continue to believe that a painting or a sculpture can only incidentally be considered a matter of taste, and that it can only be defended if it is capable of promoting abstract knowledge in the strict sense of the term."[4] This text is perfectly clear, and though it expresses one of the major principles of Surrealist thought, it would not appear to contain anything that the learned member of the French Institute could object to. It states that art cannot have as its only goal the pleasure it affords the eye (as decorative art would claim), that it is committed to divining the unknown, and that, beyond all fixed knowledge and routine common sense, it foresees a vision of things that science initially bridles at but comes around to in the end.

It is quite possible to imagine that those arts that ceased to be derivative ones only "outlawed" themselves because they had a deeper instinct for the law, only disengaged themselves from nature in order to get behind surface appearances and bring to light a truth that still remained hidden from everyday understanding. The reasoning of traditionalist critics displays this strange anomaly: They accept in general that art precedes science, yet it is in the name of the science of the past, and of a worldview that science has made popular, that they condemn new artistic movements. They recognize the foresight of which art is capable, yet they consider suspect those forecasts that do not have the blessing of traditional knowledge. It would be well worth asking whether in fact the most up-to-date scientific knowledge does not see itself reflected in the "deformed," decomposed, unserviceable universe to which art has accustomed our eyes. Artistic genius sacrifices (and sacrifice must be understood literally here, as a sacred act) the world that habit has organized and that practical life reinforces. It sets back into eternal motion elements whose organization will be made subject to other laws. Initially, all we see is its destructive power, but in fact, the ruins that it appears to pile on top of each other in barbaric fashion are already the constructions and the real forms that our laggard gaze will recognize later on.

—December 23, 1943

A World in Ruins

The latest novel by Georges Magnane, *Harvest Feast*,[1] is a brilliant book by a very talented author. It is interesting, too, for the way it reveals what themes today's writers feel driven to adopt and how, even if their own instincts do not incline them to adopt a tragic worldview, they nonetheless feel obliged to respond to tragedy and express what is fateful about it. *Harvest Feast* is the story of a man who is pursued by horror. Having come through the war, he is taken on at harvest time by some farmers. At first we know nothing about him, and it is only because a state of extreme unease makes each of his actions appear strange, and because of the alarming look in his eyes, his reserve, and his furious appetite for work that we catch a glimpse of the deep misfortune that has affected his life. Later, we learn that Olivier has killed someone. During the retreat he killed his sergeant, and if this was not premeditated, if he struck in self-defense and in order to defend someone else, he nonetheless knows that he was fundamentally committed to that death, to that chance misfortune, and that he accepts it and henceforth sees in it the shape of his destiny. The memory of his act takes possession of him. Does he feel remorse? No, he does not consider that his story has a moral side; but he is alone, his extreme experience has set him apart, it is as if he were lost, and each day he becomes a little more lost in a world where no one can join him. The manner in which he himself projects outward, through a new act of violence, the blind instinct to which he is compelled to yield, is of almost no importance. To all appearances he is the victim of bad luck; people think that at a dance, he killed a man who was his rival for the only person to whom he feels close; the hunt is on for him; he flees; but his innocence is that of a guilty man: He is being hunted for a crime he did not commit, and he flees without knowing what crime he is being accused of. He vainly takes refuge in the forest. He struggles vainly against hunger, thirst, exhaustion, and delirium. It is in vain that the proof of his innocence finally emerges, that people come to his assistance, that he is about to be rescued; just as all the misunderstanding is dispelled, he stumbles, falls into a ravine, and is killed.

Georges Magnane has divided his book into two parts; first, a series of monologues introduces its hero; the farmer he works for, the farmer's wife, the farmhand, the children, and so on all circle around the tragic character, and through their own confessions they provide us with knowledge of this man who cannot reveal what he is. The second part tells the story of the flight into the forest, of obsession and inescapable bewilderment, until the inevitable catastrophe occurs. Here it is easy to identify a form that has been made popular by American writers and allowed them to convey a world of madness and horror in all of its reality. It is thus a borrowing, but as we said recently when discussing Louis-René des Forêts's novel,[2] it is a legitimate borrowing that does not even necessarily reflect any direct influence, and that should be judged on its results, on the expressive power that an author derives from it. What is remarkable about *Harvest Feast* is the fact that its author readily uses monologues as a procedure, so that they become a mode of exposition rather than a means of communication. It is clear that he does not claim to express the inner language of the characters to whom he gives voice: His farmers often talk in a highly literary fashion and prove capable of detailed description and nuanced observation that are far removed from anything their circumstances would allow. In some respects, this intrusion of literature into the inner monologue is not unjustified. It has long been known that the inner cries and demented, troubled voices that are supposed to be a faithful reproduction of every movement of the mind are in fact totally unrelated to any sort of psychological realism; that they are only true in literary terms; that they do not express the workings of the mind directly, but translate or evoke them according to conventions that are often quite unrealistic. Magnane takes what is conventional even further while observing certain precautions; he uses monologues the way writers do in the theater, and his successive inner narratives call to mind the ancient chorus, those phantoms who comment on an action that they do not understand.

Perhaps it is all the more disappointing that these conventions ultimately fail to achieve their purpose. It is clear that the novelist[3] has sought to bring us gradually closer to his hero, to reveal him to us without shedding light on him, to make him accessible to us by showing him to be inaccessible to others. We can never obtain a direct account of him. And the writer himself has no power to act as an intermediary between him and us. But these precautions are almost too visible. They are more a reflection of an author's stratagems than a sign of helplessness in the face of inexorable truth. The sober, measured monologues become literary masks, and they distance us from the tragedy without conveying to us what must be unbearable about it. The narrative section produces the same impression in us from another angle. It has many qualities. The flight through the forest, the descriptions of trees, the twisting and turning of a man who is lost inside his own misfortune as if in a dream, all these difficult episodes are composed with remarkable skill and literary instinct, and they exemplify what is often called a happy turn of phrase. The fact is, however, that this happy quality remains somewhat detached from the terrifying misfortune it is used to describe. It is too obvious that the author writes well, that he enjoys writing and that luck is on his side. As a result, the sense of misfortune into which we would willingly sink alongside his hero is simply dispelled. For a novelist, his chosen subject is not just any subject, and a universe that is falling apart before a wounded gaze is not fundamentally a tragic one: People live there, it is possible to live there, and it is only a passing anomaly that transforms the clear, honest world where living possesses all its significance into a world of darkness.

One thing is certain, however: Horror cannot simply be given its due. Whoever talks about it and is content just to talk about it, however seriously he does so, will always ultimately appear frivolous, the way the Voltaire of the tragedies is frivolous when compared to Racine, for example. That, it is to be feared, is the weakness of *Harvest Feast*. Nonetheless, if the theme of catastrophe was imposed on the writer by external circumstance, if it is so acutely contemporary and authentic that even a novelist who is not predisposed to choose it has been obliged to use it and take it to its utmost conclusion, then this obligation should be seen as a sign, and be acknowledged not just as a revelation about where literature is tending, but as one that concerns the meaning of our world. Like Alexandre Vialatte's *Faithful Shepherd*, which was reviewed in these pages earlier in the year,[4] Magnane's hero encounters anguish and obsession in war; and yet each of them refuses to explain his fate in terms of the particular circumstances in which they were involved. They understand that what they have seen and done was inevitable, that the veil of appearances simply tore, and that through the desolation of what happened they came into contact with something more profound that they can no longer either endure, or reject, or avoid. It is thus that the world in ruins—the truth of the world—appears to them, and henceforth they must live without purpose, without hope, as they await an outcome that will itself be merely a ridiculous misunderstanding.[5]

—December 30, 1943

Notes

INTRODUCTION

1. Maurice Blanchot, "Intellectuals under Scrutiny," trans. Michael Holland, in *The Blanchot Reader*, ed. Michael Holland (Oxford: Blackwell, 1995), 206–27. First published as "Les intellectuels en question," *Le Débat* 29 (March 1984): 3–28.

2. In November, Pétain attempted to distance himself from Laval by giving back to the National Assembly the plenary powers it had granted him in 1940. Laval opposed this, Hitler instructed Pétain not to proceed, and Pétain obeyed. His power at this point effectively disappeared.

3. In 1993, Blanchot wrote, "The war with Russia was giving us new hope (1943)." See Maurice Blanchot, "For Friendship," in *Political Writings, 1953–1993*, trans. Zakir Paul (New York: Fordham University Press, 2010), 136.

4. Ibid. The term is Blanchot's.

5. For details of the Jeune France project and Blanchot's time at the *Nouvelle Revue Française*, see my introductions to Maurice Blanchot, *Into Disaster* and *Desperate Clarity*, trans. Michael Holland (New York: Fordham University Press, 2014).

6. Maurice Blanchot, letter to Francis Ambrière, July 14, 1943. In Fonds Francis et Madeleine Ambrière, Bibliothèque de l'Institut, Paris (MS 7943 Correspondance de guerre). Ambrière spent the war in a German prison camp. Blanchot refers to him briefly in "The Search for Tradition." See *Into Disaster*, 41.

7. Letter dated September 11, 1981, in Maurice Blanchot, *Lettres à Vadim Kozovoï* (Paris: Éditions Manucius, 2009), 54.

8. Letter dated July 14 [1984], ibid., 122.

9. He was nominated for the Prix Goncourt for *Thomas l'obscur* but did not win. In the light of that, something he said about Charles-Louis Philippe gains further resonance: "He does not receive the Prix Goncourt, but this failure leads to greater fame than any trivial success would have done." At the private level, he continued to participate in the meetings at which George Bataille had been seeking since 1942 to establish a "Collège socratique." See Georges Bataille, "Le Collège socratique," in *Oeuvres complètes* (Paris: Gallimard, 1973), 8:279–92.

10. Maurice Blanchot, *Comment la littérature est-elle possible?* (Paris: Corti, 1942); "How Is Literature Possible," trans. Michael Syrotinski, in *The Blanchot Reader*, 49–60.

11. Maurice Blanchot, *Faux pas*, trans. Charlotte Mandell (Stanford: Stanford University Press, 2001). In "For Friendship" Blanchot recalls "the shock mixed with irritation" that he felt when he learned that Gallimard wanted to publish *Faux pas* (134); the letter to Francis Ambrière of July 14 cited in note 6 reveals that this was not just a retrospective judgment: "Since Gallimard insisted on publishing some of my *Journal des Débats* chronicles as a book, I feebly agreed to the [Corti] project even though I continue to feel that it is of no interest."

12. Relations between Blanchot and Brasillach were always difficult. In the letter that Jean-Luc Nancy published in 2011 in a volume entitled *Maurice Blanchot. Passion politique* (Paris: Galilée), Blanchot wrote: "Brasillach, who was separated from me by a reciprocal dislike, not to say a hatred, was a far from untalented representative of the most dangerous illusions of a 'joyful' fascism" (51). In 1977, Blanchot wrote a letter to Maurice Nadeau in which he elaborated on these difficult relations: "hostility verging on hatred . . . kept me well away from Brasillach, who represented what was the essence of fascism and anti-Semitism. During the Occupation, it

was *Je suis partout*, whose editor Brasillach was (I am not accusing him personally, I can't be certain) that denounced me to the Gestapo, almost costing me my life" (letter dated April 17, 1977, trans. Michael Holland, in "Responses and Interventions," *Paragraph* 30:3, "Blanchot's Epoch," November 2007, 18–19). It is instructive to compare the authors reviewed by Blanchot in 1943 and those that were the subject of Brasillach's reviews in the newspaper *Le Petit Parisien* in 1943. While there is a certain overlap, there are also significant divergences. Alongside Blanchot's reflections, Brasillach's chirpy self-indulgence appears shallow. See Gérard Sthème de Jubécourt, *La chronique littéraire de Robert Brasillach dans Le Petit Parisien* (Paris: La Pensée Universelle, 1985).

13. This argument is driven home more pointedly when Blanchot writes, referring to Faulkner, "We can see no reason whatsoever why a French writer should have denied himself the right to use this foreign technique for his own purposes."

14. During 1941, his avowed ambition was to found a journal devoted to poetry. Further details on this subject may be found in my introduction to *Into Disaster*, 4.

15. "Unknown Romantics," in ibid., 169–70.

16. Ibid., 170. (Italics mine.)

17. See "After Rimbaud," in Blanchot, *Faux pas*, 144 (translation modified).

18. In April 1942, Blanchot evoked "what is necessarily implacable and harsh about the forms of a universe grounded in the imagination. . . . There is no more demanding taskmaster than the imagination." "Stories of Childhood," in *Desperate Clarity*, 50.

19. Twenty years later, in March 1964, Blanchot wrote an article entitled "The Apocalypse Is Disappointing" in response to Karl Jaspers's reflections on the atomic bomb. See Maurice Blanchot, *Friendship*, trans. Elizabeth Rottenberg (Stanford: Stanford University Press, 1997), 101–8.

NICHOLAS OF CUSA

1. Maurice de Gandillac, *La philosophie de Nicolas de Cuse* (Paris: Aubier-Montaigne, 1941); Nicolas de Cuse, *Oeuvres choisies* (Paris: Aubier, 1942).

THE CORRESPONDENCE OF MADAME DE LA FAYETTE

1. Mme de La Fayette, *Correspondance*, ed. André Beaunier (Paris: Gallimard, 1942).

2. Mme de La Fayette, *Le triomphe de l'indifférence*, ed. André Beaunier (Paris: Corti, 1937); *Mercure de France* 4 (October 15, 1937).

THE BOOK

1. André Lejard, *Le livre. Les plus beaux exemplaires de la Bibliothèque nationale* (Paris: Éditions du Chêne, 1942); *The Art of the French Book from Early Manuscripts to the Present Time*, trans. Philip James (London: P. Elek, 1947).

A NOVEL AND A TALE OF WAR

1. Alexandre Vialatte, *Le fidèle berger* (Paris: Gallimard, 1942).

2. Antoine de Saint-Exupéry, *Pilote de guerre* (Paris: Gallimard, 1942); *Flight to Arras*, trans. William Rees (London: William Heinemann, 1995).

3. Antoine de Saint-Exupéry, *Vol de nuit* (Paris: Gallimard, 1931); *Night Flight*, trans. Stuart Gilbert (London: Desmond Harmsworth, 1932).

CHARLES-LOUIS PHILIPPE

1. Émile Guillaumin, *Mon compatriote Charles-Louis Philippe* (Paris: Éditions Bernard Grasset, 1942).

NOVELS OF THE LAND

1. Charles-Ferdinand Ramuz, *Aimé Pache, peintre vaudois* (Paris: Grasset, 1943).

2. Paule Lavergne, *Le maître* (Paris: Gallimard, 1942).

3. Charles-François Landry, *Brume de printemps* (Paris: Corrêa, 1942); Charles Exbrayat, *Jules Matrat* (Paris: Gallimard, 1942).

TOCQUEVILLE'S *RECOLLECTIONS*

1. *Souvenirs d'Alexis de Tocqueville*, ed. Luc Monnier (Paris: Gallimard, 1942); *The Recollections of Alexis de Tocqueville*, trans. George Lawrence (London: Macdonald, 1970).

2. Both the *Débats* article and the *Chroniques littéraires* have "*poétique*" here. From the context, it would seem, however, that "*politique*" is what was intended.

SYMBOLISM AND THE POETS OF TODAY

1. Albert-Marie Schmidt, *La littérature symboliste* (Paris: Presses Universitaires de France, 1942).
2. Robert Ganzo, *Poèmes* (Paris: Gallimard, 1942).
3. Jean Tardieu, *Le témoin invisible* (Paris: Gallimard, 1943).
4. This translation first appeared in *Mesures* in October 1935, and then in Jean Tardieu, *Accents. Poèmes, suivis d'une traduction de L'Archipel de Hölderlin* (Paris: Gallimard, 1939).
5. Michel Fardoulis-Lagrange, *Sébastien, l'enfant et l'orange* (Paris: René Debresse, 1942).

ON MONTHERLANT'S PLAY

1. Henri de Montherlant, *La reine morte, ou Comment on tue les femmes* (Paris: Gallimard, 1942); *Queen After Death*, trans. Jonathan Griffin, in *The French Theatre Since 1930*, ed. Oreste F. Pucciani (Waltham, Mass.: Xerox College Publishing, 1954). Also in Henri de Montherlant, *The Master of Santiago and Four Other Plays* (London: Routledge & Kegan Paul, 1951).

THE ROMANCE OF MARIE DORVAL AND VIGNY

1. Marie Dorval, *Lettres à Alfred de Vigny*, ed. Charles Gaudier (Paris: Gallimard, 1942).

NOVELS

1. Pierre Van der Meulen, *L'enfant du Bois Plauquet* (Paris: Plon, 1943).
2. Henri Thomas, *Le précepteur* (Paris: Gallimard, 1942).
3. Henri Thomas, *Travaux d'aveugle* (Paris: Gallimard, 1941).
4. Maria Le Hardouin, *La voile noire* (Paris: Corrêa, 1943).

MACHIAVELLI

1. Augustin Renaudet, *Machiavel. Étude d'histoire des doctrines politiques* (Paris: Gallimard, 1942).
2. Machiavel, *Le Prince* (Paris: Garnier Frères, 1941).

ELOQUENCE AND LITERATURE

1. Martin Stanislas Gillet, *L'éloquence sacrée* (Paris: Corrêa, 1943); Maurice Garçon, *Tableau de l'éloquence judiciaire* (Paris: Corrêa, 1943); Anatole de Monzie, *Mémoires de la Tribune* (Paris: Corrêa, 1943).
2. Speech to the Chamber of Deputies, March 8, 1918, "Je fais la guerre." Whether inadvertently or by design, Blanchot refers to this speech in his article as "Faire la guerre" (make war).
3. Paul Valéry, "Choses tues, " in *Tel quel, Oeuvres complètes* (Paris: Gallimard, 1960), 2:479.

ON JOUHANDEAU'S WORK

1. Marcel Jouhandeau, *Les miens* (Paris: Gallimard, 1943); *Nouvelles chroniques maritales* (Paris: Gallimard, 1943). The latter work can be found in *Marcel and Elise*, trans. Martin Turnell (London: Longman, Green and Co, 1955) as part of *Chronicle of Married Life*, 83–151.
2. This is the beginning of the article. The rest appears in the chapter of *Faux pas* entitled "Chaminadour," (227–33).

THE THIRTEEN FORMS OF A NOVEL

1. Roland Cailleux, *Saint Genès ou la vie brève* (Paris: Gallimard, 1943).
2. This is a clear—and barbed—reference to Robert Brasillach's novel *Les sept couleurs* (Paris: Plon, 1939).

FROM PRAISE TO SOVEREIGNTY

1. Georges Dumézil, *Servius et la fortune* (Paris: Gallimard, 1943).

RELIGIOUS POETRY

1. Dominique Aury, *Anthologie de la poésie religieuse française* (Paris: Gallimard, 1943).

2. Thierry Maulnier, *Introduction à la poésie française* (Paris: Gallimard, 1939); Dominique Aury, *Poètes précieux et baroques du XVIIe siècle* (Angers: J. Petit, 1941). Blanchot reviewed Aury's book in the *Débats* on June 3, 1942. The article is included in *Faux pas* with the title "The Baroque Poets of the Seventeenth Century," 122–27.

3. In *From the Theorems of Master Jean de La Ceppède: LXX Sonnets*, ed. Keith Bosley (Manchester: Carcanet, 1993), 27.

4. In Laurent Drelincourt, *Sonnets chrétiens sur divers sujets*, ed. Julien Goeury (Paris: Honoré Champion, 2004), 146.

5. In Martial de Brives, *Les oeuvres poétiques et sacrées*, ed. Anne Mantero (Grenoble: J. Milon, 2000).

NOVELS

1. Paul Valéry, *Tel quel*, in *Oeuvres complètes* (Paris: Gallimard, 1960), 2:479.

2. Maxence Van der Meersch, *Corps et âmes* (Paris: Albin Michel, 1943); *Bodies And Souls*, trans. Eithne Wilkins (London: Pilot Press, 1948).

3. Alice Rivaz, *Nuages dans la main* (Lausanne: La Guilde du livre, 1940; Paris: René Julliard/Sequana, 1943).

4. André Dhôtel, *Le village pathétique* (Paris: Gallimard, 1943).

5. The *Débats* article and the *Chroniques littéraires* have "*sans effet*" (without effect). "*Sans effort*" (without effort) makes more sense in context.

6. Dominique Brejon de Lavergne, *Le coeur anachronique* (Paris: Gallimard, 1943).

FRENCH SUITE

1. Claude Roy, *Suite française* (Paris: René Julliard/Sequana, 1943).

2. Louis Aragon, "Controverse sur le génie de la France," in *Controverses sur le génie de la France, Cahiers du Rhône* 5 (Novembre 1942).

3. Paul Valéry, "La pensée et l'art français," in Paul Valéry et al., *La France et la civilisation contemporaine* (Paris: Flammarion, 1941), 18. Blanchot quotes this passage in "France and Contemporary Civilization," in Maurice Blanchot, *Into Disaster*, 30.

4. Paul Valéry, "Images de la France," in *Regards sur le monde actuel* (1931), *Oeuvres complètes*, 1:1005; *Reflections on the World Today*, trans. Francis Scarfe (London: Thames & Hudson, 1951), 105.

HOFFMANN'S FANTASTIC

1. E.T.A. Hoffmann, *Le chat Murr*, trans. Albert Béguin (Paris: Gallimard, 1943).

2. Albert Béguin, *L'âme romantique et le rêve* (Paris: Corti, 1939).

ON THE *SONG OF ROLAND*

1. Émile Mireaux, *La Chanson de Roland et l'histoire de France* (Paris: Albin Michel, 1943).

KIERKEGAARD AND AESTHETICS

1. Søren Kierkegaard, *Ou bien . . . Ou bien*, trans. F. Prior, O. Prior, and M. H. Guignot (Paris: Gallimard, 1943).

THE ART OF THE SHORT STORY

1. Jean Fougère, *Visite* (Paris: Éditions du Pavois, 1943).

2. Colette, *Le képi* (Paris: Fayard, 1943); *The Kepi*, in *The Stories of Colette*, trans. Antonia White (London: Secker & Warburg, 1958).

3. Marcel Aymé, *Le passe-muraille* (Paris: Gallimard, 1943); *The Man Who Walked Through Walls*, trans. Sophie Lewis (London: Pushkin Press, 2012).

4. Marius Richard, *La naissance de Phèdre* (Paris: Éditions Colbert, 1943).

THE RELIGION OF RABELAIS

1. Lucien Febvre, *Le problème de l'incroyance au XVIe siècle. La religion de Rabelais* (Paris: Albin Michel, 1943); *The Problem of Unbelief in the Sixteenth Century: The Religion of Rabelais*, trans. Beatrice Gottlieb (Cambridge, Mass.: Harvard University Press, 1982).

WOMEN NOVELISTS OF TODAY

1. Germaine Beaumont, *Agnès de rien* (Paris: Plon, 1943).
2. Gabrielle Cabrini, *La résurrection des morts* (Paris: Gallimard, 1943).
3. Henri Alain-Fournier, *Le Grand Meaulnes* (Paris: Émile Paul Frères, 1913); *The Lost Estate (Le Grand Meaulnes)*, trans. Robin Buss (London: Penguin, 2007); Dominique Rolin, *Les marais* (Paris: Denoël, 1942); for Blanchot's review of this novel, see *Desperate Clarity*, 111–13; Jean Cocteau, *Les enfants terribles* (Paris: Grasset, 1929); *The Holy Terrors*, trans. Rosamund Lehman (New York: New Directions, 1955).
4. Marguerite Duras, *Les impudents* (Paris: Plon, 1943).
5. Marion Delbo, *Monsieur Durey* (Paris: Denoël, 1943).
6. Elsa Triolet, *Le cheval blanc* (Paris: Denoël, 1943); *The White Horse*, trans. Mervyn Savill (London: Hutchinson International, 1951).

MONTESQUIEU'S TRAVELS

1. For Blanchot's review of this, see "The Art of Montesquieu," in *Into Disaster*, 34–39.
2. Montesquieu, *Histoire véritable* (Paris: Gallimard, 1942).
3. *Voyages de Montesquieu* (Paris: Stock, 1943).

A HISTORY OF FRENCH LITERATURE

1. Kléber Haedens, *Une histoire de la littérature française* (Paris: René Julliard, 1943).
2. This is a reference to Haedens's 1941 study *Paradoxes sur le roman*. For Blanchot's review of this, see "Paradoxes on the Novel," in *Into Disaster*, 131–37.

THE INFLUENCE OF THE AMERICAN NOVEL

1. Louis-René des Forêts, *Les mendiants* (Paris: Gallimard, 1943); *The Beggars*, trans. Helen Beauclerk (London: Dennis Dobson, 1948).

THE MYSTICISM OF ANGELUS SILESIUS

1. Henri Plard, *La mystique d'Angelus Silesius* (Paris: Éditions Aubier, 1943).

AUTOBIOGRAPHICAL NARRATIVES

1. Roger Caillois, *Puissances du roman* (Paris: Éditions du Sagittaire, 1942).

2. The *Chroniques littéraires* (in the *Débats* version) mistranscribes "*nos*" (our) as "*ses*" (his).

3. Julien Blanc, *Seule, la vie. . .* (Paris: Gallimard, 1943); Pierre Molaine, *Samson a soif* (Paris: Corrêa, 1943).

4. Jules Vallès, *L'enfant* (Paris: Bibliothèque-Charpentier, 1879); *The Child*, trans. Douglas Parmée (New York: NYRB Classics, 2005); *Le bachelier* (Paris: Bibliothèque-Charpentier, 1881); *L'insurgé* (Paris: Bibliothèque-Charpentier, 1886); *The Insurrectionist*, trans. Sandy Petrey (Englewood Cliffs, N.J.: Prentice Hall, 1971).

HISTORY AND THE MASTERPIECE

1. Gaston Roupnel, *Histoire et destin* (Paris: Éditions Bernard Grasset, 1943).

2. Gaston Roupnel, *Histoire de la campagne française* (Paris: Grasset, 1932).

3. Léon Émery, *Chefs-d'oeuvre, introduction à l'humanisme* (Paris: Aubier-Montaigne, 1942).

4. Victor Bérard, *La résurrection d'Homère, I: Au temps des héros* (Paris: Grasset, 1930), 17.

A STUDY OF THE APOCALYPSE

1. R. P. Henri-Marie Féret, *L'Apocalypse de saint Jean, vision chrétienne de l'histoire* (Paris: Éditions Corrêa, 1943); *The Apocalypse*

Explained, trans. Elizabeth Corathiel (London: Blackfriars Publications, 1958).

LA FONTAINE WITHOUT THE *FABLES*

1. Jean Giraudoux, *Les cinq tentations de Jean de La Fontaine* (Paris: Grasset, 1938).

2. La Fontaine, *Oeuvres diverses*, ed. Pierre Clarac (Paris: Gallimard, 1943).

3. Jean de Lafontaine, *Adonis*, trans. David Glixon (London: Rodale Press, 1957), 75 (translation modified).

BARON D'HOLBACH

1. Pierre Naville, *Paul Thiry d'Holbach et la philosophie scientifique au XVIII*[e] siècle (Paris: Gallimard, 1943).

2. See "Vigils of the Mind," in Blanchot, *Desperate Clarity*, 144–51.

3. Bernard Groethuysen, *Origines de l'esprit bourgeois en France*, 2 vols. (Paris: Gallimard, 1927); *The Bourgeois: Catholicism versus Capitalism in Eighteenth-Century France* (London: Barrie & Rockliffe, 1968).

THE PURE NOVEL

1. "Problèmes du roman," ed. Jean Prévost, *Confluences* 21–24 (1943).

2. André Gide, *Les faux-monnayeurs* (Paris: Gallimard, 1995 [1927]); *The Counterfeiters with the Journal of "The Counterfeiters,"* trans. Dorothy Bussy and Justin O'Brien (New York: Knopf, 2012 [1951]), 205 (translation modified).

3. Ibid., 187–88 (translation modified).

4. Friedrich Gundolf (Gundelfinger) (1880–1931) was a German-Jewish literary scholar. The Nazis banned his books in 1933. By citing him, Blanchot is thus defying the prevailing laws of censorship. He cites him in similar terms in his 1945 article "A Note on Malraux," but with reservations: "Such distinctions leave us rather mistrustful." See Maurice Blanchot, *The Work of Fire*, trans. Charlotte Mandell (Stanford: Stanford University Press, 1995), 209.

5. Gide, *The Counterfeiters*, 352–53 (translation modified).

THE LAMENT OF THE SHADOW

1. "The Shadow," in Friedrich Nietzsche, *Thus Spake Zarathustra*, trans. Thomas Common (Mineola, N.Y.: Dover, 1999), 195.

2. See *Oeuvres complètes du Pseudo-Denys l'Aréopagite*, trans. Maurice de Gandillac (Paris: Aubier, 1943; rpt. 1980); and *Le bienheureux Henri Suso*, trans. Jeanne Ancelet-Hustache (Paris: Aubier-Montaigne, 1943).

3. Marius Grout, *Passage de l'homme* (Paris: Gallimard, 1943), winner of the 1943 Prix Goncourt; *When the Man Passed By*, trans. Emerson Lamb (New York: Vantage Press, 1962).

4. Selma Lagerlöf, *Jerusalem*, trans. V. S. Howard (Auckland: Aeterna, 2010 [1914]); *The Holy City: Jerusalem II*, trans. V. S. Howard (Whitefish, Mont.: Kessinger, 2007 [1918]).

5. For Blanchot's review of this work see "Paradoxes on the Novel," in *Into Disaster*, 131–37.

6. Jacques Audiberti, *Le retour du divin* (Paris: Gallimard, 1943).

7. This article is the third to appear on the first page of the *Journal des Débats*, under the heading "Chronique de la vie intellectuelle" (Chronicle of Intellectual Life).

THE NOVEL OF THE GAZE

1. Simone de Beauvoir, *L'invitée* (Paris: Gallimard, 1943); *She Came to Stay*, trans. Yvonne Mayse and Roger Senhouse (London: Secker & Warburg, 1949).

2. For Blanchot's review of Jean-Paul Sartre's play *The Flies*, see "The Myth of Orestes," in *Faux pas*, 59–64.

TRADITION AND SURREALISM

1. This article and the following one are the last to appear on the first page of the *Débats*.

2. Louis Hourticq, *L'art et la science* (Paris: Flammarion, 1943).

3. André Lejard, *Les tapisseries de l'Apocalypse de la cathédrale d'Angers* (Paris: Albin Michel, 1942).

4. André Breton, "Distances," in *Les pas perdus* (Paris: Gallimard, 1924), 174; "Distance," in *The Lost Steps*, trans. Mark Polizzotti (Lincoln: University of Nebraska Press, 1996), 104 (translation modified).

A WORLD IN RUINS

1. Georges Magnane, *Gerbe Baude* (Paris: Gallimard, 1943).

2. See "The Influence of the American Novel" in this volume.

3. Both the *Débats* article and the *Chroniques littéraires* have "*conférencier*" (lecturer) here. In the recently discovered typescript of the article, however, the word is "*romancier*" (novelist).

4. See "A Novel and a Tale of War" in this volume.

5. This article and the two others that Blanchot devotes to Magnane in the *Journal des Débats* are discussed in Michael Holland, "Blanchot, Magnane and 'the chance of a rigorous language,'" in *Georges Magnane: la plume et le sport*, ed. Thomas Bauer (Reims: Presses Universitaires de Reims, 2015), 213–26.

Index